# A CHRISTIAN PHILOSOPHY

# A Christian Philosophy

*16*

## LAWRENCE E. LYNCH

*St. Michael's College, University of Toronto*

*CHARLES SCRIBNER'S SONS · NEW YORK*

Printed in the United States of America

Library of Congress Catalog Card Number 67–21341

# Acknowledgments

The author wishes to make grateful acknowledgment for permission to quote from the works indicated below. Authors are listed in alphabetical order, and the selections are also identified in the references for each chapter. Unless otherwise noted, publishers are located in New York.

Aristotle, *The Oxford Translation of Aristotle,* various dates. Reprinted by permission of the Clarendon Press, Oxford.

Cassirer, Ernst, *An Essay on Man,* copyright 1944 by Yale University Press, New Haven, Conn. Reprinted by permission.

Comte, Auguste, *The Positive Philosophy,* trans. by Harriet Martineau. Reprinted in 1896 by G. Bell & Sons, Ltd.; originally published in Bohn's Library by G. Bohn & Sons Ltd.

Cox, Harvey, *The Secular City,* copyright © 1965 by The Macmillan Company. Reprinted by permission.

de Chardin, Teilhard, *The Future of Man,* trans. by Norman Denny, 1964, by permission of William Collins Sons & Co. Ltd., London and Toronto. Also with the permission of Harper & Row, Publishers, Inc.

Dennis, Nigel, *Cards of Identity,* 1960, permission by A. M. Heath & Company Ltd., for Weidenfeld and Nicolson Ltd., London. Also with the permission of Vanguard Press, Inc.

Descartes, René, *The Philosophical Works of Descartes,* trans. by Elizabeth S. Haldane and G. R. T. Ross (1911), 1931, by permission of Cambridge University Press, Cambridge.

Durant, Will, *The Age of Faith,* from *The Story of Civilization,* Vol. 4, copyright 1950, by Simon and Schuster, Inc. Reprinted by permission.

Fichte, Johann Gottlieb, *The Vocation of Man,* trans. by Roderick M. Chisholm, copyright 1956 by Bobbs-Merrill Company, Inc. Reprinted by permission.

Forbes, R. J., "Power," from *A History of Technology,* ed. Charles Singer, et al., Vol. II, 1956, the Clarendon Press. Reprinted by permission of the Clarendon Press, Oxford.

Gilson, Etienne, *The Christian Philosophy of St. Thomas Aquinas,* © copyright 1956 by Etienne Gilson. Reprinted by permission of Random House, Inc.

————. *The Spirit of Medieval Philosophy*, trans. by A. H. C. Downes, copyright 1936 by Charles Scribner's Sons. Reprinted by permission and also by permission of Sheed and Ward, London.

Hegel, G. W. F., *Philosophical Propadeutik*, trans. by G. E. Mueller, in Hegel, *Encyclopedia of Philosophy*, 1959. Reprinted by permission of Philosophical Library.

————. *The Phenomenology of Mind*, 1961, by permission of George Allen & Unwin Ltd., London.

Heidegger, Martin, *An Introduction to Metaphysics*, trans. by Ralph Mannheim, copyright 1961 by Yale University Press, New Haven, Conn. Reprinted by permission.

————. *Being and Time*, trans. by John Macquarrie and Edward Robinson, 1962, by permission of Basil Blackwell, Oxford, and of Max Neimeyer Verlag, Tübingen.

Kahn, Eugen, "An Appraisal of Existential Analysis," *The Psychiatric Quarterly*, Vol. 31, April 1957 and July 1957. Reprinted with the permission of the author and of *The Psychiatric Quarterly*.

Kant, Immanuel, *Critique of Practical Reason*, trans. by Lewis W. Beck, copyright 1956 by Bobbs-Merrill Company, Inc. Reprinted by permission.

————. *Critique of Pure Reason*, trans. by Norman Kemp Smith, 1929, St. Martin's Press, Inc., New York, Macmillan & Co., Ltd., London. Reprinted by permission.

————. *Fundamental Principles of the Metaphysics of Morals*, trans. by T. K. Abbott, copyright 1949 by Bobbs-Merrill Company, Inc. Reprinted by permission.

Kierkegaard, Søren, *Philosophical Fragments*, trans. by David F. Swenson and revised by Howard V. Hong. Reprinted by permission of the Princeton University Press. Copyright © 1936, 1962 by Princeton University Press.

Leff, Gordon, *Medieval Thought: St. Augustine to Ockham*, 1958. Permission granted by Penguin Books Ltd., Middlesex.

Marcel, Gabriel, *The Philosophy of Existence*, trans. by Manya Harari, 1949. Reprinted by permission of Philosophical Library.

May, Rollo, Ernest Angel and Henri F. Ellenberger, eds., *Existence*. Copyright 1958 by Basic Books, Inc. Reprinted by permission.

Nietzsche, Friedrich, *The Joyful Science*, 1929. Permission granted by George Allen & Unwin Ltd., London.

————. *The Portable Nietzsche*, translated and edited by Walter Kaufmann. Copyright 1954 by the Viking Press, Inc. Reprinted by permission of the Viking Press, Inc.

Plotinus, from *The Philosophy of Plotinus*, Representative Books from the *Enneads*. Selected and translated with an Introduction by Joseph Katz. Copyright, 1950, by Appleton-Century-Crofts, Inc. Reprinted by permission of Appleton-Century-Crofts, Inc., Division of Meredith Publishing Company.

Russell, Bertrand, *History of Western Philosophy*, copyright 1945 by Bertrand

Russell. Permission granted by George Allen & Unwin Ltd., London, and by Simon and Schuster, Inc.

————. *Human Knowledge,* Copyright 1948 by Simon and Schuster, Inc. Permission granted also by George Allen & Unwin Ltd., London.

————. *Logic and Knowledge,* 1956. Permission granted by George Allen & Unwin Ltd., London.

————. *Mysticism and Logic,* 1959. Permission granted by George Allen & Unwin Ltd., London.

St. Augustine, *The City of God,* trans. by Marcus Dods, 1871–76, T.&T. Clark, Edinburgh. Also by permission of Hafner Publishing Company.

St. Peter Damian, *Selected Writings on the Spiritual Life,* trans. by Patricia McNulty, 1959. Reprinted by permission of Faber and Faber Ltd., London.

St. Thomas Aquinas, from *Basic Writings of Saint Thomas Aquinas,* edited by Anton C. Pegis. Copyright 1945 by Random House, Inc. Reprinted by permission of the publisher.

————. *Commentary on Boethius' De Trinitate,* trans. by Armand Maurer C.S.B., 1953. Permission granted by Pontifical Institute of Mediaeval Studies, Toronto.

————. *On Kingship,* trans. by Gerald B. Phelan and I. T. Eschmann, 1949. Permission granted by Pontifical Institute of Mediaeval Studies, Toronto.

————. *On the Truth of the Catholic Faith* (*Summa Contra Gentiles*), Book I, translated and with an Introduction and Notes by Anton C. Pegis. Copyright © 1955 by Doubleday & Company, Inc. Reprinted by permission of the publisher.

————. *On the Truth of the Catholic Faith* (*Summa Contra Gentiles*), Book II, translated and with an Introduction and Notes by James F. Anderson. Copyright © 1956 by Doubleday & Company, Inc. Reprinted by permission of the publisher.

————. *On the Truth of the Catholic Faith* (*Summa Contra Gentiles*), Book III, translated and with an Introduction and Notes by Vernon J. Bourke. Copyright © 1956 by Doubleday & Company, Inc. Reprinted by permission of the publisher.

————. Quoted from the *Summa Theologica,* trans. by the Fathers of the English Dominican Province; 1947, Benziger Brothers, Inc., publishers and copyright owners. Also with the permission of Burns & Oates Ltd.

————. *Truth: St. Thomas Aquinas,* trans. by Robert W. Mulligan, James V. McGlynn and Robert W. Schmidt, 1952–1954, by permission of Henry Regnery Company, Publishers, Chicago.

Santayana, George, *Realms of Being,* One-Volume Edition. Copyright 1942 by Charles Scribner's Sons. Also by permission of Constable Publishers, London.

Sartre, Jean-Paul, *Being and Nothingness,* trans. by Hazel Barnes, 1957, by permission of Methuen & Co. Ltd., London; from *L'Etre et le Neant* de Jean-Paul Sartre © Editions Gallimard, 1943. Permission also granted by Literary Masterworks, Inc., for Philosophical Library.

————. *In Camera* [*No Exit*], trans. by Stuart Gilbert, 1946. Reprinted by permission of Hamish Hamilton Ltd., London, and of Alfred A. Knopf, Inc.

————. *The Flies*, trans. by Stuart Gilbert, 1946. Reprinted by permission of Hamish Hamilton Ltd., London, and of Alfred A. Knopf, Inc.

Schlick, Moritz, "The Turning Point of Philosophy," in *Philosophy, Religion and Science*, trans. by Charles H. Monson Jr., © 1963, Charles Scribner's Sons. Reprinted by permission of Albert M. Schlick and Mrs. Barbara van de Velde.

Spinoza, Benedictus, *Ethics*, trans. by Andrew Boyle, Everyman's Library edition, 1938. By permission of J. M. Dent & Sons Ltd., London, and by E. P. Dutton & Co., Inc.

# Preface

The history of *A Christian Philosophy* serves as a useful background against which the general character and structure of the work may be better appreciated. For just as history plays a major role in the philosophical arguments unfolded in its pages, so too does it help to explain the book's genesis as well. In the fall of 1961 the producers of the Canadian Broadcasting Corporation's program *University of the Air* suggested a series of eight half-hour radio broadcasts on Scholastic philosophy. Throughout the discussion that followed many of the ambiguities and misunderstandings surrounding the term "Scholastic philosophy" emerged, and it was finally decided to take the person and work of St. Thomas Aquinas as the theme instead. My assignment was to interpret St. Thomas' thought for listeners unacquainted with medieval methods and vocabulary, and to present that interpretation in language readily understandable to the average non-academic radio listener. The talks were subsequently broadcast on the Trans-Canada Network as well as on several independent Canadian and American stations. In 1963 the series appeared as a book under the title *Christian Philosophy*.

The present book retains the basic argument and organization of its predecessor; it differs from the earlier version in the amplification of the argument, the addition of materials more suited to a book than to the air waves, and in title. For it must be borne in mind that the medium of radio imposes a definite form on the materials, determines how evidence is to be most effectively presented, and sets rigid time-limits, measured in seconds, to each chapter. Conceived now as a book, it has become possible to re-structure individual parts of the general argument, add the texts that serve to bolster the historical evidence and illustrate various points, and supply explanatory notes, glossary and biographies. In its new form the work is directed more to the needs of the undergraduate student seeking an overall view of an historically important philosophical position that retains germs of insight significant for our own times. The new title,

A *Christian Philosophy*, is a more exact expression of the view presented throughout the earlier radio talks: while the thought of St. Thomas does constitute a *Christian philosophy*, it remains *a* Christian philosophy. One need not think in the way Aquinas did nor defend the same philosophical conclusions to be an authentic Christian philosopher.

Although it is an amplification of simpler materials, the book remains but a sketch of a viable Christian philosophy. An effort has been made to distinguish the essentials of St. Thomas' philosophical speculation within the setting in which it developed historically. As a living reality his thought was fed by theological insight and grew in a cultural context marked by a distinct science and a definite social organization; if his philosophical principles are to live in our own day they must also be nourished by theological speculation and assimilate vastly different cultural materials. What is presented here, then, is little more than an outline of philosophical principles, not a developed philosophical position. A Christian philosophy making use of those principles and viable in the twentieth century has hardly begun to appear. Contemporary religious experience and theological reflection, the physical and life sciences, human knowledge about man himself have provided rich materials for philosophical work, but St. Thomas' principles have scarcely begun to organize those materials into a living body of contemporary Christian speculation. *A Christian Philosophy* presents St. Thomas in dialogue with modern and contemporary thinkers in the hope that some readers may be inspired to engage in this work of the Christian philosopher. St. Thomas for too long has been pictured as alive only in the Church; he must at last begin to appear in the market-place, standing on his own intellectual credentials.

The dialogue remains, however, a dialogue; both sides make their own unique contribution to the discourse. Modern man's great concern is with religious and moral questions, and he will not be content with metaphysical and merely speculative answers. Those answers are important, and some effort has been made in the pages that follow to indicate that metaphysical convictions do ultimately stand behind practical solutions. But acceptance of metaphysical views in our own day will be more readily forthcoming after practical plans, based on such views, have proven themselves beneficial to everyday human living.

Here St. Thomas has been poorly served by his followers. He has all too often been presented as metaphysician or epistemologist; too rarely has he been introduced as a *moral* thinker. It may very well be that in our modern dialogue phenomenology, phenomenological anthropology and existential philosophy will enable friends of St. Thomas to formulate and develop the philosophical dimensions of his moral thinking, as idealism aided them in understanding his approach to being and truth in an earlier day. Existence, the being of things, substance, the nature and accessibility of truth are unquestionably fundamental philosophical realities; but so are man's being, his freedom, the being he lives and experiences in his orientation to goodness and the realization of his possibilities, his life with other human persons, his being before God. It is for this reason that *A Christian Philosophy* tries to bring St. Thomas into especially intimate discourse with Martin Heidegger, Jean-Paul Sartre, Friedrich Nietzsche and Søren Kierkegaard. For without in any way assenting to the positivist conviction that metaphysical speculation is out-dated or, at worst, nonsense, it does remain true that contemporary thought is much more involved in solving man's psychological and moral problems, both personal and social. Hopefully this small book may inspire some students to work through the new materials provided by the behavioral and social sciences with the eye of the philosopher and in the light of St. Thomas.

L.L.

*January 15, 1968*

# Contents

Note to the Reader    xv

*Chapter I*
Scholastic Philosophy    3

*Chapter II*
Christian Philosophy    23

*Chapter III*
The Christian as Philosopher    43

*Chapter IV*
Philosophic Knowledge of Reality    68

*Chapter V*
Human Being    101

*Chapter VI*
Man's Being Free    134

*Chapter VII*
Man's Social Being    174

*Chapter VIII*
Philosophic Knowledge of God    204

Notes    235
Biographies    251
Suggested Reading    273
Index    275

# Note to the Reader

In view of the fact that *A Christian Philosophy* hopes to serve the needs of the general reader and students, texts have been quoted from English versions most readily available to such readers. Thus, Aristotle has been quoted from the edition of Richard McKeon, *The Basic Works of Aristotle* (New York, Random House, 1941). Usually book and chapter are cited and the standard Bekker number is provided so that the texts can be identified in other editions. Also in the notes, for the sake of convenience, Francis Bacon, Thomas Hobbes, John Locke, David Hume and John Stuart Mill are quoted from *The English Philosophers from Bacon to Mill*, edited by Edwin A. Burtt (New York, The Modern Library, 1939). It will be cited as: Ed. E. A. Burtt, p.—.

Various English editions of St. Thomas' works have been used. Whenever possible texts have been selected from the edition of Anton C. Pegis, *Basic Writings of Saint Thomas Aquinas*, Vol. 1–2 (New York, Random House, 1945). Otherwise the following editions have been used:

*Summa Theologiae* (cited as *S.T.*) in the translation of the Fathers of the English Dominican Province (London, Burns, Oates and Washbourne Ltd., 1947).

*Summa Contra Gentiles* (cited as *S.C.G.*) in the translation of Anton C. Pegis, James F. Anderson, Vernon J. Bourke, Charles O'Neil in *On the Truth of the Catholic Faith* (Garden City, Hanover House, 1955–1956).

*Quaestiones Disputatae de Veritatae* (cited as *On Truth*) in the translation of Robt. W. Mulligan, James V. McGlynn, Robt. W. Schmidt in *Truth: St. Thomas Aquinas* (Chicago, Henry Regnery Co., 1952–1954).

*De Regno* (cited as *On Kingship*) in the translation of Gerald B. Phelan and I. Th. Eschmann, O.P. (Toronto, Pontifical Institute of Mediaeval Studies, 1949).

*In librum Boethii de Trinitate* (cited as *On Boethius' De Trinitate*) (1) in the translation of Armand Maurer, C.S.B. (Toronto, Pontifical

Institute of Mediaeval Studies, 1953); (2) in the translation of Sr. Rose Emmanuella Brennan (St. Louis, B. Herder Book Co., 1946).

Where passages from the Bible are used in the text of the book, the Confraternity Text has been used—the Jerusalem Bible appeared in English too late for changes to be made; where biblical passages occur in texts that are being quoted, the translator's text is preserved.

The argument rests very heavily on historical evidence and therefore a great many names appear that are unfamiliar to most readers. By way of explanation a series of brief biographies is added, so that one may place important figures in time and place; in most instances some indication is given as to additional books that might be consulted if the reader should want additional information. A similar problem arises in connection with technical philosophical terms, so a small effort has been made to solve it by providing a brief gloss for some unusual terms in the index.

For convenience, these abbreviations for several references have been used in the notes.

St. Thomas, *S.T.* I, 46, 1 refers to the *Summa Theologiae* of St. Thomas Part I, question 46, article 1.

St. Thomas, *In VIII Phys.*, lect. 2 refers to St. Thomas' commentary on the *Physics* of Aristotle, book VIII and lecture 2 of St. Thomas' exposition.

Plotinus, *Enneads* V. 1. 7 refers to the collection of philosophical treatises written by Plotinus and arranged in groups of nine by Porphyry. In the example the reference is to the fifth collection, par. 7 of the first treatise.

Aristotle, *Metaphysics* Z, 6, 1032a4. refers to Aristotle's *Metaphysics*, Book Zeta, chapter 6. In the Bekker numbering used in all standard editions the exact text is at line 4 of page 1032a.

*Div. Nom. ii* refers to a work of Dionysius Areopagita (Denis the Areopagite), *On Divine Names*, chapter 2.

*P.G.* 3, 872 refers to the monumental collection of patristic and medieval writing edited by Migne and published in Paris from 1857–1866 under the title *Patrologiae cursus completus, Series Graeca* in 162 volumes. The reference is to volume 3, column 872.

*P.L.* 145, 697 B–C refers to the monumental collection of patristic and medieval writing edited by Migne and published in Paris under the title *Patrologiae cursus completus, Series Latina* (1844–1864) in 221 volumes. The reference is to volume 145, column 697, parts B and C.

*AHDLM* XIX (1952), p. 135 refers to a journal of medieval studies published by J. Vrin in Paris under the title *Archives d'histoire doctrinale et littéraire du moyen âge.* The reference is to volume XIX for the year 1952, page 135.

S.P.C.K. refers to the Society for the Propagation of Christian Knowledge in London, England.

Translations by the author are of the selections being used, not of the entire work from which a selection has been taken.

Emphasis is as it appears in the selections unless it is stated in square brackets that it has been added. The style of selections has been retained, except for the use of quotation marks which has been standardized throughout.

# A CHRISTIAN PHILOSOPHY

# CHAPTER I

# *SCHOLASTIC PHILOSOPHY*

. . . Nowadays, all the old means of self-recognition have been swept away, leaving even the best people in a state of personal dubiety. Even dispossession, the surest means of bringing home the naked identity, has disappeared. Very wisely, governments all over the world have sought to stop this rot before the entire human population has been reduced to anonymous grains. They give you cards, on which they inscribe in capital letters the name which your fading memory supplies before it is too late. It is their hope that by continually reading and re-reading your *name*, you will be able to keep your hold on a past that no longer exists, and thus bring an illusion of self into the present. As you see, the authorities have been obliged to reverse the normal procedure—which is, of course, first to create a world and *then* to name the things that inhabit it. Now, by doing the naming first, they hope creation will follow as a result of association and suggestion. This, as you know, is the method followed by women who want to have babies.

"This method has its dangers, of course; we all know mothers who have dreamed-up an Agnes and, on being delivered of a Horace, have stubbornly brought them up as Agnes; and something of the same kind may result from the authorities' efforts at present. But that is not my point at the moment. What I want to emphasize is this: don't lose your name again, Mrs. Chirk. Don't, at least, lose the cards on which that name is written. Not only would you yourself be left nameless, but people have been known to pick up such lost cards, put them in a wallet with their own, and start a hopeless tangle of selves that spreads like a bush fire. . . .[1]

Many critics of contemporary life, sociologists and anthropologists alike, have remarked on the phenomenon of identification cards so characteristic of North American life. They point out that practically every phase of our daily routine is covered by a card: social security cards, insurance cards, etc. Many people, indeed, appear to feel that all the possibilities of their personalities have not been uncovered until they have

a full range of such cards! Young people are said to be searching franti-
cally for an "identity" and only feel that they have found one when they
have slipped noiselessly into their proper slot in life. Academic failures
are called "drop-outs;" apparently their cards have dropped onto the
sorting-room floor, having failed to find a suitable pigeon-hole. Comput-
ers sort us out and batteries of tests reveal our true selves. In short, the
mystery of personality has given way to the clarity of the card-file.

A similar scientific card catalogue system of identification is applied
to our studying and teaching. Thus, novels are "explained" by being dis-
sected and "understood" by being classified into suitable genres; for some
quite unknown reason paintings become more "meaningful" or "significant" when identified with a particular school. And philosophers yield
up their hidden secrets when they are branded with a particular "ism."
The moment a writer is classified as a realist or empiricist, analyst or
idealist, a wave of satisfaction comes over the reader. Now he can talk
about him—not in virtue of what he has written or because the reader
has finally succeeded, after much effort of his own, in re-discovering the
painfully thought out nuances of the man's insights, but because he has
been tagged and labelled like a dead specimen of butterfly neatly pinned
to the collector's board. And, as might be expected, the number of tags
needed to keep the collection tidy increases as knowledge of the differences, marking specimen off from specimen, grows.

Thus it has been with the period that vaguely intervenes between Saint
Augustine in the fifth century A.D. and Erasmus at the end of the fifteenth century, the period it has been fashionable to call the Dark Ages.
Until a hundred years ago very little was known about the important
figures of that period, and what was known was esteemed of little worth.
They were "monks" and "theologians;" their thinking appeared to be re-
petitive and seemed to follow very narrow, regular patterns. Lacking
clearly-defined differences, they required a single identification card,
"Scholastic." Research during the past fifty years, however, has changed
all of that and today a whole range of cards would be needed to play
the game that way. If one is satisfied with the "understanding" that comes
from categorizing, rather than with the understanding that is the product
of philosophical thinking, he must be able to fit scores of individuals and
highly distinct thinkers into a wide spectrum of slots. We cannot use the
term "Scholastic" indiscriminately today.

Whenever I hear a contemporary speak of "Scholastic philosophy," I
am reminded of the familiar story of Alice's strange experiences with the
looking-glass insects in *Through the Looking Glass*. The conversation
between Alice and the Gnat runs as follows:

"What sort of insects do you rejoice in, where *you* come from?" the Gnat inquired.

"I don't *rejoice* in insects at all," Alice explained, "because I'm rather afraid of them—at least the large kinds. But I can tell you the names of some of them."

"Of course they answer to their names?" the Gnat remarked carelessly.

"I never knew them to do it."

"What's the use of their having names," the Gnat said, "if they won't answer to them?"

"No use to *them*," said Alice, "but it's useful to the people that name them, I suppose." ²

In their own way, philosophers are very much like Alice's insects—very often they, too, refuse to answer to their names, the names proving more "useful to the people that name them" than to the philosophers they name.

A few years ago Etienne Gilson, French philosopher and historian of ideas, returned to Toronto after a lecture tour in South America and remarked rather wryly to a friend: "They thought that I was an existentialist! Everywhere I went, I was introduced as an existentialist." It was undoubtedly useful—and, perhaps, even profitable!—to hold up the card "Existentialist" to classify, identify or advertise the lecturer. But Gilson was not prepared to answer to the name. In his own case, Martin Heidegger, one of the most influential of contemporary philosophers in Germany, has reacted in similar fashion to the same tag. He, too, refuses it, especially if he is expected to answer to it along with Jean-Paul Sartre, high priest of existentialism. Heidegger explains his opposition in these words:

Sartre expresses the basic principle of Existentialism in this way: "Existence precedes essence". Here he is taking *existentia* and *essentia* in the sense of metaphysics which ever since Plato has said: *essentia* precedes *existentia*. Sartre turns the proposition around. However, turning a metaphysical proposition around, it remains a metaphysical proposition. In this statement he persists, with metaphysics, in forgetting the truth of Being. . . . Sartre's proposition about the precedence of *existentia* over *essentia* justifies, however, the name "Existentialism" as a suitable title for his philosophy. However, this basic principle of "Existentialism" bears not the slightest resemblance to that expression in *Sein und Zeit*.³

On his side Gilson would undoubtedly reject Heidegger's reasons while joining him in refusing to answer to "Existentialist." He would question the assertion that metaphysics after Plato gave *essentia* precedence over *existentia* and the view that metaphysics has to forget the truth of Being. But both Heidegger and Gilson would agree that *Existenz* and *esse* are not *existence*. They would, therefore, forego the tag "Existentialist."

The identity card "Scholastic," too, is more useful to the one who uses it than it is satisfactory to the one named. Many answer it only out of fear that a worse name might be concocted for them—as Alice herself was to say when she reached the inner woods where things have no names. As she tells the story:

> This must be the woods where things have no names. I wonder what'll become of *my* name when I go in? I shouldn't like to lose it at all—because they'd have to give me another, and it would be almost certain to be an ugly one. But then the fun would be trying to find the creature that had got my old name! That's just like the advertisements, you know, when people lose dogs—*"answers to the name of "Dash:" had on a brass collar"*—just fancy calling anything you met "Alice" till one of them answered! Only they wouldn't answer at all, if they were wise.[4]

Fancy everyone calling out 'Scholastic' till someone answered—"they wouldn't answer at all, if they were wise!" For in vulgar usage the term "Scholastic" does not have the most agreeable connotation. The dictionary defines Scholastic (as an adjective) as:

> 1. Pertaining to or characteristic of scholars, education, or schools.
> 2. Pertaining to or characteristic of the medieval schoolmen; hence, precise, pedantic.[5]

And considering it as a noun, it says:

A schoolman of the Middle Ages; hence, a pedant.[6] Playing out the dictionary game still further and tracing back the word "pedant", we find something even less flattering:

> Pedant. A scholar who makes needless and inopportune display of his learning or who insists upon the importance of trifling points of scholarship.[7]

Happier the philosopher who stays with Alice in the woods where things have no names!

Professional as well as popular historians of philosophy do their best to make the name "Scholastic" even more unwelcome. Each seems to find the core of Scholasticism in something different. Thus, John Dewey, the

American philosopher who wielded such a powerful influence over American thought and educational theory a few years back and who continues to sway educational practice, in one place reiterates the characteristics we have found in our dictionary definition. Dewey says Scholasticism is:

> . . . any mode of thought characterized by excessive refinement and subtlety; the making of formal distinctions without end and without special point.[8]

Another description will undoubtedly strike a responsive chord in some circles. Friedrich Paulsen, in the introduction to his work *Immanuel Kant*, sets forth certain marks of Scholasticism as it appears to him. Here is what Paulsen writes:

> If Scholastic philosophy is at present experiencing a kind of revival in the schools of Catholicism, this is due, not so much to its inner vitality as to its supposed fitness to serve an ecclesiastical political system, which, through the favor of circumstances—*patientia Dei et stultitia hominum*, an old Lutheran would say—has attained again in our time to unexpected power. Moreover, there still remains the question whether continuance of existence is in general something of which a philosophy can boast. Perhaps fruitfulness is a better characteristic and this the Kantian philosophy shows; it still gives rise to new systems of thought. Thomism, on the contrary, though of course a great achievement for its own time, yields today nothing except unfruitful repetitions. It does not set free the spirit, it enslaves it, which of course is just its intention.[9]

In Paulsen's view, then, Scholasticism is distinguished by these marks: first, it is a tool of ecclesiastical-political control; second, it enslaves the spirit—and it is intended to do so; third, it is identified with Thomism.

Bertrand Russell, after making an invaluable contribution to the understanding of mathematical thinking and to the logic derived from it, has turned his attention to the history of Western thought. In discussing Scholasticism he ascribes both chronological and doctrinal characteristics to it. Russell writes:

> Scholasticism, in its narrowest sense, begins early in the twelfth century. As a philosophical school, it has certain characteristics. First, it is confined within the limits of what appears to the writer to be orthodoxy; if his views are condemned by a council, he is usually willing to retreat. This is not to be attributed entirely to cowardice, it is analogous to the submission of a judge to the decisions of a Court of Appeal. Second, within the limits of orthodoxy,

Aristotle, who gradually became more fully known during the twelfth and thirteenth centuries, is increasingly accepted as the supreme authority; Plato no longer holds the first place. Third, there is a great belief in "dialectic" and in syllogistic reasoning; the general temper of the scholastics is minute and disputatious rather than mystical.[10]

These points are noteworthy in Russell's description: first, Scholasticism is "a philosophical school;" second, it begins in the twelfth century; third, Aristotle, not Plato, is its supreme authority "within the limits of orthodoxy."

A popular historian, Will Durant, included here because of the wide public his writings on successive stages of Western thought and culture have commanded, places the essence of Scholasticism in its "attempt to establish the faith by reason." According to Durant:

> Scholasticism was a Greek tragedy, whose nemesis lurked in its essence. The attempt to establish the faith by reason implicitly acknowledged the authority of reason; the admission, by Duns Scotus and others, that the faith could not be established by reason shattered Scholasticism, and so weakened the faith that in the fourteenth century revolt broke out all along the doctrinal and ecclesiastical line. Aristotle's philosophy was a Greek gift to Latin Christendom, a Trojan horse concealing a thousand hostile elements.[11]

For the moment we shall leave, without further comment, Durant's statement that "the attempt to establish the faith by reason implicitly acknowledged the authority of reason." For what, indeed, does it mean? That reason is to prove what faith believes? But that would seem to *destroy* belief, and it does seem odd for any man of faith to attempt that! And what *is* the authority of reason? Its authority would seem best acknowledged when it establishes conclusions of reason, not articles of faith. But these are questions to which we shall return later in discussing the notion of Christian philosophy.

Finally, let us consult the definition of Scholasticism given by a well-respected contemporary historian of medieval thought, Gordon Leff. He is somewhat more careful than Durant when he comes to describe the essence of Scholasticism. It is "the *application* of reason to revelation." Leff writes as follows:

> Scholasticism has long been seen as an attitude or state of belief which takes Christian revelation for its subject; to others it is a method of disputation, and this has been its distinguishing trait;

while others have regarded it as the rational aspect of belief, a philosophy in its own right.

While none of these is necessarily self-exclusive, in my view Scholasticism was essentially the application of reason to revelation. It was an outlook in which rational enquiry was governed by the assumptions of faith, and faith was supported by the power of reason. Both were indispensable, and to separate them, or to neglect their inherent unity is, I believe, to do violence to Scholasticism.[12]

Let us now examine in somewhat greater detail certain common themes that recur in these several definitions. First, Scholasticism is a school or a philosophy; second, it is "medieval;" third, it is "Aristotelian."

In many ways some of the very scholars who have undertaken the task of defending what they have called "Scholastic philosophy" are to blame for treating it as though it had a doctrinal unity. If we go back to the early days of modern scholarship concerned with the history of medieval thought, an instructive story begins to unfold. Barthélemy Hauréau was one such historian and, writing in his *Histoire de la philosophie scolastique,* he described Scholasticism as a philosophy and sought to define it chronologically by referring to the *time* at which it flourished. Hauréau wrote:

Scholastic philosophy is the philosophy professed in the schools in the Middle Ages from the establishment of the school to the day in which the outside philosophy, the spirit of novelty disengaged from the bonds of tradition, came to dispute with it and withdraw from its control the minds of men.[13]

Maurice de Wulf, who in later years was to become one of the most authoritative and widely-read historians of medieval thought, disputed this description on two counts. First, the definition is incomplete because it is restricted to the Middle Ages and ignores the neo-scholastics of the fifteenth and sixteenth centuries; second, it rules out common doctrines and conceives of Scholasticism extrinsically by referring only to the time it flourished. On the contrary, De Wulf writes:

Now we believe a completely different idea should be formed of the philosophy of the Schools. Scholasticism is a clearly marked body of doctrine. It did not spring suddenly from the brain of a man of genius. It is an organism that developed through the centuries with a slow and steady progression. Weak of constitution and indecisive in form from the ninth to the twelfth centuries, Scholasticism attained the fulness of its expansion in the thirteenth century; it wasted away during the fourteenth and fifteenth centuries to be invigorated in the sixteenth century.[14]

And defining its doctrinal unity more clearly, he says:

> . . . in order to understand Scholasticism it is not enough to characterize it by the processes that have been the means of propagating it, or by the language its doctors used. One must look to their lectures, collect their teachings, and cull out the fundamental ideas that dominate their philosophy.
> Is this synthesis possible? We have no doubt about it. But to be complete it would require at the outset a colossal job of analysis and would find its place on the very last page of a general history of Scholastic philosophy.[15]

This task of sifting through history to discover a synthesis of fundamental ideas has resulted in a whole stream of textbooks bearing as their title some variation of the designation "Scholastic Philosophy." They include: J. K. Kleutgen, *La philosophie scolastique exposée et defendue* (Paris, 1869); Elie Blanc, *Traité de la philosophie scolastique* (Lyon, 1889); François Picavet, *La scolastique* (Paris, 1893); Sebastian Reinstadler, *Elementa Philosophiae Scholasticae* (Freiburg, 1901); J. J. Urraburu, *Compendium Philosophiae Scholasticae* (Madrid, 1902–4); Maurice de Wulf, *Introduction á la philosophie néo-scolastique* (Louvain, 1904). The last appeared in English and inspired a whole series of manuals on logic, ontology, etc. by De Wulf's translator, Peter Coffey, each written from the "Scholastic standpoint."

The result of this "colossal task of analysis" has been a synthetic body of doctrine such as no medieval doctor ever taught! The task of synthesizing St. Thomas Aquinas and John Duns Scotus, two of the most penetrating and productive thinkers of the later thirteenth and early fourteenth centuries is, indeed, colossal. As represented in the modern editions of their writings, St. Thomas' works fill twenty-five volumes in the Parma edition of 1862–1870. Duns Scotus' works take up twenty-six volumes in the so-called Vives edition of 1891. Add to that the formidable production of St. Bonaventure, Siger of Brabant, Henry of Ghent, Giles of Rome and Godfrey of Fontaines, and the period 1250–1350 presents a tremendous challenge to analysis. But the physical obstacles are as nothing compared to the intellectual problems; analysis is relatively simpler than the task of *synthesis*. The most formidable difficulty is the basic differences in the respective doctrines. These differences make reconciliation impossible. Thus, to take but a few examples, Aquinas and Scotus held quite divergent views of such philosophic fundamentals as the meaning of being, the concept of "common nature," the reality of things, the being of matter, the character of understanding as action or quality, the subject of metaphysics, the ways open to the human intellect as it strives to gain some conviction about God's existence. Later research has proven that De Wulf oversimplifies the facts when he writes:

> We bring this preliminary analysis to a close at this point. We are content to show that it is possible to give a *doctrinal* definition of Scholasticism. On the great theorems all the doctors are in agreement. Beyond that, certain divergences come to light.[16]

Little wonder, then, that a public image of Scholasticism as *a* philosophy has been created when scholars have deliberately tried to synthesize *a* philosophy from the disparate elements of several incompatible philosophies. Unity in faith or similarity in theological ambition do not guarantee philosophical identity. Indeed, one may well wonder what the image of Scholasticism would have been if its creators had not been so overwhelmed by monolithic Catholicism and *had* recognized differences in medieval *theologies*.

The image of Scholastic philosophy as a seamless garment soon breaks down under historical research. Careful investigation reveals the profound philosophical differences between one philosophy and the next. Abelard, Roscelin and William of Champeaux provide very different answers to questions like these: What reality must one assign to the notion signified by the word "man?" What justification is there for using a *general* name like "man" if there are only *individual* men? Roscelin is said to have defended the general position that individual things alone exist. Consequently, only this or that man, John or Peter, is real. When a person calls each one of them a "man," he has brought a new individual into existence, namely, this uttered sound "man." The only reality, then, that he attached to *man* is the being it has in the sound one makes with his voice. William of Champeaux took quite a different view: a universal species, *man*, corresponds to the word "man" and it is wholly present in each individual man. The species is present in each individual "indifferently," and this lack of difference justifies the use of a common name. Thus, John and Peter are *not* different as man and, consequently, each can be called a "man." Abelard, contrary to each of these views, claimed that universality belongs to words, not to things. For while individual men alone exist, each one *is man*. They have a common status (not essence) as men. The word "man" is said of many individual men and is, therefore, universal; it can justifiably be said of each individual because each has the status of being man. There is precious little unanimity in evidence between these three doctrines!

To cite another example, St. Thomas was one of St. Albert's students as Abelard had been a student of William of Champeaux, yet Aquinas gave quite a different account of human knowledge than his master did. Each account finds its place in a very different philosophical outlook. St. Albert was above all concerned with accommodating the apparently divergent views of Plato and Aristotle, Averroës and Avicenna in a single, coherent doctrine, and his world of human experience was peopled with individual substances, each distinct from the other in its particular and peculiar union of form and matter. St. Thomas was less concerned with reconciling the views of his predecessors than with using their conclusions as stepping-stones to a deeper understanding of reality, and his was a world of *existing entities*. Thus, St. Albert concluded that man is a composite of soul and body wherein the soul is in itself an incorporeal substance, but in relation to the body it is a mover or source of activity; to St. Thomas each man is *one being* who derives his unity above all from his act of existing, and his soul is primarily a *form* through which being comes to the individual. The result is that human knowledge is viewed differently by the two saints. St. Albert seeks to explain how a substance like the human soul knows *intelligible* entities, and this is accomplished by an agent intellect gradually reducing the potentiality of a possible (initially a "material") intellect to the fuller act represented by scientific knowledge. St. Thomas, on the other hand, is concerned with understanding how a human *being* with a form like the human soul knows *existing* entities, and he explains that this is done through the senses, and the intellect's abstracting activity, but above all by its ability to judge. For St. Thomas human knowing remains radically incomplete until it has passed judgment on the act of existing realities. So, although master and disciple, the two differ in their general philosophies and interpretations of human knowing.

Illustrations could be continued almost endlessly. Duns Scotus was convinced that St. Thomas' way of proving God's existence would not work—as, indeed, it would not within Scotus' philosophical framework! A demonstration that draws its validity from the order of existing sensible realities soon loses it when interpreted within a realm of possible essences. And William of Occam, in seeking to defend his own theology of divine omnipotence, worked to destroy the very metaphysical foundations that Aquinas and Scotus had built for their philosophies and theologies. For Occam felt that any structure of essence or nature, standing between the individual entity and God, was not only needless and arbitrary but positively hostile to God's freedom.

In short, whenever a person comes upon so-called Scholastic philosophers, he is well advised to look for their differences rather than to assume their similarities—let alone their identities! Will Durant recognizes this very clearly, for even while deploring the Aristotelianism of Scholasticism he writes:

> Obviously it is a mistake to think of "the" Scholastic philosophy as a dreary unanimity of opinion and approach. There were a hundred Scholastic philosophies. The same university faculty might harbor a Thomas honoring reason, a Bonaventure deprecating it, a William of Auvergne (1180–1249) following Ibn Gabirol into voluntarism, a Siger of Brabant teaching Averroism.[17]

If Scholasticism is not a doctrinal unity, is it true to say that it is Aristotelian? Most of the historians we have quoted would answer "Yes." And once again there is very good reason for such an attitude. Certainly the development of philosophy in the schools of the eleventh and twelfth centuries was greatly dependent on Aristotle—particularly on the logic of two of his works, the *Prior Analytics* and the *Posterior Analytics*. Most of the great philosophical questions of the thirteenth century were posed by the reading of Aristotle's writings, *On the Soul, Physics, Metaphysics* and *Nicomachean Ethics*, at the universities of Paris and Oxford when these texts became available for the first time. Moreover, one has but to examine the writings of those days to discover the exalted position Aristotle held even among those Christians who saw in his writings a grave danger to the faith. He was "*The* Philosopher;" and to many medieval philosophers and theologians rejecting Aristotle was tantamount to rejecting human reason. The very words in which the great disputes of the thirteenth and fourteenth centuries were carried on were largely Latin versions of Aristotle's own terminology. Turning to our own day, the manuals and textbooks that seek to communicate this Scholastic philosophy give every appearance of claiming Aristotle's authority. Look at a few of the titles: De Maria, *Philosophia Peripatetico-Scholastica;* Joseph Gredt, *Elementa Philosophiae Aristotelico-Thomistica.* Open one of these books and the eye immediately falls on a formulation of argument that people have long since identified, either rightly or wrongly, with Aristotle: major, minor, major probatur, minor probatur, conclusio. It appears to have, in short, all the rigid formality of strict syllogistic reasoning.

Now much of this argument is superficially true, but its very obviousness hides many important truths. For one thing it assumes a great many things. First, it assumes that there is common agreement about the interpretation of the historical Aristotle, i.e. the Aristotle who studied with

Plato and taught in the Lyceum. Second, it assumes that the Aristotle who was so influential in the schools of the thirteenth century was that same Aristotle. Third, it assumes that there was some agreement about interpreting the Aristotle who did reach the thirteenth century. And finally, it assumes that the conclusions drawn from *that* Aristotle, in handling the philosophical questions of the thirteenth century, were largely uniform. History should make the wary pause over each of these assumptions.

On the first point one has only to read the works of contemporary interpreters of Aristotle—Jaeger, Von Arnim, Mansion, Oggioni, Taylor, Ross, Owens, Wilpert, Décarie, Van Ivanka, Merlan—to note a wide range of varying opinions concerning many notions vital to the understanding of Aristotle's thought; for example, the subject of first philosophy, the meaning of "substance" (οὐσία) and "being as being" (ὂν ᾗ ὂν), the causality of the Prime Mover, etc. On the second point, to say that it was *that* historical Aristotle who was so influential in the thirteenth century is to ignore the synthesis Arabic thinkers of the tenth and eleventh centuries sought to make of Aristotle, Plato, Plotinus and Proclus, a synthesis which was transmitted to the Latin scholars of Paris and Oxford. On the third point, that there was some agreement about interpreting the Aristotle who *did* reach the thirteenth century, it is a most chastening experience to read William of Occam and Thomas Aquinas as they interpret Aristotle. One then begins to appreciate the so-called "agreement" reached among medieval interpreters of Aristotle. Finally, the assumption that the conclusions medieval thinkers drew from the Aristotle they *did* know were fairly uniform is most dangerous. It implies that those men merely drew consequences suggested in Aristotle's writings and did *not* do their own independent thinking. As an antidote let us follow the mental struggles of St. Bonaventure, St. Albert, Roger Bacon and Roger Marston as they tried to explain what Aristotle had in mind in speaking of intellect as in some way separable from the human soul.

In his work *On the Soul* Aristotle was concerned with understanding how ψῡχή or soul is present in living bodies and, towards the end of his investigation, with explaining the presence of a divine element, νοῦς or intellect, in the living bodies of human beings. He had this to say:

> . . . mind, as we have described it, is what it is by virtue of becoming all things, while there is another which is what it is by virtue of making all things: this is a sort of positive state like light; for in a sense light makes potential colours actual colours. Mind in this sense is separable, impassible, unmixed, since it is in its essential nature activity.[18]

What precisely did Aristotle mean by this statement? What is this "light?" In what sense is it "separable?" How is it conjoined to the soul? A long list of Greek, Arabic and Jewish interpreters wrestled with the problem and advanced different solutions before the Christian masters of the thirteenth century tackled it. Thus about 850 A.D. the Arab Alkindi said that Aristotle's statement meant that there is one intellect for all men and it is the agent that properly causes our knowledge. Later, at the beginning of the eleventh century, Avicenna interpreted Aristotle to mean that intellect is separable in the sense of constituting a separate, active substance that poured forth intelligible forms into individual human souls. Each soul, according to Avicenna, has the capacity (he called it a "material intellect") of being suitably prepared to receive the forms from without. About a hundred and fifty years later still another influential Arabic interpreter, Averroës, agreed that Aristotle intended to teach that intellect is separable as a distinct substance; he disagreed with Avicenna in denying that each soul has its own intellect. According to Averroës each of us has only an imagination or disposition, physical and destructible in character, to receive intelligible forms from the separated intellect. These were the main explanations with which the Christian doctors had to work. Which one was correct? Above all, which one could most easily be reconciled with the doctrine of illumination taught by their great Christian teacher, St. Augustine?

The accommodations made by the main masters of the thirteenth century were varied and ingenious. Thus, according to St. Albert, there is no separated intellect except God; rather, each soul has its own agent intellect and it functions *within* the soul as Averroës' separated intellect functioned *outside* the soul. Roger Bacon gave a different solution. Each soul, he contended, has an intellect that is called "agent intellect" when it is concerned with intelligible realities and does not need sense-knowledge, and "possible intellect" when it does turn its concern to sensible things. Above each intellectual soul is God, and He acts as a kind of separate intellect bestowing intelligibility and reality on all that exists. St. Bonaventure in turn differs somewhat in attributing a kind of abstractive function to the possible intellect. For him each human soul has a possible intellect whose task it is to pick out the universal elements present in sensible data. But the soul can only perform that task with the illuminating assistance of an agent intellect. Abstraction, however, is only needed when the soul is concerned with sensible, worldly entities. When it wishes to know itself or God, it has recourse to higher powers. Here it comes under the regulative action of God's ideas, and the soul then becomes capable of certain (i.e. irrefutable) knowledge. God, then, acts as a kind of separate intellect bestowing *certitude* on human knowledge. In this

way Aristotle is brought into harmony with St. Augustine. And Roger
Marston pretty well agrees: each soul has its own possible and agent
intellect, but the agent intellect can only operate under the influence of
a higher, separate intellect that the theologians call God. Each of these
masters, then, tried to find his way through the maze of possible interpretations suggested by the various commentators on Aristotle. In so doing each sought his own solution and thereby provided us with a variety
of philosophical positions.

As for St. Thomas Aquinas, it is fascinating and instructive to watch
him wrestling with texts in which Aristotle arrives at conclusions that
seem at variance with things Aquinas accepted as true by faith. Take one
very striking example, the question of the eternity of the world. St. Thomas
was perfectly familiar with the questions Aristotle posed at the beginning
of book eight of his *Physics:*

> It remains to consider the following question. Was there ever a be-
> coming of motion before which it had no being, and is it perishing
> again so as to leave nothing in motion? Or are we to say that it
> never had any becoming and is not perishing, but always was and
> always will be? Is it in fact an immortal never-failing property of
> things that are, a sort of life as it were to all naturally constituted
> things? [19]

And St. Thomas had also followed the arguments Aristotle had developed
which come to this conclusion:

> Let this conclude what we have to say in support of our contention
> that there never was a time when there was not motion and never
> will be a time when there will not be motion.[20]

Now what was St. Thomas to say? Could he not simply proclaim that
Aristotle was wrong in teaching the eternity of motion because such a
conclusion contradicted his faith? Perhaps he could have done so, but in
fact he did not. Instead he subjected Aristotle's arguments to careful rational scrutiny to determine the status and validity of those arguments.
In book eight of his *Physics* Aristotle shows how motion is eternal; St.
Thomas is quick to point out, however, that whatever is eternal in *duration* may still require a cause of its *being.* Consequently, he contends,
Aristotle is not saying that motion is uncaused because it is eternal. It
may be eternal *and* caused. Moreover, he goes on, in the *Physics* Aristotle is treating motion as it would be treated in natural philosophy, and
therefore in the proofs he gives concerning its eternity he uses the definition of motion given by the *physicist,* i.e. motion is "the act of a thing

capable of motion insofar as it is such." He is concerned, then, with the causes that are found in motion and among things capable of motion. In this context Aristotle concludes that motion is eternal. But, according to St. Thomas, Aristotle does not touch the question of the cause of the very *being* of motion. That would be a problem for the metaphysician to examine and in doing so he would have to use quite different principles. So in St. Thomas' view Aristotle does not *demonstrate* about the uncaused *being* of motion. This is the way St. Thomas himself states the case:

> Therefore it is clear that what Aristotle proves here, namely that every motion needs a mobile subject, is not against the tenets of our faith. For it has already been stated that the universal production of things, whether they are said to be from eternity or not from eternity is not motion or change. For it to be motion it would be necessary that something be otherwise now and before. But then something would exist before and it would not be a *universal* production of things. And that is what we are talking about now. . . . Thus, therefore, if some particular being comes into being, it does not do so from absolute non-being, but if the whole of being comes into being, and that is what it means for being as being to come into being, it is necessary that it come into being from absolute non-being. If we are to call this a *becoming*, it is to use the word equivocally, as has been said before.[21]

Averroës, therefore, as one of the foremost and most widely respected commentators on the text of Aristotle, is wrong in extending Aristotle's argument from motion to becoming and making it contrary to the faith. Averroës' argument is briefly as follows: there must always be a subject of becoming just as there is of motion. Therefore the world of motion could not have come into being from nothing. According to St. Thomas it is not a valid argument because becoming applies where there is a previous subject and implies, therefore, change. Now change belongs to particular things; one particular being changes into another particular being. But the production of the *whole* of being *as being* is not a change or a becoming. Therefore the argument about a subject necessarily preceding a becoming does not apply, and what Aristotle said about the eternity of motion does not constitute a demonstration establishing a conclusion contradictory to any tenet of the faith. Treating the same discussion of the *Physics* in his *Summa Theologiae*, St. Thomas sums up his evaluation of Aristotle's arguments in this way:

> Nor are Aristotle's arguments absolutely demonstrative, but only relatively, viz. as against the arguments of some of the ancients who

asserted that the world began to be in some actually impossible ways. This appears in three ways. First, because both in *Physics* VIII and in *De Caelo* I he premises some opinions, such as those of Anaxagoras, Empedocles and Plato, and brings forward arguments to refute them. Secondly, because wherever he speaks of the subject, he quotes the testimony of the ancients, which is not the way of a demonstrator, but of one persuading of what is probable. Thirdly, because he expressly says that these are dialectical problems which he cannot solve demonstratively, as, *whether the world is eternal.*[22]

In short, St. Thomas concludes that Aristotle is arguing in book eight of the *Physics* as a dialectician weighing the opinions of his predecessors; he is not concerned with demonstrating conclusively that the world is eternal. St. Thomas is intent upon remaining Aristotle's faithful expositor even in such a difficult question; he did not take the texts at their surface-meaning but sought, rather, to interpret them in as favorable a light as possible. So, like the other masters we have looked at, St. Thomas did not slavishly accept interpretations of Aristotle handed down by tradition. Even as renowned a commentator as Averroës came in for careful rational scrutiny and philosophical rebuttal. All of these men tried to understand Aristotle for themselves, and their interpretations were as varied as their own philosophical positions; St. Thomas was more intent upon understanding reality, and if Aristotle and his commentators could help in that work, so much the better. If they could not, new principles had to be formulated or old ones re-thought. Consequently, in reading these medieval masters it is dangerous to stop at superficial similarities in language and assume that the words they use have exactly the same meaning they are intended to convey in Aristotle or one of his interpreters. Meanings, even of the common terms used by Aristotle, have to be sought and fixed within the context of the individual master's own thought, whose so-called Aristotelianism is in no sense univocal.

The view that Scholasticism is Aristotelian not only makes these assumptions, but it also overlooks several important facts. To make the method of the Scholastics merely an application of Aristotle's logic is to overlook the contributions Boethius made to the logic of the Schools; it is to forget the influence of grammarians like Priscian, Donatus and their commentators, and of such canonists as Gratian and Huguccio. To see in Aristotle the only authority for philosophers at Paris and Oxford is to pass over the enduring reverence in which St. Augustine was held. Augustine wielded an influence as potent as Aristotle's but of quite a different kind—the influence of Christian wisdom. Let us be aware, then, of the dangerous ambiguities attaching to the term "Aristotelian," and refrain from transmitting those ambiguities to Scholastic philosophy.

Paulsen, in the text we have quoted earlier, gives still another meaning to Scholasticism. It is "Thomism," he says. This is quite a common identification, but one that usually (in popular rather than academic circles) may stem from ignorance—ignorance of the existence of any other outstanding medieval philosopher besides St. Thomas Aquinas. However, if it becomes clear from what has already been said that there were *many* philosophical positions taken in the schools of the Middle Ages, then identifying Scholasticism with any one of them is obviously faulty definition. Even if the identification be granted, one might still ask: What is Thomism? To whom do we usually apply the word "Thomist?"

Everyone will agree, I think, that the name does designate the thought of St. Thomas in some way or other; not everyone will agree to restrict it to that designation. And even when it is used in a restricted way so that only Thomas Aquinas is intended, the term may still apply either to his theological doctrine or to his philosophical teachings, or to both at once. In this context it is instructive to note that the title of Etienne Gilson's exposition of Aquinas' thought underwent a change in translation. In French it bore the title *Le Thomisme*, which might lead one to believe that it dealt with Aquinas' theological and philosophical speculation; in English it became *The Christian Philosophy of Saint Thomas Aquinas*. In more popular common usage, however, "Thomism" is usually used to indicate philosophical teaching, but it is not reserved in such a way as to designate *St. Thomas'* philosophical views only. The result is that it has come to mean many things and to apply to scholars teaching many different, often opposite, doctrines.

Thus in our day it has become fashionable to speak of a "living Thomism" or a "Neo-Thomism" and to mean thereby a collection of doctrines originally conceived in seed in the intellect of Aquinas, nurtured in the minds of Cajetan, John of St. Thomas, Suarez and the commentators of Salamanca and Coimbra, and bearing progeny of varying shapes and sizes in our own day in the writings of Maréchal, Van Steenberghen, Yves Simon, Jacques Maritain and a host of others. It is a Thomism that has developed in the course of a long and continuing attempt to discuss philosophical questions raised by Descartes, Locke, Hume, Kant, Hegel, Kierkegaard, Husserl, Bergson, Heidegger and others, to re-think concepts used by St. Thomas or incorporate new concepts into the structure of his thought, and to suggest answers in the light of the insights he provided. This Thomism has not only tried to provide criticisms of other views, but to develop constructive positions and assert positive solutions

to philosophical problems current at whatever time the particular Thomist
lived. Canon Van Steenberghen, for instance, describes such a Thomism
in this way:

> We believe that up to the present time it has not been sufficiently
> shown that Thomistic philosophy is far more than a collection of
> philosophical doctrines grouped in orderly fashion about theology
> and serving that sacred science. Thomism is a strict philosophical
> system, well able to face up to the most brilliant systems of modern
> philosophy. It is possible, and today it is absolutely indispensable,
> to expound Thomism in a way that will satisfy the strictest require-
> ments of a critical and systematic philosophy.[23]

This is a view of Thomism not shared by all who would call themselves
Thomists; nor are the doctrines associated with that Thomism always
shared by other Thomists. For it is important to bear in mind that, even
having recourse to Aquinas for the insights with which to work, there is
no guarantee that those insights will be interpreted identically nor that
the conclusions reached about a variety of philosophical questions will
be identical. An excellent example of contemporary Thomists holding
contrasting views is the controversy that raged throughout the 1930's and
1940's in the field of what has come to be called epistemology. At issue
was the fundamental principle of our human knowledge of sensible realities. Must a Thomist start his philosophical interpretation of human knowing with a sensible, singular, existing thing? Or may he start with consciousness, in the manner of Descartes' *cogito?* Or will Kant's sensible
intuition do? The controversy set Msgr. Noel, Picard, Fr. Maréchal, Canon
Van Steenberghen, Maritain, Simon and Gilson at odds and produced a
huge flow of philosophical writing expressing various Thomistic points of
view. In similar fashion the philosophical understanding of the human
person, the meaning of "the common good," the nature of philosophy of
nature and its relationship to metaphysics and the natural sciences, the
very work of the metaphysician, the function of judgment in human
knowing, and many other subjects have led many philosophers who call
themselves "Thomists" to defend opposed doctrines. When "Thomism" is
used in this context it actually covers a multitude of philosophical positions. So when a person is asked: What is the Thomistic view on this or
that question?, the only correct answer is: "Well, Maritain says . . . ,"
or "Van Steenberghen holds . . ."

The term "Thomism," then, is a thoroughly ambiguous one and tells
us very little about the philosophical view held by any individual thinker.
It is a particularly fruitless exercise to follow Paulsen's example and speak
of Scholasticism as Thomism. For one thing, St. Bonaventure, Roger Ba-

con, Siger of Brabant, Henry of Ghent, John Duns Scotus and William of Occam might merit the name Scholastic in one way or another, but none of them is a Thomist; and for another, Thomism (even when the term is applied to St. Thomas) is not a Scholasticism. Jacques Maritain and Etienne Gilson both explain why, and they use much the same terms. Gilson writes:

> Whatever one thinks of it himself, it is beyond doubt that St. Thomas's entire thought has turned, at first intention, towards the knowledge of the concrete existent given in sensible experience and of the first causes of that datum, whether they are sensible or not. From his metaphysics to his ethics, the whole philosophy . . . is evidence of it. That is why it is and remains a philosophy properly so called and not, in the pejorative sense which is so common, a "Scholasticism." Every philosophy engenders its scholasticism, but these terms designate two specifically different facts. Every philosophy worthy of the name starts from the real and returns to it. Philosophy degenerates into scholasticism immediately it is applied to formulae set forth to be explained—as though those formulae rather than the things they illuminate, were reality itself—rather than taking the concrete existent as object of reflection so as to penetrate it and constantly illumine it further . . . St. Thomas's doctrine could degenerate into a scholasticism every time it is cut off from the object whose sole object it is to illumine. That is no reason to believe it is a scholasticism, for Thomism's object is not Thomism, but the world, man and God attained as existents in their very existence.[24]

And Maritain states his case in strikingly modern terms:

> The Thomist philosopher is dubbed *scholastic*, a name derived from his most painful affliction. Scholastic pedantry is his peculiar foe. *He* must constantly triumph over his domestic adversary, the Professor.
> The Thomist philosophy, therefore, is, in the sense just explained, an *existential* philosophy.[25]

Identification cards, then, are of little avail in real philosophical discussion; "Scholastic," "Aristotelian," "Thomist," "Neo-Scholastic," do little to clarify the philosophical position they are intended to designate. In what follows we shall attempt to avoid tag-names and categorical classifications. Instead, we shall try to relive a person's doctrine, the doctrine of Thomas Aquinas (realizing that reliving involves feeding on his thought, assimilating his principles and insights, and reproducing them in a contemporary setting). In making St. Thomas the subject of our investigation it is not our aim merely to learn and repeat the formulae he used, nor to discover how those formulae fit together to form a systematic and coherent whole. We shall try to see how St. Thomas reacted to the world; we shall be concerned, too, with discovering whether or not we can react similarly.

An immediate danger, however, looms up to challenge our whole enterprise from the very start. It may be formulated in this brief question: when we are examining St. Thomas' thought, are we witnessing the reactions of a theologian or a philosopher? Bertrand Russell will insist that there is little of the philosopher in St. Thomas, and we must carefully examine that viewpoint. Russell writes:

> There is little of the true philosophic spirit in Aquinas. He does not, like the Platonic Socrates, set out to follow wherever the argument leads. He is not engaged in an inquiry, the result of which it is impossible to know in advance. Before he begins to philosophize, he already knows the truth; it is declared in the Catholic faith. If he can find apparently rational arguments for some parts of the faith, so much the better; if he cannot, he needs only fall back on revelation. The finding of arguments for a conclusion given in advance is not philosophy but special pleading. I cannot, therefore, feel he deserves to be put on a level with the best philosophers either of Greece or modern times.[26]

In Russell's evaluation we are brought face to face with those attempts to accommodate faith and reason that many have seen to constitute the very essence of Scholasticism. Is St. Thomas eliminated from serious philosophical consideration because he was a Christian and a theologian? Our problem is neatly set in the term "Christian philosophy." Does it hide an inner contradiction like "square circle?" Can a Christian theologian philosophize? Can philosophy be Christian and remain philosophy?

# CHAPTER II

# CHRISTIAN PHILOSOPHY

What we have said about security in faith as one position in regard to the truth does not imply that the biblical "In the beginning God created heaven and earth" is an answer to our question. Quite aside from whether these words from the Bible are true or false for faith, they can supply no answer to our question because they are in no way related to it. Indeed, they cannot even be brought into relation with our question. From the standpoint of faith our question is "foolishness."

Philosophy is this very foolishness. A "Christian philosophy" is a round square and a misunderstanding. There is, to be sure, a thinking and questioning elaboration of the world of Christian experience, i.e. of faith. That is theology. Only epochs which no longer believe in the true greatness of the task of theology arrive at the disastrous notion that philosophy can help to provide a refurbished theology if not a substitute for theology, which will satisfy the needs and tastes of the time. For the original Christian faith philosophy is foolishness. To philosophize is to ask "Why are there essents rather than nothing?" [1]

Historical realities, in the form of the vast diversities in philosophical principle and conclusion taught by medieval thinkers, stand opposed to any univocal usage of the term "Scholastic philosophy." But the effort to sort out the ambiguities involved in using such an identity-card inevitably brings one face to face with another historical reality, Christian philosophy. For according to many of the historians we have consulted above, one of the central features of so-called Scholasticism is the attempt many Christians made throughout the Middle Ages to bring reason to bear on their Christian beliefs. However, that very attempt immediately raises this fundamental question: Can a man still claim to be doing the work of a philosopher if he has committed his intellect to revealed Christian truth in faith? One eminent historian puts it this way:

> We may make use of philosophy to facilitate the acceptance of religious dogma, and then we assimilate philosophy to apologetics; or

we may allow rational conclusions to be judged by their accord
with dogma, and then we are at once in theology; or perhaps, in
order to get over these difficulties we may make up our minds to
say that "Christian philosophy" simply means "true philosophy," and
then there is no more reason why this philosophy should be discovered and professed by Christians than by unbelievers or anti-Chris-
tians; or we may finally call a philosophy "Christian" simply because it is compatible with Christianity, but then, if this compatibility be a mere fact, and due to nothing but a purely rational
working out of first principles, the relation of this philosophy to
Christianity remains just as extrinsic as in the preceding case, and
if, on the other hand, the compatibility results from some special
effort to achieve it, we are back at once in theology and apologetics.
And so we go around: it looks as though we were trying to define,
in distinct terms, a contradictory concept; . . .[2]

It would be very difficult to put the case against Christian philosophy
with greater precision and cogency. Yet the argument we have just presented is not the work of a scholar unsympathetic to the notion he is
examining; it is, rather, an honest statement of the counter-argument by
a man who has *defended* the validity of Christian philosophy for over
thirty years: Etienne Gilson. He asks: Why defend a notion that appears
contradictory and has given rise to endless controversy?

An historian's experience led him to do so. Early in his academic career
Gilson was engaged in the purely scholarly task of trying to understand
the antecedents of the thought of René Descartes, the great seventeenth-
century French philosopher. Gradually he found himself pushed back, by
the inexorable instinct of an historian, to Suarez (in the late sixteenth
century), Scotus (in the fourteenth century), Thomas Aquinas and Bonaventure (in the thirteenth century), Bernard (in the twelfth century),
Augustine (in the fifth century), and finally to Plotinus and even earlier
Greek philosophers. In the process Gilson realized that the formulation
of many philosophical questions had undergone a change during the long
interval between classical ancient thought and the rise of modern ra-
tionalistic and scientific speculation. So he asked himself: Why? Was it
because philosophy had undergone a change as *philosophy* during the
so-called Age of Faith? If so, perhaps the philosophy or philosophies that
had wrought such a change should be given the name "Christian philosophy."

Gilson has not hesitated to use that name; indeed, he has written books
specifically bearing it in their titles: *History of Christian Philosophy in
the Middle Ages, The Christian Philosophy of St. Thomas Aquinas, The
Christian Philosophy of St. Augustine.* But even in the early years of his

career challengers arose to contest his defense of the notion. Thus, in 1928 Emile Bréhier gave three lectures at Brussels in which he addressed himself to the question: Is there a Christian philosophy? Bréhier gave the categorical answer: no, there is not. The debate was continued in 1931 and in subsequent years and soon brought Maurice Blondel, Léon Brunschwicg, Jacques Maritain, Pierre Mandonnet, Fernand van Steenberghen and a host of others into the lists.[3] To appreciate the direction the debate took and the central issues involved, one must have clearly in view the formulation Bréhier gave to the questions he asked. In the symposium held in 1931 he asked: What is the *intellectual* vocation of Christianity? What *positive* part has Christianity played in the development of philosophic thought? Did Christianity *create* its own philosophy? [4] [Emphasis added.]

Let us make the central issue crystal clear. The question is not this one: Was there *any* philosophy in the thought of St. Augustine and St. Thomas—philosophy that they deemed compatible with their faith? On *that* question Bréhier is quite clear. There is, indeed, philosophy in these two medieval Christians' writings. But Bréhier adds:

. . . there is not a Christian philosophy in St. Augustine at all, i.e. a concept of the universe grafted onto dogma. The only philosophy he knows, the only one we find in him, is the philosophy of Plato and Plotinus.[5]

And there is philosophy in St. Thomas' works, too. As Bréhier puts it:

In St. Thomas, philosophy is not at all a part of religion; it is the work of human reason and it does not appear as a collaborator with salvation in any way whatsoever; on the other hand, however, it is not a weapon against Christianity, either; it enters, as an integral element, into a Christian life which is no less intellectual than religious.[6]

The real question does not arise at *that* point. It is, rather, this one: Did Christianity make any contribution to that philosophy?

That is why Gilson has stated the case as he has. He is not concerned with defending a Christian philosophy that would only be a repetition of Plato or Plotinus, or perhaps an extension of Aristotle's thought—a repetition and an extension that would simply stand side by side with Christian belief. He makes no effort to defend as *philosophy* a body of conclusions that might be drawn from articles of faith or a collection of arguments intended to defend those articles. That is theology or apologetics. He takes his stand, rather, directly against Bréhier's central question: did Christianity play any positive role in the development of philosophic thought? Gilson's answer is: "Yes, it did." [7] The evidence he offers represents the results of over thirty years of intense historical and philosophic research.

As Gilson points out,[8] Christians have always been concerned with the questions philosophy has posed to them. From the very start philosophy came to them cloaked in the garb of paganism. But *must* it be pagan? Is it intrinsic to its very nature to be pagan? Or is philosophy's pagan character only an historical *fact?* Christians have always turned to St. Paul for counsel, and some of them have taken the following text to be St. Paul's final word on philosophy. In the *Epistle to the Colossians* St. Paul says:

> Beware lest any man cheat you by philosophy and vain deceit, according to the tradition of men . . . .[9]

Thus, in the third century, Tertullian found philosophy to be a rich source of heresy. As he says:

> Philosophy it is which is the material of the world's wisdom, the real interpreter of the nature and dispensation of God. Indeed, heresies are themselves instigated by philosophy. The same subject matter is discussed over and over again by the heretics and philosophers; the same arguments are involved.[10]

A similar distrust of philosophy or dialectics was often expressed during the debates of the eleventh century concerning the propriety of monks cultivating secular learning and of Christian thinkers compelling the truths of faith to undergo the scrutiny of Aristotle's logic. As Peter Damian remarks in one place,[11] if philosophy were necessary for man's salvation, God would have sent philosophers to convert the world, not fishermen! In *The Book of 'The Lord be with you'* he expresses his feelings about philosophy and secular learning in this way:

> I spurn Plato, the searcher into the hidden things of nature, who set a measure to the movements of the planets, and calculated the courses of the stars; Pythagoras, who divided the round world into its regions with his mathematician's rod, means nothing to me; I renounce the much-thumbed books of Nicomachus, and Euclid too, round-shouldered from poring over his complex geometrical problems; the rhetoricians with their syllogisms and the cavillings of the sophists are useless in this matter. Let the gymnasts shiver in their

nakedness for love of wisdom, and the peripatetics seek truth at the bottom of a well.

For I seek from you the Highest Truth, not that which lies ignobly hidden in a well, but that which rose from the earth, and, made manifest to all the world, reigns in eternal majesty in Heaven.[12]

In the twelfth century, St. Bernard expressed the conviction that philosophy was a useless undertaking for a Christian because a Christian already knows more than any philosopher.

We learn from history that there were some in former times—I believe they have very few successors, if any at all—whose all-engrossing occupation and only care it was to investigate the laws and dispositions of natural objects, so that for the most part they not merely disdained to inquire about the utility of things for human ends, but magnanimously despised them under this aspect, using only the vilest of them for food, and in the scantiest measure. These men called themselves philosophers; but in my opinion they should rather be called the slaves of curiosity and pride. . . . I rejoice to know, dearest brethren, that you belong to this third school, the school of the Holy Ghost, where you are being taught "goodness and discipline and knowledge" (*Ps.* cxviii, 66), so that each one of you can say with the Psalmist, "I have understood more than all my teachers" (*ibid.*, 99). Wherefore, O my brother, dost thou make such a boast? Is it because thou art clothed with purple and fine linen and feastest more sumptuously than anyone else? (*Luke*, xvi, 19). Or perhaps it is because thou hast understood or hast endeavored to understand the reasonings of Plato and the subtleties of Aristotle? "God forbid!" thou answerest. "It is because I have sought Thy commandments, O Lord" (*Ps.*, cxviii, 100).[13]

Fear of appearing proud has often deterred Christians from philosophy; as the author of the *Imitation of Christ* (very probably Thomas à Kempis) says:

Every man naturally desires to know, but what does knowledge avail without the fear of God? Better indeed is a humble peasant who serves God than a proud philosopher who watches the stars and neglects the knowledge of himself. He who knows himself well is vile in his own sight, and does not delight in the praises of men.[14]

A second group of Christians, on the other hand, has found advice of a totally different kind in St. Paul. From him they have learned not to suspect the deceits of philosophy, but, rather, to cultivate it. For in the *Epistle to the Romans* St. Paul says:

> For the invisible things of Him, from the creation of the world, are clearly seen, being understood by the things that are made.[15]

As a result many have been challenged to learn of God through the things He has made, and that challenge has been variously interpreted by Christians of different ages. St. Augustine, for example, interpreted it to mean that one may, indeed, gain an understanding of God through His creatures, but to do so he must first believe. It seems clear that his own personal experience led him to this view. Before his conversion to Christianity, Augustine had been in turn skeptic and Manichaean, and in each instance he had looked to reason for a satisfactory philosophy of life and had not found it. After hearing St. Ambrose at Milan, he began to give serious consideration to Christianity, but without final conviction. Augustine then turned to the books of the Platonists—mainly to Plotinus—and suddenly he realized that everything the philosophers had been trying to say had already been said in Revelation. In a passage of his *Confessions,* that has become classic, St. Augustine describes his experience:

> . . . Thou procurest for me, by the instrumentality of one inflated with most monstrous pride, certain books of the Platonists, translated from Greek into Latin. And therein I read, not indeed in the same words, but to the same effect, enforced by many and varied reasons, that, In the beginning was the Word, and the Word was with God, and the Word was God. The same was in the beginning with God. All things were made by Him: and without Him was not any thing made that was made. That which was made by Him is life. . . .[16]

In short, when St. Augustine read certain passages from the *Enneads,* in which Plotinus describes the two highest beings (that he called the One and Intellect), he was certain that he was reading the opening passages of St. John's Gospel. Only the words were different, and the statements of Plotinus were supported by "many and varied reasons." Compare these two texts and try to share the Saint's impression:

We call Intelligence the Image of the One. Let us explain this. It is its image because that which is begotten by the One must possess many of its characteristics and re-

In the beginning was the Word, and the Word was with God; and the Word was God. He was in the beginning with God. All things were made through him, and with-

semble it, as light resembles the sun. But the One is not Intelligence. How then can it produce Intelligence? By its turning towards itself the One has vision. It is this vision which constitutes Intelligence. . . . Intelligence has in itself consciousness of the power to produce and to define Being out of itself by means of the power it derives from the One. It sees that Being is a part of that which belongs to the One and proceeds from it, that it owes all its force to the One, and that it achieves Being because of the One.[17]

out him was made nothing that has been made. In him was life, and the life was the light of men.[18]

Even St. Paul's *Epistle to the Romans*, which we quoted earlier, appeared in Plotinus as well. For in a later passage in the *Confessions* Augustine says:

. . . Having read those books of the Platonists, and being admonished by them to search for incorporeal truth, I saw Thy invisible things, understood by those things that are made . . . .[19]

From this experience St. Augustine drew a lesson that has inspired a long line of Christian thinkers from his day to our own: unless you believe, you will not understand. It was a lesson he might already have learned from the Prophet Isaias! [20] In St. Augustine's eyes, the best way to reason about God is to be found in the thought of Plato and Plotinus: to understand God, turn to the things of nature (conceived as the Platonists would conceive them in their philosophies) and discover what those things tell us about Him. Sometimes, however, the actual texts and arguments of Plato and Plotinus are not enough, and then reason must create the concepts and arguments needed to understand the faith. And so we have the example of St. Anselm in the twelfth century.

St. Anselm was a faithful disciple of the ideal that Augustine has set before us; he was, however, a consummate logician as well. Saint Augustine had found that Plotinus expressed the essentials of St. John's Gospel, but "enforced by many and varied reasons;" Saint Anselm set out to discover in the logic and grammar of his day "necessary reasons" for the things he believed. Convinced of the primacy of faith, Anselm did not seek to submit it to the examination of reason nor to replace it with rational arguments; but likewise convinced of the worth of reason, he sought to find the point where reason and dialectics would do their own full work and produce rational arguments that would converge on the truths of faith. Thus he developed his famous speculation about God's existence. The God St. Anselm *believed* to exist may well be defined by a *logician* as "the greatest conceivable being." Now a logician approaching such a concept armed with his principle of contradiction, must conclude that it would be contradictory for the being so conceived not to exist.[21] And so there is a necessary reason for saying that the God in whom the Christian believes must exist.

This argument is the work of a logician provided with the concept of God given in Christian faith. To call it an ontological argument is a gross misunderstanding and a grievous misnomer. St. Anselm did not know Christian Wolff; he had no idea of an ontology that would explore the implications of a general notion of being. St. Anselm was a realist and for him essences were real; an essence that included all being in its reality could not help but exist. Such an essence *must* exist; others, that do not include such a fulness of reality, may or may not exist. God, being such an essence, must exist. Later, when St. Thomas[22] and Kant[23] undertake to criticize that argument, they do not do so on the grounds that Anselm's notion of God is taken from faith; they criticize it, rather, because the conclusion does not follow rationally and philosophically—as *they* understand reason and philosophy. In short: they evaluate a *philosophical* argument in the light of philosophical procedures that, they feel, were violated.

In the thirteenth century a new prospect opened up as Aristotle became known to Christian thinkers as a natural philosopher, metaphysician and moral philosopher.[24] Previously Aristotle had been known to Boethius and Abelard for the "old logic" of the *Categories* and *Perihermeneias* and, later in the twelfth century, for the "new logic" of the *Prior* and *Posterior Analytics*, the *Topics* and *Elenchics*. But during the first quarter of the thirteenth century when Latin translations of the *Physics*, *Metaphysics* and *Nicomachean Ethics* became available in Paris, a new Aristotle became known to Christian scholars and new possibilities for Christian speculation opened up. The prospect was this: use the philosophical tools Aristotle has developed and see what understanding they can give us of our faith. For is not Aristotle the master of human reason? And has he not taught us that human knowledge must start with the individual things we find around us in the sensible world? Why not follow him as he sought the highest cause of the motion he observed in things? Aristotle found such a cause in a mover that is itself not moved; perhaps the Christian could gain some understanding of the God in whom he believes if he were to follow a similar course.

Now that was an enticing prospect. It was, however, soon to prove that it was fraught with many pitfalls. For suppose, in following the path marked out by Aristotle, we were to find that the universe was *eternal,* that the mover or movers were *indifferent* to the affairs of men, that men were thoroughly *mortal* (their souls included!), that man's happiness was to consist in the exercise of *civic virtue.* What would the Christian do then? Leave Aristotle alone? But, then, how gain understanding? Go part of the way with Aristotle but only accept conclusions that do not immediately contradict the faith and reject those that do? That is not a very consistent position! Indeed, it is a position open to this very grave danger: a person of greater intellectual perspicacity might very well prove that the so-called "innocent" conclusions are necessarily consequent upon the more "threatening" ones! Surely *that* would be a most precarious position for a Christian to occupy.

A stronger position would be to seek some accommodation with Aristotle. That was precisely the ambition of Siger of Brabant who taught in the Faculty of Arts in the University of Paris during the latter half of the thirteenth century. Siger was convinced of the validity of Aristotle's reasoning, but he was also a believing Christian. His solution—and one that may appear strange to our eyes (although *he* sincerely held it)—was that we must not seek *truth* from human reason; all that one can get from rational speculation is *necessary conclusions.* For *truth* one must have recourse to faith.

Although St. Thomas was Siger's contemporary at Paris and just as thoroughly appreciated the contribution Aristotle and human reason might make to understanding, he thoroughly disagreed with Siger's solution to the problem of relating faith to reason. St. Thomas' own position depends on carefully distinguishing between the various ways truth can exist in the human reason. So before we begin to explore St. Thomas' thought to discover the role philosophy plays in his thinking, we should be quite clear in our own minds about the way he conceives truth is present in faith, theology and the various sciences. Quite often he speaks of faith as concerned with simple, everlasting, first truth or as a knowledge of things not seen. Here is a typical example:

> Faith implies assent of the intellect to that which is believed. Now the intellect assents to a thing in two ways. First, through being moved by its very object, which is known either by itself (as in the case of first principles, which are held by the habit of understanding), or through something else already known (as in the case of conclusions which are held by the habit of science). Secondly, the intellect assents to something not through being sufficiently moved to this assent by its proper object but through an act of choice,

whereby it turns voluntarily to one side rather than to another: and
if this be accompanied by doubt and fear of the opposite side,
there will be opinion, while if there be certainty and no fear of the
opposite side, there will be faith. Now those things are said to be
seen which, of themselves, move the intellect or sense to knowledge
of them. Wherefore it is evident that neither faith nor opinion can
be of things seen either by the senses or by the intellect.[25]

The result of such an argument, when taken in isolation from the rest of
his discussion of faith, is likely to give the impression that St. Thomas
overly-intellectualizes faith and makes it a work or possession of the intellect alone.

It is true that he does make the act of belief reside primarily in the intellect as in its subject,[26] but in estimating his overall position we should
not overlook this fact: St. Thomas makes his own the definition St. Paul
gives of faith: "Faith is the substance of things to be hoped for, the evidence of things not seen" (Hebrews, xi, 1). And in interpreting that text
St. Thomas points out how all the various definitions given by St. Augustine, St. John Damascene and Dionysius find accommodation in the definition St. Paul gives. The intellect does, indeed, act when it gives its assent in believing; it is, however, determined to the object to which it
assents in virtue of a command given by the will. The act of faith, then,
has a two-fold order: first, it is ordered to the will's object, i.e. to whatever is good and is marked with the character of an end; second, it is
ordered to the intellect's object, i.e. to whatever is true. And inasmuch as
faith is a *theological* virtue having God as its object, it has the same being, God, as both object and end. Thus, for example, faith does have first
and eternal truth as its *object* (as Dionysius had said)[27] insofar as that
truth is not *seen* by man's intellect. But that very same truth is also the
*end* of the intellect and faith, precisely as of things *not seen*, is a truth-
to-be-hoped-for. God is not only a being in whose existence one may
believe, He is also a being to be sought after by the intellect in love—
and love is only satisfied by laying hold of its object's *being*. In short, the
intellect's truth is not merely an object to be known, it is also a good to
be possessed. And it is as a good that the intellect's truth becomes a good
or end commanded by the will. Materially, then, faith is of the intellect,
but formally it is of the will and charity. St. Thomas explains it in this
way:

As appears from what has been said above, voluntary acts take their
species from their end, which is the will's object. Now that which
gives a thing its species functions as a form in natural things. Therefore the form of any voluntary act is, in a manner, the end to which

that act is directed, both because it takes its species from it, and because the mode of an action should correspond proportionately to the end. Now it is evident from what has been said that the act of faith is directed to the object of the will, i.e. the good, as to its end; and this good which is the end of faith, viz. the divine Good, is the proper object of charity. Therefore charity is called the form of faith, in so far as the act of faith is perfected and formed by charity.[28]

So for St. Thomas faith is not simply of the intellect, nor is it merely concerned with knowledge; it is just as much an act stemming from the will and is just as truly an act of love. One might speak of it as a knowledge gained from love, love of God and eternal life. As a virtue of the intellect, faith makes the intellect capable of easily and readily following the commands of the will to know God because that is what is good for the intellect. St. Thomas uses an analogy to express his thought on this point:

Faith is not in the speculative intellect absolutely, but according as it is subject to the command of the will, just as temperance is in the concupiscible appetite according as it participates in some way in reason. Now when the good of any power requires that that power be subject to some higher power so as to follow its command, not only must that higher power be perfected so that it commands or directs correctly, but the inferior, too, must be perfected that it may obey promptly. Hence, a person who has a right reason but an unruly concupiscible appetite, does not have the virtue of temperance because he is beset by passions, even though he is not carried away by them. Thus he does not perform the work of the virtue easily and pleasantly, and this is required by a virtue. For this temperance must be present, the concupiscible appetite must itself be perfected by a habit so that it is subject to the will without any difficulty. In this way the virtue of temperance is said to exist in the concupiscible appetite. Similarly, in order that the intellect follow the will's command promptly, there must be some habit in the speculative intellect. This is the divinely infused habit of faith.[29]

In short, the human intellect does assent firmly and with conviction to truths about God and eternal life revealed in faith, but in saying this it should be kept in mind that it is only part of the story, the material part. The assent is due to the will and is a true act of love.

Now for St. Thomas some truths are simply of faith; for example, truths about the Incarnation and the Trinity; other truths may be of faith for some and of science for others, for instance, the existence of God. Those truths that are held by faith cannot be held by the same intellect through science. St. Thomas expresses it in this way:

All science is derived from self-evident and therefore *seen* principles; wherefore all objects of science must needs be, in a fashion, seen. Now as stated above (A.4) it is impossible that one and the same thing should be believed and seen by the same person. Hence, it is equally impossible for one and the same thing to be an object of science and of belief for the same reason. It may happen, however, that a thing which is an object of vision or science for one, is believed by another: since we hope to see some day what we now believe about the Trinity, according to I *Cor.*, xiii, 12: "*We see now through a glass in a dark manner: but then face to face:*" which vision the angels possess already; so that what we believe, they see. In like manner it may happen that what is an object of vision or scientific knowledge for one man, even in the state of a wayfarer is, for another man, an object of faith, because he does not know it by demonstration. Nevertheless that which is proposed to be believed equally by all, is equally unknown by them all as an object of science: such are the things which are of faith simply. Consequently, faith and science are not about the same thing.[30]

A person may take those truths of faith as starting points for reflection and try to gain some understanding of them. And then one is doing theology, a part of sacred doctrine. St. Thomas states:

Sacred doctrine is a science. We must bear in mind that there are two kinds of science. There are some which proceed from principles known by the natural light of the intellect, such as arithmetic and geometry and the like. There are also some which proceed from principles known by the light of a higher science: thus the science of optics proceeds from principles established by geometry, and music from principles established by arithmetic. So it is that sacred doctrine is a science because it proceeds from principles made known by the light of a higher science, namely, the science of God and the blessed. Hence, just as music accepts on authority the principles taught by the arithmetician, so sacred doctrine accepts the principles revealed by God.[31]

Consequently, the study of God that is a part of sacred doctrine is a science, not because it proves truths of faith, but because it takes its principles from a higher science and uses the logic of scientific argument. St. Thomas is quite outspoken, in fact, in his criticism of those who would try to *prove* an article of faith. He says:

. . . that the world began to exist is an object of faith, but not of demonstration. And it is useful to consider this, lest anyone, presuming to demonstrate what is of faith, should bring forward reasons that are not cogent, so as to give occasion to unbelievers to laugh, thinking that on such grounds we believe things that are of faith.[32]

And again:

> The reasons employed by holy men to prove things of faith are not demonstrations, they are either persuasive arguments showing that what is proposed to our faith is not impossible, or else they are proofs drawn from the principles of faith, i.e. from the authority of Holy Writ, as Dionysius declares (*Div. Nom.*, ii). Whatever is based on these principles is as well proved in the eyes of the faithful as a conclusion drawn from self-evident principles is in the eyes of all.[33]

Finally, according to St. Thomas, science is possible—even a science of God apart from the theology that is a part of sacred doctrine—when reason finds its starting point in natural principles, i.e. in the things of the sensible world. This is how St. Thomas explains it:

> Sciences are diversified according to the diverse nature of their knowable objects. For the astronomer and the physicist both prove the same conclusion—that the earth, for instance, is round: the astronomer by means of mathematics (i.e. abstracting from matter), but the physicist by means of matter itself. Hence there is no reason why those things which are treated by the philosophical disciplines, so far as they can be known by the light of natural reason, may not also be treated by another science so far as they are known by the light of divine revelation. Hence the theology included in sacred doctrine differs in genus from that theology which is part of philosophy.[34]

Let us pause now and summarize the main points in the view St. Thomas is presenting:

(a) Faith is of things not seen. The intellect accepts them for reasons other than evidence presented by the human intellect's natural objects—sensible things.

(b) Some truths are *simply* of faith—e.g. the Incarnation, Trinity etc.; others may be of faith for some men, of science for others—e.g. the existence of God.

(c) Truths held by faith cannot be held by the same intellect through science.

(d) Theology (as a part of sacred doctrine) may be a science in the sense that it employs the logic of demonstration and proceeds from principles derived from faith; it is *not* a science in the sense that it proves truths of faith by demonstrations proceeding from natural principles of reason.

(e) Science, apart from the science of theology (as part of sacred doctrine), is possible when reason finds its starting point in natural principles, i.e. in the things of the sensible world. In this sense there is even a science of theology different in kind from the theology derived from truths of faith.

With that as our preparation, let us now come to the central point of our discussion, Christian philosophy. Is there room for philosophy in St. Thomas' economy of human knowledge? Did St. Thomas actually develop a philosophy? What part did Aristotle and the other recognized philosophers play in St. Thomas' philosophizing? And finally, to answer Bréhier's question: Did Christianity play an important role in the development of Aquinas' philosophy?

The first question concerns the order of essences. Is there any contradiction between what St. Thomas understands philosophy to be and what human knowledge is? Human knowledge as *science* differs in the certitude of its principles and conclusions from opinion and takes some characteristic of sensible things as its subject—color, heat, figure, life, growth—and seeks to understand why it is as it is. Philosophy does exactly that. It differs from other scientific disciplines in that its subject is more fundamental and the causes it seeks are more universal in their effects. But in all that is essential to it, philosophy is in no way contradictory to the nature of human knowledge; it is but one of many human sciences. And what the philosopher does is *not* what the theologian does. Thus, in discussing the question: Is faith a virtue?, St. Thomas shows how clearly he differentiates between the philosopher's treatment of a fundamental human problem, human happiness, and the theologian's consideration of the same question:

> The ultimate good that the philosopher reflects upon is one thing, the one the theologian ponders is another. Anything proportioned to a human power is deemed to be the ultimate good by the philosopher, and it consists in an act of man himself. Thus, he says that happiness is an operation. According to the philosopher, then, an act whose principle is a virtue is called good absolutely insofar as it is suited to a power because it perfects it. So whenever the philosopher discovers a habit that elicits such an act, he says it is a virtue— whether it exists in the intellective part of man, for example, science and similar intellectual virtues whose act is the good of the power itself, namely, reflecting on what is true; or in the affective part, for example, temperance, fortitude and the other moral virtues. The

theologian, on the other hand, considers the ultimate good to be something that surpasses the capacity of nature, to wit, eternal life, as has been stated before. So he does not think that the good exists absolutely in human acts because he does not place the end in such acts. He places it, rather, in the order to that good which does constitute the end. So he asserts that only that act is completely good that is proximately ordered to the final good, i.e. that is meritorious of eternal life. And the theologian says that every such act is the act of a virtue, and any habit that elicits such an act is called a virtue.[35]

Philosophy, then, is an accomplishment of human reason contemplating natural things; it is not theology but may exist in the human intellect alongside theology.

The second question concerns the *existence* of philosophy rather than its nature. Did St. Thomas actually philosophize? We have seen that he recognized the *possibility* of philosophy side by side with the other human sciences. But did he *actually* develop a philosophy? Well, St. Thomas did recognize that philosophy exists and he tells us, for instance, that the philosophers have proved demonstratively that God exists.[36] And he himself actually did undertake the same philosophical task. Moreover, on page after page of his writings he has reasoned about the things of nature—bodies, animals, man, his body, sensible and intellectual knowledge, freedom—with a view to gaining necessary, scientific knowledge. And the Averroists, the most ardent philosophers and rationalists of his day, recognized St. Thomas' eminence in philosophy. One of their greatest representatives, Siger of Brabant, spoke of St. Thomas along with St. Albert as "men pre-eminent in philosophy." [37] Surely it must be deemed special pleading to say that a man like Siger really did not know what philosophy was and who was or was not a philosopher. It really is quite pointless to retort that St. Thomas was called a theologian, not a philosopher, by many of his contemporaries. For to these men a philosopher was usually a pagan (like Plato or Aristotle) or an infidel (like the Arabian philosophers Averroës and Avicenna).[38] St. Thomas was a Christian and a theologian. But that is not to say that there was no philosophy in the thought of St. Thomas the theologian. Although philosophy is one thing and theology quite another, the person who is a theologian may very well philosophize.[39] This is exactly what St. Thomas was and did. He expressly states the role that philosophy can play in the work of the theologian, and he gives us the reason for his position:

Thus, in sacred doctrine we are able to make a threefold use of philosophy:

1. First, to demonstrate those truths that are preambles of faith. Such are the truths about God that can be proved by natural reason—that God exists, that God is one; such truths about God or about His creatures, subject to philosophical proof, faith presupposes.
2. Secondly, to give a clearer notion, by certain similitudes, of the truths of faith, as Augustine in his book *De Trinitate* employed many comparisons taken from the teachings of the philosophers to aid understanding of the Trinity.
3. In the third place, to resist those who speak against the faith, either by showing that their statements are false, or by showing that they are not necessarily true.[40]

That is philosophy in the hands of the *theologian*, but to be used it must first exist *as philosophy*. And the reason it can so exist is, according to St. Thomas, that faith does not destroy the natural capacities of human reason but perfects them:

> . . . gifts of grace are added to those of nature in such a way that they do not destroy the latter, but rather perfect them; wherefore also the light of faith, which is gratuitously infused into our minds, does not destroy the natural light of cognition, which is in us by nature.[41]

Strangely enough, many of St. Thomas' contemporaries felt that he went too far in his use of philosophy! Roger Bacon, in describing the seven sins that had come to befoul the studies of his day, described the first sin in this way: philosophy predominates in theology.[42] As Bacon put it:

> The greater part of the questions in the *Summae* of theology is pure philosophy.[43]

There was too much discussion of being, human knowledge, the movers of the planets, and so on, in theological works to suit his taste!

Let us now turn to our third question: What part did Aristotle and the other recognized philosophers play in St. Thomas' philosophizing? In answering this question we must be careful to distinguish St. Thomas the *expositor* of Aristotle's thought from St. Thomas as he philosophizes in his own name. As an interpreter of what Aristotle *said*, St. Thomas is concerned with being as faithful as possible to Aristotle's *text* (as he had it!) and to *his* thought. When St. Thomas philosophizes himself, he is concerned with the truth which reason can discover in things. In this context he may at one time, as we have already seen, evaluate Aristotle's arguments as dialectical or probable rather than demonstrative or surely convincing; at other times he may make Aristotle intend things Aristotle never intended. For we must understand that St. Thomas uses Aristotle as an authority but only so that he can speak in Aristotle's name when the truth he, i.e. St. Thomas, sees in things warrants it. Aristotle's name does not yield philosophic proof, things do; if Aristotle has said the same thing, even though for different reasons, so much the better. But while Aristotle is such an authority for St. Thomas, he is certainly not the only authority. If philosophers like Plato, Gabirol or Averroës (respectively Greek, Jewish and Arabic) advance arguments or provide insights that are useful to Aquinas' search for philosophical knowledge, he will take them even though they may not be Aristotelian at all. But a reader of St. Thomas' text must be careful when St. Thomas is writing in his own name, using terms or arguments taken from other sources. St. Thomas uses a whole range of terms—"being," "act," "form," "cause," "mover"— that might come from Aristotle, Avicenna or Gabirol. But they are given a completely different philosophic meaning *proper* to St. Thomas' own thought. Plato and Aristotle can stand side by side in St. Thomas, not as threads in a loosely woven eclecticism, but completely transformed. This transformation can, however, only be understood in terms of the answer to our fourth question: Did Christianity play an important role in the development of Aquinas' philosophy?

According to the Old and New Testaments, God showed Himself to be a divinity far different from any of the divinities of Greek mythology or the pagan religions. He was seen to be a unique divinity, the one and only God, not one of many gods; a God bearing the name "Jahweh," instead of a name men might know from human experience ("Sun," "Moon," "Earth," "Thunder"); a God of love who brought forth beings out of nothingness, rather than a god who merely presides over human destinies. And men were challenged to understand the mysteries of this God. If they were *not* philosophers, they might see a law-giver in God, one to worship, a jealous God on whom men's lives and happiness depended; if they *were* philosophers, they might try to understand Him as the philosophers had tried to comprehend their divinities. As we have seen, St. Augustine tried to understand the Trinity of Persons he found in *his* God by having recourse to the trinity of substances Plotinus had discovered in his reflections on nature. St. Thomas, too, tried in the self-same spirit to understand God with the help of the philosophers, and mainly of Aristotle. He soon discovered, however, that the intellectual tools the philosophers had devised could not uncover the riches of meaning he found in the world revealed to him as the handiwork of God. Having looked at the world as Aristotle and Plato saw it (an eternal world of things that merely change in shape and size, that move from place to place, or that find their explanation in an ideal world), he now saw that it was a world of things that need not be, that have no *necessary* reason within them that they exist. The concepts that Aristotle had devised to formulate his world of eternally moving things (matter, form, substance, potency) or the principles Plato had suggested to understand the world of becoming (form, participation) could not capture the reality of *existing* things. New philosophical concepts, principles and demonstrations had to be fashioned, and the only models St. Thomas had at his disposal for philosophic work were Greek in origin. So he had to work with the tools he had; the use he made of them and the new meaning he injected into them had to remain, however, strictly philosophical. Thus, a new doctrine of matter or actuality could not be drawn from and established by the evidence of the Scriptures or the authority of holy men. If a new meaning were to be found for ancient concepts, it had to come from consulting the very same sources of evidence Aristotle had consulted in developing his doctrine of form from the antecedents Plato had provided, namely, the world of things examined sensibly and rationally. Where Aristotle would consult the ancient physicists in his search, St. Thomas would look to Averroës and the Arabic scientists for help. And if form were to be understood as a mere *principle* of material being rather than as substance, it had to be in virtue of rational, philosophical evidence. Ultimately the very fundamental structure of being itself had to be re-examined: What is the basic structure of being? Why do we call things "beings?" Rational and sensible evidence convinced St. Thomas that unless things exist, nothing can be said of them. Do material things exist? Reason and sense convinced him that they *do*. Does man, as a distinct kind of material being, exist? Human experience convinced him that he does. Does God exist? Philosophical experience assured him that He does. In short: St. Thomas' experience as a *Christian* led him to re-examine current views of the world, the structure of things, the composition of man, his freedom and destiny, his ultimate happiness and the cause from which he sprang. That experience led him to ask *philosophical* questions (in addition to many other different kinds of questions) about these things and to search for philosophical answers grounded in viable philosophical evidence. It enabled him to gain a glimmer of human understanding of the revelation of God as "The Being Who is;" Christian experience led him to ask the meaning of that "name," but philosophical meditation upon things *as beings* (i.e. as existents, as things that *are*) brought him to a *human* knowledge of God insofar as that was possible. And just as the Greek concern for *being*—and in our own day Martin Heidegger defines *Dasein* by its fundamental concern for *Sein* (being)—led St. Thomas to develop new philosophical concepts, so, too, has the Christian pre-occupation with *love* led many Christians today to seek philosophical understanding of the God of love in the analysis of the human experience of love. As a consequence we are witnessing in the works of Gabriel Marcel, for instance, the fashioning of new philosophical concepts inspired by a Christian's experience, but developed with true philosophical (phenomenological) tools. St. Thomas' philosophical work is, then, but one example of Christian philosophy; it is one way—and there are certainly others—in which the Christian, who happens to be possessed of philosophical skills, can seek philosophical answers to questions prompted by Christian faith rather than by Euclidean geometry, Newtonian physics, Freudian psychology or Marxist economics.

Christianity, then, did play a fundamental role in the development of St. Thomas' philosophy. And philosophy has never recovered from the touch of Revelation first felt in the early Fathers. For in spite of the fact that their experience as scientists—whether as geometrician, mathematician or physicist—has prompted them to ask many of their philosophical questions, Descartes, Malebranche, Leibnitz, Spinoza, Locke, Kant and Hegel all philosophize with the God of Revelation in mind. Indeed, it is tragic to see Martin Heidegger deny the reality of Christian philosophy while trying to find an answer to a question that has come from Christian speculation:[44] Why is there something rather than nothing? And one of Jean-Paul Sartre's most annoying philosophical problems arises from his view of God, the Christian God, as *causa sui!* [45] Indeed, could anything be more Christian—and more tragic—than Sartre's man trying to *be* such a *causa sui!*

Finally, two comments are in order in connection with Bertrand Russell's statement quoted earlier: "He [i.e. Aquinas] is not engaged in an inquiry, the result of which it is impossible to know in advance." This statement is only superficially true. Before St. Thomas philosophized he did not "know" that God existed—he *believed* it. For although he was certain of it at the dictate of his will, he did not understand it philosophically and could not prove it rationally. In that sense Aquinas did *not* know God's existence. On his own side, Lord Russell "knew" his mathematical conclusions before he began to philosophize about them— not through his will or faith, but through mathematical reasoning; but he only *understood* them philosophically after he had created his wonderful logical analysis of mathematical thinking. Previous attempts to understand numbers certainly helped, but Lord Russell had to fashion his own philosophical arguments; St. Thomas found some help in his predecessors' work but he, too, had to construct his own philosophy before he *understood*. To do so he had to philosophize just as truly in his own way as Lord Russell had to do in his.

This leads to a second comment. Lord Russell says: "The finding of arguments for a conclusion given in advance is not philosophy." St. Thomas would have been perplexed at discovering a conclusion given *before* the argument. But if the statement merely means that a proposition, given first as *true*, was then *proved*, St. Thomas would agree that it is not philosophy. He would probably have called it bad theology! The real question is this: Where do the arguments come from? The philosopher uses various means, depending upon his philosophical convictions, to reach conclusions about what he is convinced is real. St. Thomas was convinced of this conclusion, among many others: *What* anything is, i.e. its essence (an individual man's humanity), is *real* only because a unique act of existing makes the *individual* real. Aristotle did not think so, nor did Plato. It represents a philosophical conclusion St. Thomas himself reached. One may disagree with that philosophical conclusion, but it remains an authentic philosophical conclusion—unless one believes, as Lord Russell apparently does, that philosophy has nothing to say about being!

Here we are brought to the next step in our inquiry. What is philosophy? What is philosophy for St. Thomas? Down to this point we have tried to understand the reasons for calling his thought a *Christian* philosophy; let us now try to see how he goes about his work in philosophy.

# CHAPTER III

# *THE CHRISTIAN AS PHILOSOPHER*

As for me, in stretching my canvas and taking up my palette and brush, I am not vexed that masters should have painted before me in styles which I have no power and no occasion to imitate; nor do I expect future generations to be satisfied with always repainting my pictures. Agreement is sweet, being a form of friendship; it is also a stimulus to insight, and helpful, as contradiction is not; and I certainly hope to find agreement in some quarters. Yet I am not much concerned about the number of those who may be my friends in the spirit, nor do I care about their chronological distribution, being as much pleased to discover one intellectual kinsman in the past as to imagine two in the future. That in the world at large alien natures should prevail, innumerable and perhaps infinitely various, does not disturb me. On the contrary, I hope fate may manifest to them such objects as they need and can love; and although my sympathy with them cannot be so vivid as with men of my own mind, and in some cases may pass into antipathy, I do not conceive that they are wrong or inferior for being different from me, or from one another. If God and nature can put up with them, why should I raise an objection? But let them take care; for if they have sinned against the facts (as I suspect is often the case) and are kicking against the pricks of matter, they must expect to be brought to confusion on the day of doom or earlier. Not only will their career be brief and troubled, which is the lot of all flesh, but their faith will be stultified by events, which is needless and eternal ignominy for the spirit.[1]

As an historical reality St. Thomas' Christian philosophy came into existence within theology. In company with many other Christians who have experienced a similar need, St. Thomas felt impelled to gain some understanding of his faith. That compulsion inspired him to discover or create concepts and arguments that would throw light on the knowledge he had gained by believing. His search turned his mind to the things he found in the sensible world around him, and he evolved a body of philosophical conclusions in trying to understand why they existed and why they existed *as* they did.

Not so, Bertrand Russell objects. Those concepts and conclusions are not worthy of the name philosophy at all. In Russell's estimation St. Thomas' philosophizing is not a free inquiry because he could not follow reason wherever it led him; St. Thomas could not seriously ask and face the questions intellectual curiosity might suggest, so it is not philosophy but special pleading. St. Thomas is not objectively seeking the truth, but arguing a case handed him by Christian belief. We must, then, come face to face with the vital and challenging question Russell is raising: In what sense can St. Thomas' Christian *philosophy* claim to be *philosophical?*

Before attacking this question directly, let us clear away several side-issues that might intrude themselves to becloud the real problem. In the first place, when St. Thomas' philosophy is said to be a Christian philosophy, it is not implied that it is the only Christian philosophy. Indeed, several Christian philosophies made their appearance within medieval thought alone. As has already been pointed out, St. Augustine had to re-interpret many concepts Plotinus used and re-think many of his philosophical conclusions. Thus, emanation, reminiscence, ideas and matter as Plotinus conceived them did not find a ready place in a world freely created from nothingness and within which each man came into being (after not having previously existed) and through which he had to gain new knowledge for the first time. And although Plotinus' conclusions about his trinity—One, Intelligence and Soul—did stimulate Augustine's mind, it soon became clear to him that they were not really congruent with the Christian Trinity—Father, Son, Holy Spirit. His re-examination produced philosophical concepts and conclusions markedly different from those of his predecessors. William of Occam tried to understand God's freedom and omnipotence with the conceptual tools furnished by Aristotle, but in the process he found it necessary to eliminate traditional concepts of divine ideas, natures and essences. They stood between God and the individual and, therefore, appeared to interfere with the divine freedom. As a consequence, he had to re-define knowledge, science, habit, truth and many other ancillary philosophical notions. In the process he developed the most radical empiricism that had appeared down to that point in history. And by a strange irony of history, Occam's doctrines have attracted the interest of many analytical philosophers of our own time, even though those doctrines were initially inspired by faith and found their true place within a theologian's speculation!

In our own day Gabriel Marcel considers his reflections to be a Christian philosophy, and yet his reflections are totally different from St. Thomas'. In one sense, Marcel's claims are considerably more radical than any we would try to make; for example, the claim that at this period in man's experience philosophy *must* be Christian if it is to be philosophical. His reasons are most interesting. According to Marcel philosophy must deal with human existence and it must do so in a manner that might be loosely termed phenomenological, i.e. the philosopher should not try to *define* human existence but, rather, to *describe* human reactions to reality—whatever reality may be apart from those reactions. Defining love, friendship or loyalty really destroys them by making them abstract objects rather than *lived experiences*. When experience is examined as it is actually lived, it is found to be quite different from the experience one might have of a world of timeless, unchangeable essences. Time and the accumulations of past experience enter to give experience quite a different meaning. Consequently, it is Marcel's view that today men exist and experience the world and other human beings in a way that has been fundamentally affected by 2,000 years of Christian experience. So if we are to describe reality as it is actually experienced by men in their present situation, the description must be Christian. Marcel writes:

> Now, as at any other time, the philosopher is placed in a given historical situation from which he is most unlikely to abstract himself completely; he would deceive himself if he thought that he could create a complete void both within and around himself. Now this historical situation implies as one of its essential data the existence of the Christian fact—quite independently of whether the Christian religion is accepted and its fundamental assertions are regarded as true or false. What appears to me evident is that we cannot reason today as though there were not behind us centuries of Christianity, just as in the domain of the theory of knowledge, we cannot pretend that there have not been centuries of positive science.[2]

Marcel is convinced, then, that Christianity *must* enter into modern philosophical speculation and that his is a Christian philosophy. The claim made in this book, however, is not nearly as broad as that; it would limit itself to these two points: first, philosophy *may* be Christian and remain truly philosophical; second, there may be *many* Christian philosophies and the instance under examination, the philosophy of St. Thomas, is but *one* way of philosophizing open to the Christian.

This at once suggests a second preliminary clarification. Saying that philosophy in St. Thomas' thought is Christian does not imply that philosophy *must* be Christian if it is to be philosophy. That would be totally at odds with the argument as it has unfolded down to this point: Christian philosophy is an *historical* reality. Being Christian affects the status or condition of philosophy—let us say, the way philosophy *exists;* it does not alter its nature or character as philosophy. Philosophy as such is always human reason's search for and convictions about what is most fundamental in reality. But the moment an individual philosopher actually undertakes that search at a point in time, differences in the condition or status of philosophy begin to appear. For what, indeed, is reality? Is it, as Plato thought, the permanent as contrasted with what is always changing? Is it, as it was for Aristotle, the form of some sensible thing? Is it an individual material thing that we sense? Is it a physical event? Or do we, as Descartes did, call real anything about which we can be most certain, a reality that we cannot doubt, i.e. thinking itself? Is it experience, whether sensible or moral? The way reality has presented itself to various philosophers in successive periods of time has issued into a long line of philosophies, each of a different hue: the philosophies of Plato, Aristotle, Plotinus, Occam, Descartes, Hume, Kant, Hegel, Russell. Each of these attempts to understand reality has made it necessary either to adapt old tools or to improvise and create new ones to do the job.

For example, Aristotle developed the tool of logical demonstration to explore a world of eternal species, but that method was to prove useless—indeed, an obstruction—to Francis Bacon as he sought to invent the arts that would command nature in action. The old Organon had to give way to a new Interpretation of Nature. As Bacon states:

Having thus coasted past the ancient arts, the next point is to equip the intellect for passing beyond. To the second part therefore belongs the doctrine concerning the better and more perfect use of reason in the inquisition of things, and the true helps of the understanding; that thereby (as far as the condition of mortality and humanity allows) the intellect may be raised and exalted, and made capable of overcoming the difficulties and obscurities of nature. The art which I introduce with this view (which I call Interpretation of Nature) is a kind of logic; though the difference between it and the ordinary logic is great, indeed immense. For the ordinary logic professes to contrive and prepare helps and guards for the understanding, as mine does; and in this one point they agree. But mine differs from it in three points especially, viz., in the end aimed at, in the order of demonstration, and in the starting point of the inquiry.[3]

And the chains of definitions Leibnitz found it necessary to construct so as to understand substance as he saw it—independent, windowless blocks of reality, monads, each reflecting everything else in nature— would never work when applied to Newtonian reality interpreted, as Kant did, as so many objects experienced in space and time. Where ontology and the principles of contradiction and sufficient reason failed, Kant would create a critical analysis and develop a transcendental logic of categories and rational ideas to take over. Illustrations could be given in an almost endless series, but they would all point to this lesson: philosophy takes on many and varied guises the moment individual human intelligences begin to ponder reality in terms of what each is convinced is most real.

An immediate consequence pertinent to the present discussion is that philosophy's relationship with faith undergoes parallel changes as it alters its own character—as, indeed, does the very formulation of what faith itself is! Is it a kind of knowledge or insight into the things of God? Superstition? Mythology? The will to accept various moral postulates or ideas? Personal engagement? The encounter of a sinful creature with a good, transcendent God? An inferior moment in the mind's consciousness, subordinate to philosophical insight? Pose the question: What is faith? to St. Thomas, Hume, Kant, Hegel or Kierkegaard and each answer will vary. The replies will reflect the conviction each man has about the fundamental character of reality. The result is that each will see a somewhat different relationship between philosophy and faith. Consequently, Bertrand Russell's objection, that St. Thomas' thinking is not a real philosophy, has to be understood in the light of Lord Russell's own conception of what philosophy is and of what reality truly is.

Russell is convinced that "the world contains *facts*, which are what they are whatever we may choose to think about them, and there are also *beliefs*, which have reference to facts and by reference to facts are either true or false." Now facts are not *things* like Socrates, the rain or the sun; a fact is, rather, a state of affairs or whatever is expressed by a whole sentence. Thus, for example, if a person says: "It is raining," the condition of weather that makes the statement true or false is a fact. To quote Russell:

I mean by a "fact" something which is there, whether anybody thinks so or not. If I look up a railway time-table and find that there is a train to Edinburgh at 10 a.m., then, if the time-table is correct, there is an actual train, which is a "fact." The statement in the time-table is itself a "fact," whether true or false, but it only *states* a fact if it is true, i.e. if there really is a train. Most facts are independent of our volitions; that is why they are called "hard," "stubborn," or "ineluctable." Physical facts, for the most part, are independent, not only of our volitions, but even of our existence.[4]

As a biological organism, man must always be adapting to facts. As Russell says:

> The whole of our cognitive life is, biologically considered, part of the process of adaptation to facts. This process is one which exists, in a greater or less degree, in all forms of life, but is not commonly called "cognitive" until it reaches a certain level of development. Since there is no sharp frontier anywhere between the lowest animal and the most profound philosopher, it is evident that we cannot say precisely at what point we pass from mere animal behaviour to something deserving to be dignified by the name of "knowledge." But at every stage there is adaptation, and that to which the animal adapts itself is the environment of *fact*.[5]

And beliefs are states of an organism that result from encountering facts:

> I propose, therefore, to treat belief as something that can be pre-intellectual, and can be displayed in the behaviour of animals. I incline to think that, on occasion a purely bodily state may deserve to be called a "belief." For example, if you walk into your room, in the dark, and someone has put a chair in an unusual place, you may bump into it, because your body believed there was no chair there. But the parts played by mind and body respectively in belief are not very important to separate for our present purposes. A belief, as I understand the term, is a certain kind of state of body or mind or both. To avoid verbiage, I shall call it a state of an organism, and ignore the distinction of bodily and mental factors.[6]

In its most developed form belief is displayed by the assertion of a thought in a sentence, and it is in this form that belief is considered by the philosopher. And inasmuch as there is a "continuity of mental development from the amoeba to *homo sapiens*," [7] belief is characterized by an inherent and inevitable vagueness. It is the job of the philosopher to analyse such complex patterns as they are seen in sentences, and to clarify them. So Lord Russell speaks of his aim in this way:

> The process of sound philosophizing, to my mind, consists mainly in passing from those obvious, vague, ambiguous things that we feel quite sure of, to something precise, clear, definite.[8]

Philosophy, then, is concerned with statements and its task is to give a logical analysis of them; the philosopher can never rest easy with any unexamined statements, words, concepts or pre-conceptions, whether they belong to the field of mathematics, science, metaphysics, morality or religion. Mind, matter, consciousness, knowledge, causality and will must all come under the scrutiny of logical analysis before they can form part of an exact science.

Now how did Russell view this logical tool he is wielding? It was the result, as he himself tells us, of his philosophy of mathematics, i.e. of his reflections on the nature of numbers and of mathematical reasoning:

This course of lectures which I am now beginning I have called the Philosophy of Logical Atomism. Perhaps I had better begin by saying a word or two as to what I understand by that title. The kind of philosophy that I wish to advocate, which I call Logical Atomism, is one which has forced itself upon me in the course of thinking about the philosophy of mathematics, although I should find it hard to say exactly how far there is a definite logical connexion between the two. . . . As I have attempted to prove in *The Principles of Mathematics*, when we analyse mathematics we bring it all back to logic. It all comes back to logic in the strictest and most formal sense. In the present lectures, I shall try to set forth in a sort of outline, rather briefly and rather unsatisfactorily, a kind of logical doctrine which seems to me to result from the philosophy of mathematics—not exactly logically, but as what emerges as one reflects: a certain kind of logical doctrine, and on the basis of this a certain kind of metaphysics.[9]

And in briefly outlining his own philosophical development, Russell once again pointedly relates his philosophy to mathematical thinking:

A few words as to historical development may be useful by way of preface. I came to philosophy through mathematics, or rather through the wish to find some reason to believe in the truth of mathematics. . . . At Cambridge I read Kant and Hegel, as well as Mr. Bradley's *Logic*, which influenced me profoundly. For some years I was a disciple of Mr. Bradley, but about 1898 I changed my views, largely as a result of arguments with G. E. Moore. I could no longer believe that knowing makes any difference to what is known. Also I found myself driven to pluralism. Analysis of mathematical propositions persuaded me that they could not be explained as even partial truths unless one admitted pluralism and the reality of relations. An accident led me at this time to study Leibnitz, and I came to the conclusion (subsequently confirmed by Couturat's

masterly researches) that many of his most characteristic opinions
were due to the purely logical doctrine that every proposition has
a subject and a predicate. This doctrine is one which Leibnitz
shares with Spinoza, Hegel and Mr. Bradley; it seemed to me that,
if it is rejected, the whole foundation of the metaphysics of all these
philosophers is shattered. I therefore returned to the problem which
had originally led me to philosophy, namely, the foundations of
mathematics, applying to it a new logic derived largely from Peano
and Frege, which proved (at least so I believe) far more fruitful
than that of traditional philosophy.[10]

Those researches issued into a magnificent creation: a new logical tool
fashioned to clarify all statements as one would analyse a mathematical
formula or expression. Each word, phrase or sentence was to be treated
as a number or equation, its quantitative and relational aspects reduced
to simple components for clarification. Use of that tool has resulted in
a novel analysis of philosophical and scientific statements.

It is in the light of this logical approach that St. Thomas appears, in
Lord Russell's view, to be uttering nonsense when he speaks of God's
existence or of the existence of things in the sensible world. For God
and things are not facts; and there is nothing whatsoever that you can
say of them (i.e. of God or things) that in any way corresponds to
"existence." As Russell states the case:

Existence. When you take any propositional function and assert of
it that it is possible, that it is sometimes true, that gives you the
fundamental meaning of "existence." You may express it by saying
that there is at least one value of $x$ for which that propositional
function is true. Take "$x$ is a man," there is at least one value of $x$
for which this is true. That is what one means by saying that "There
are men," or that "Men exist." Existence is essentially a property of
a propositional function. It means that that propositional function is
true in at least one instance. If you say that "There are unicorns,"
that will mean that "There is an $x$, such that $x$ is a unicorn." That
is written in phrasing which is unduly approximated to ordinary
language, but the proper way to put it would be "$(x$ is a unicorn$)$
is possible." We have got to have some idea that we do not define,
and one takes the idea of "always true," or of "sometimes true," as
one's undefined idea in this matter, and then you can define the
other one as the negative of that. In some ways it is better to take
both as undefined, for reasons which I shall not go into at present.
It will be out of this notion of sometimes, which is the same as the
notion of possible, that we get the notion of existence. To say that
unicorns exist is simply to say that "$(x$ is a unicorn$)$ is possible." [11]

The conviction that existence does not belong to *things* but to propositional functions *only* is a conclusion that Lord Russell reached by thinking as a mathematician and using his own method of logical analysis. If St. Thomas were able to read Russell's statements he would probably repeat comments he had made in quite a different context, namely, that the mathematician *abstracts* from the being of things and is not concerned with existence as the first act of beings. But existence does not apply *solely* to the being of things; it also refers to the truth of propositions. Consequently, if the mathematician, thinking as a mathematician, *does* use the term existence, it can *only* refer to mathematical propositions and their verifiability, as we would say today. There would be a measure of agreement here. And as far as God's existence is concerned, St. Thomas does not claim to know *that* philosophically; philosophy cannot yield the beatific vision. His claim is, rather, as we shall see later, that he is certain of this: the proposition "God exists" is true, and there are philosophical reasons for that certainty.

Lord Russell also insists, as we have seen, that inquiry is not free in St. Thomas' philosophy because the conclusion is prescribed in advance. Philosophy must be an unfettered and uncompromising examination of *all* preconceptions; keeping one realm of belief, the world of faith, as a sacred preserve is quite opposed to the free philosophical spirit. But what is faith in Russell's view?

Religion, or mysticism as Russell prefers to speak of it, has left its mark on all philosophies from Plato to Bergson that have tried to develop a philosophical doctrine consistent with such belief. He finds four main marks of mystical philosophy, each a direct result of religion: first, belief in insight as against discursive analytic knowledge; second, a belief in unity and a refusal to admit opposition or division anywhere; third, a denial of the reality of time; fourth, a belief that evil is mere appearance, an illusion produced by the divisions and oppositions of the analytic intellect. The overall consequence, in Russell's eyes, is that ever since Plato philosophy and science have been divorced. The remedy, if we are to bring philosophy and science into harmonious relationship once more, is to proclaim philosophy's freedom from mysticism; it must become as objective as physics, chemistry and astronomy:

In philosophy, hitherto, ethical neutrality has been seldom sought and hardly ever achieved. Men have remembered their wishes, and have judged philosophies in relation to their wishes. Driven from the particular sciences, the belief that the notions of good and evil must afford a key to the understanding of the world has sought a refuge in philosophy. But even from this last refuge, if philosophy is not to remain a set of pleasing dreams, this belief must be driven forth. It is a commonplace that happiness is not best achieved by those who seek it directly; and it would seem that the same is true of the good. In thought, at any rate, those who forget good and evil and seek only to know the facts are more likely to achieve good than those who view the world through the distorting medium of their own desires.[12]

Mysticism, then, imposes a variety of attitudes and concepts that render the free inquiry enjoyed by the natural sciences impossible to philosophy. So philosophy has to proclaim its independence of *that* faith.

When philosophy does so, however, does it really gain and enjoy the freedom of inquiry that Lord Russell claims for it? When philosophy is not tied to faith, it may still remain tied to mathematics or the physical sciences; it cannot treat realities as *they* reveal themselves but only as mathematical entities. Philosophy is not free to look at existence because mathematics is not concerned with it! If philosophy does not try to understand the truths of faith, it does work to understand the technical truths of science. Whereas St. Thomas had insisted that one is foolish to try to treat all realities using the *same* method for different kinds of entities, instead of being free to seek differing truths in diverse things using a variety of tools, Lord Russell is committed to one method and one truth, namely, the method and truth of mathematics. In short, Russell is propounding a philosophy that results from his conviction, itself the consequence of a mathematician's reflections, about what reality is: the events that a mathematico-physical science proclaims to be real. Submitting St. Thomas' Christian philosophy for examination as philosophy does not mean that Russell's philosophy is *not* philosophy—St. Thomas would welcome into philosophy any method and any truth that might come to light in a hitherto unexplored corner of reality. He himself did very little to pry into the secrets of quantity, number and the logic of mathematics—not because they were not valuable, but because he was a theologian concerned above all with God. Yet philosophy itself may be inspired as well by one non-philosophic conviction (faith) as by another non-philosophic conviction (mathematical knowledge). But when it is inspired by Christian faith it does not cease to be philosophy.

And now for a third and last preliminary observation. In St. Thomas' thought philosophy is not and cannot constitute a system. As we have already seen in a preliminary fashion, and as we shall see later in greater detail, St. Thomas' philosophic search is directed towards understanding (by intellect and reason) what individual things are as *existents,* what man as an existent is, what God is as an existing reality. A system, on the contrary, implies a view of reality as an integrated, unified, consistent and, usually, logical whole. As caught up in a vast network of necessarily-connected relations, each individual thing is understood as having a determined reference to and dependence on everything else. For St. Thomas each and every being has its own principles that account for its reality; they are *not* logically or essentially inter-related. Their relations are ultimately a consequence of freedom—God's freedom and that of individual men—rather than of a determined nature. He is only too clear about the distinct way in which things exist as individual entities in a created world, as constrasted with their existence as abstract concepts in a logical world of thought. St. Thomas stands at the opposite pole from the wonderfully intelligible and rationally satisfying accounts of reality produced by Spinoza and Hegel, for instance. And he does so precisely in virtue of his basic philosophical principle: the act of existing as constitutive of the being of whatever is real. Allowing reality to announce itself as *existing* permits it to reveal varied facets that would be beclouded by systematic impositions. Philosophy has to accommodate itself to the variety of reality by respecting the various ways in which reality exists: reasoning proper to the understanding of the *quantitative* characteristics of reality must differ from the reasoning proper to the understanding of its properly *existential* characteristics. In short, respect for the existence of things introduces a remarkable flexibility into St. Thomas' thought. He is not confined to thinking of the world of natural science but free to extend his consideration to the worlds of morality, art and metaphysics as well.

With these clarifications out of the way, let us now turn to the main questions confronting us: In what sense is St. Thomas' thought *philosophical?* To shed light on this central issue, let us ask three more limited questions:

First, what does St. Thomas say philosophy is?

Second, how is philosophy related to other branches of knowledge?

Third, what principles does philosophy use in its attempt to understand reality?

St. Thomas speaks of philosophy in many ways. It is wisdom, the love of wisdom, the science of things in their highest causes, the science of first causes. Now each of these definitions is of Greek origin and may seem rather strange, misleading and even contradictory to the modern eye. When St. Thomas calls philosophy a wisdom, he is drawing our attention to a specifically Greek model of knowledge, but the meaning of that model will become clearer if we look at a simple illustration. A person inexperienced in the various building-trades might stroll down the street past a building under construction and only notice

that each of the workmen was going about his task in his accustomed
way. A carpenter or bricklayer, observing the same scene, would see
the work through a more experienced eye; he would be in a position
to judge how well carpenters and bricklayers on the job were doing
their work. He would be wiser than the casual observer. A building-
contractor, on the other hand, would understand why the work was
done in a definite order; he would know how preparations were being
made by the workers on hand for the subsequent work of the plumbers
and electricians. An architect would have a still more comprehensive
view of the whole project having, indeed, planned several such buildings himself. Now each of these men would be wiser than the next,
each would have a view of the building that would be more comprehensive and fundamental than the next—even though the architect might
not be able to lay bricks!

Now with just such an example in mind, St. Thomas speaks of the
wise man as the one who has a total view of reality—not in the sense
of knowing every individual thing in the world, but as having a knowledge of the basic principles and causes at work in them.

> . . . a truth which is known through another is understood by the
> intellect, not at once, but by means of the reason's inquiry, and is
> as a *term*. This may happen in two ways: first, so that it is the last
> in some particular genus; secondly, so that it is the ultimate term of
> all human knowledge. And, since *things that are later knowable
> in relation to us are knowable first and chiefly in their nature,* hence
> it is that that which is last with respect to all human knowledge is
> that which is knowable first and chiefly in its nature. And about
> these truths is *wisdom,* which considers the highest causes, as is
> stated in *Metaph.* i. Therefore, it rightly judges and orders all truths,
> because there can be no perfect and universal judgment except by
> resolution to first causes.[13]

It is, then, the wise man's function to bring order into knowledge in
virtue of basic principles that he gradually comes to know; his responsibility is to judge and defend the knowledge that results from seeing
things in the light of more specialized causes—even as the architect
can understand buildings in the light of basic structural principles and
from that vantage-point judge and defend what the contractor or carpenter is doing. Today we have very largely lost this view of knowledge
because we are better acquainted with the extremely specialized knowledge of the physicist, chemist and biochemist. The root of our difficulty,
however, goes much deeper than this: the meaning we associate with
the term science is quite different from the meaning St. Thomas had in

mind. We are not accustomed to calling philosophy "wisdom" or "science," let alone speaking of the moral sciences or defending theology as a science. But St. Thomas does just that:

> Whatever is based on these principles [i.e. principles of faith] is as well-proved in the eyes of the faithful, as a conclusion drawn from self-evident principles is in the eyes of all. Hence again, theology is a science.[14]

Many questions immediately arise in a person's mind as he reads such expressions today. How does one go about conducting an experiment in theology? Who ever heard of a laboratory for theological research? Did anyone ever succeed in measuring God? What would a theological law be? Would anyone dare to predict when God would act in some particular way, or that someone might expect to have an experience of Him at a precise time or in a definite place? Obviously we have come to define science in a way very different from the way in which St. Thomas used the term. And the difference in definition makes it difficult to understand him when he speaks of philosophy as a science.

Today we identify science with the work of the chemist or physicist working experimentally in his laboratory to measure the observable effect of heat, cold or strain on metals, or the reaction of one chemical substance on another so as to arrive at a general formulation or law of their behavior. In broad terms we usually associate experimentation, measurement, calculation, hypothetical reasoning and verification with the scientific enterprise. As Claude Bernard describes the process:

> In the experimental method we never make experiments except to see or to prove, i.e., to control or verify. As a scientific method, the experimental method rests wholly on the experimental verification of a scientific hypothesis. We obtain this verification with the help, sometimes of a fresh observation (observational science), sometimes of an experiment (experimental science). In the experimental method, the hypothesis is a scientific idea that we submit to experiment. Scientific invention consists in the creation of fortunate and fertile hypotheses; these are suggested by the feeling or even the genius of the men of science who create them.
>
> When an hypothesis is submitted to the experimental method, it becomes a theory, while if it is submitted to logic alone, it becomes a system. A system, then, is an hypothesis with which we have connected the facts logically with the help of reason, but without experimental, critical verification. A theory is a verified hypothesis, after it has been submitted to the control of reason and experimental

criticism. The soundest theory is one that has been verified by the greatest number of facts. But to remain valid, a theory must be continually altered to keep pace with the progress of science and must be constantly resubmitted to verification and criticism as new facts appear.[15]

On this basis we restrict what we call scientific knowledge to our knowledge of sensible phenomena, of events in space, time, or space-time, of substances, qualities or appearances that can be measured. The main standard we apply to determine success or failure in the operation is successful prediction.

Now all the branches of knowledge traditionally associated with theology and philosophy run counter to this trend. Theology, having God as its subject, would seem to violate all of the requirements set out above. If a person is convinced that theology does give some valid insight into God and His actions, he hesitates today to call the insight knowledge, let alone scientific knowledge. He contents himself, rather, with calling it a moral conviction or a religious conviction. Or if he does want to point up the more speculative character of theology and indicate the *knowledge* it involves, he would probably use some such expression as "scholarly conclusion." It would also seem inappropriate to think of metaphysics as scientific knowledge. Indeed, its usual statements about being, essence, potency and substance would appear either meaningless, because the terms lack any conceivable experimental foundation, or tautological, because the terms in the statements are endlessly repetitious and add nothing new to our store of information. Ethics and moral philosophy present similar difficulties. Can a human act remain distinctively human and free while being *predictable* in any meaningful way? How can one *measure* the goodness of any act that he performs? Must not ethical concepts and moral laws somehow escape the order of space-time and belong to a purely intelligible order? How, then, can they be scientific? Freedom and morality would appear antithetic to the whole scientific enterprise. And yet St. Thomas *does* apply the term "science" to metaphysics and theology as well as to astronomy. What, then, does *he* think science is?

Science is but one of several different kinds of cognition that St. Thomas distinguishes on the basis of the certitude with which various conclusions are held. St. Thomas says:

. . . What is comprehended is perfectly known; and that is perfectly known which is known so far as it can be known. Thus, if anything which is capable of scientific demonstration is held only by an opinion resting on probable proof, it is not comprehended. For instance, if anyone knows by scientific demonstration that a triangle has three angles equal to two right angles, he comprehends the truth; whereas if anyone accepts it as a probable opinion because wise men or most men teach it, he does not comprehend the thing because he does not attain to that perfect mode of knowledge of which it is intrinsically capable.[16]

Science, then, is the comprehension of an object that results from demonstration and it differs in certitude from opinion and probable cognition. Faith, in its intellectual aspects, falls somewhere in between science and opinion, but it is clearly different from science. St. Thomas compares faith, science and opinion in this way:

On the part of the means, perfect and imperfect knowledge are exemplified in the knowledge of a conclusion through a demonstrative means, and through a probable means. On the part of the subject, the difference between perfect and imperfect knowledge applies to opinion, faith and science. For it is essential to opinion that we assent to one of two opposite assertions with fear of the other, so that our adhesion is not firm; to science it is essential to have firm adhesion with intellectual vision, for science possesses certitude which results from the understanding of principles; while faith holds a middle place, for it surpasses opinion insofar as its adhesion is firm, but falls short of science as it lacks vision.[17]

The reason science represents a firmly-held conviction is that the intellect has been moved by intellectual evidence to assent to a conclusion; faith is different. For while the man of faith does, indeed, assent to a given truth, he does so because of his *will*. His intellect is not moved by evidence; rather, his will moves his intellect out of love. Science, then, is a certain knowledge, i.e. knowledge held with certitude and conviction, but it is the result of demonstration. And while similar to the knowledge one has of principles—for example, the axioms of geometry—it differs from that understanding in its discursiveness. Science and the understanding of principles are both certain; science alone is demonstrative knowledge, i.e. knowledge resulting from strict proof.

Now science, according to St. Thomas, does not constitute a single body of knowledge marked by the use of a univocal or universally valid method that might be consistently applied to all realities. It is, rather, a *habit* of the intellect, and each science has its own unique method. Truth is strictly proportionate to the capacities of various objects to reveal themselves more or less convincingly. As St. Thomas puts it:

. . . they are in error who try to proceed in the same way in these three parts of speculative science.[18]

And he does not expect to gain the same degree of certitude about all objects. Indeed, he is quite blunt in saying that the method of mathematics is most likely to bring the human intellect its greatest certainty:

> For since learning is nothing else than receiving science from another, we are then said to proceed according to the mode of learning when our method leads to certain knowledge, which is called science. Now this occurs particularly in the mathematical sciences. For since mathematics is intermediate between natural and divine science, it is more certain than either.[19]

The reason is, as he goes on to explain, that natural science is concerned with understanding sensible, moving things, and inasmuch as they are material and individual, a great many things have to be known (and known in the world of motion where innumerable contingencies have to be examined) before knowledge is at all secure:

> Now since natural science deals with things that are mobile and which lack regularity, its knowledge is less certain; for its demonstrations frequently hold good only in the majority of cases because things sometimes happen differently. And so too the more a science draws close to particular things, as do practical sciences like medicine, alchemy and ethics, the less certain they can be because of the multitude of factors to be taken into account in sciences of this sort, the omission of any one of which leads to error, and because of their variability.[20]

Mathematical sciences, on the contrary, are concerned with such objects as the order of the parts of numbers (units in arithmetic) or figures (points in geometry). The mathematician is not worried in the least about the being or existence of the objects he is studying—indeed, he deliberately *prescinds* from considering the individual observable idiosyncrasies and the actual motions of the things in which numbers and figures may perchance be incorporated. So he does not have to keep his senses constantly fixed on the rapidly fluctuating and highly contingent behavior of moving things. His concern is with very stable realities capable of yielding quite certain knowledge. And the mathematician is in a much more advantageous position than the metaphysician who is struggling to understand objects farthest removed from sensible perception—separated substances, for instance, that cannot be found in the sensible world of motion, or essence, being, potency that can be found in the sensible world but not sensibly perceived there. For St. Thomas, then, science is of at least three generic kinds: natural, mathematical and divine or metaphysical science. Ultimately the differences between these three species are to be accounted for by the formally distinct objects each considers. The natural scientist sees a thing as a moving object, he apprehends and defines it by material and formal principles, but he judges it in accordance with the information his senses provide:

> . . . sometimes the properties and accidents of a thing revealed by the sense adequately manifest its nature, and then the intellect's judgment of the thing's nature must conform to what the sense reveals about it. All natural things, limited to sensible matter, are of this sort. So the terminus of knowledge in natural science must be in the sense, so that we judge of natural things as the sense reveals them, as is clear in the *De Caelo et Mundo* [Aristotle]. And the person who neglects the senses in regard to natural things falls into error. Furthermore, I call natural things those which are concreted with sensible matter and motion both with respect to their existence and our consideration of them.[21]

The mathematician defines in a different fashion, taking into account only the purely formal requirements of quantity. And the judgments he makes and the conclusions he reaches concerning those objects are not answerable to the senses but only, according to St. Thomas, to the demands of the imagination. Human reason working in conjunction with imagination, principles of consistent and coherent thinking applied to and verified in imaginable numbers or figures: these are the criteria that the mathematician must respect. As for the metaphysician, even though he must start his speculation with something the senses present to him, still he has to define and judge the objects he is studying in virtue of purely intellectual principles:

> It follows that with regard to divine things we can use the sense and the imagination as the beginnings of our knowledge but not as the ends of our knowledge, namely, so that we judge divine things to be such as what the sense or imagination apprehends. Now to go to something is to terminate in it. Therefore, in divine science we should go neither to the imagination nor to the sense. In mathematics, however, we must go to the imagination and not to the sense; while in the natural sciences we must rather go to the sense.[22]

Science, then, is of many different kinds, and in the order of speculative knowledge it is at its peak of intellectual perfection in first philosophy or metaphysics. The situation is quite different, however, in the order of operation, for here the main concern is either with individual things that do *not* yet exist but have to be made, or with human acts that do *not* yet exist but have to be performed. Ultimately, the termination of practical thinking, whether artistic or moral, is in something radically singular and non-existent; in the final analysis the medical doctor is concerned with preserving or restoring the health of an individual organism, John Smith's body, that is not now healthy. But in addition to the more purely practical parts of medicine that deal with symptoms and remedies, there are also more theoretical parts that teach the principles by which the physician is to be guided. Similarly, practical knowledge may be immediately concerned with making the right judgment about an act to be performed in a precise and unique set of circumstances (the only setting in which one ever acts!); but it may also be more remotely concerned with such a judgment when it tries to understand the general principles—what goodness consists in, the nature of law operative in the order of human acts, the role that virtue and passion play in making a moral decision. Understanding of that kind is proper to the moral sciences. St. Thomas states:

> Every science is in the intellect. But some sciences are of contingent things, as the moral sciences, which consider human actions subject to free choice; and again the sciences of nature insofar as they consider things generable and corruptible.[23]

Such science constitutes a perfectly valid pre-occupation for the human intelligence even though it may not bring the highest practical insights and is not sufficient of itself to give man the assurance that mastering it will bring him happiness as its reward. For even as the highest part of speculative philosophy, metaphysics, does not provide the highest theoretical insights of which man's intellect is capable, neither does moral philosophy give him the highest insights or guides of which his intellect is capable in the order of human actions. The natural, rational knowledge of metaphysics is surpassed by the knowledge of faith and the vision of Wisdom and Understanding; the precepts of moral philosophy are complemented, indeed, superseded by the liberating commands of charity. But as works of man's own native powers, metaphysics and moral philosophy represent his crowning intellectual achievements.

Before proceeding any further, let us pause briefly at this point and summarize what St. Thomas conceives science to be:

First, it is knowledge held without fear that the opposite may be true. It is *certain* and *necessary* knowledge.

Second, it is knowledge that results from reasoning rather than from intellectual vision or insight. It is *reasoned* knowledge.

Third, it is knowledge of conclusions that result from demonstration. It is *demonstrated* knowledge.

Fourth, it is knowledge in which we judge of things that are naturally known. It is *judicative* knowledge.

In this concept of science and, hence, of philosophy, the central notions are demonstration and principle. Most of the controversies concerning this way of philosophizing have revolved around these two poles. So let us try to fix them clearly in mind as St. Thomas understands them.

Demonstration is a proof or, as St. Thomas speaks of it, a syllogism that makes us know, i.e. that gives us the kind of knowledge that is certain, necessary and universal:

> The natural philosopher proves the earth to be round by one means, the astronomer by another. For the latter proves this by means of mathematics, e.g. by the shapes of eclipses or something of this sort; while the former proves it by means of physics, e.g. by the movement of heavy bodies towards the center and so forth. Now the whole force of a demonstration, which is a syllogism producing science, as is stated in the *Posterior Analytics* i, depends on the means. And consequently various means are so many actual principles according to which the habits of science are distinguished.[24]

Two points should be noted here:

First, the central role assigned to the means of demonstrating.

Second, the possibility of distinguishing various sciences by the different means of demonstrating which each uses.

What, then, is a means of demonstrating? How does it function? The means of demonstrating is the middle term of a syllogism: two terms are brought together in a conclusion through a third term, the mediating or middle term. The path to the conclusion is marked out by two premises or propositions in each of which the middle term serves as either subject or predicate. Here is an example taken from St. Thomas' writings:

> It has been shown above that every intellectual substance is incorruptible; now the soul of man is an intellectual substance, as has been shown; hence the human soul is incorruptible.[25]

The means of demonstrating may be a cause or definition, as in this example, or it may be an effect:

Demonstration can be made in two ways: one is through the cause, and is called *propter quid*, and this is to argue from what is prior absolutely. The other is through the effect, and is called a demonstration *quia;* this is to argue from what is prior relatively only to us. When an effect is better known to us than its cause, from the effect we proceed to the knowledge of the cause. And from every effect the existence of its proper cause can be demonstrated, so long as its effects are better known to us; because, since every effect depends upon its cause, if the effect exists, the cause must pre-exist.[26]

Demonstration may, then, yield a knowledge of *what* a thing is if the means is a defining property; it may yield a knowledge *that* something is so if the means is an effect. The essential thing is that a necessary relationship or some form of identity has to be established between the middle term and the other two terms, and to that end it may be necessary to *prove* that the predication *is* necessary before one can be said to have a scientific knowledge of such a conclusion. So in the example given above St. Thomas says of each premise "as has been shown before." Ultimately, then, the necessity and certitude of the conclusion depends on the necessity of the principles from which the whole proof proceeds.

Two brief comments would seem in order here. First, when St. Thomas speaks of science as a certain or evident knowledge of conclusions gained by demonstration, he is speaking *formally* of science and stating the precise way it is distinct from other kinds of cognition, for instance, sense-knowledge, opinion or faith. As a result, one might get the impression that science—and philosophy, too—is *merely* or *solely* a matter of demonstrating or of abstract reasoning. To correct such an impression we must always bear in mind St. Thomas' account of the starting-points of all the sciences. They all result from induction:

Therefore, inasmuch as we get a knowledge of universals from singular things, the conclusion is clear that the first universal principles must be known by induction. For in this way, i.e. by induction, the sense makes a universal in the soul inasmuch as the singulars are considered.[27]

In the final analysis, then, the principles of science—its definitions and basic judgments—must be traced back to memory, imagination and sense, and grasped by induction. This is true, as we have already seen, even in the case of metaphysics whose objects seem so far removed from the senses. So when St. Thomas speaks of the human intellect's power of defining, he is not assigning it a magic capability that would eliminate

long inductive or experimental process. Indeed, there are many instances where we cannot succeed in defining through essential differences and have to be content with using accidents:

> A name is said to be imposed by someone in two ways: either the name is imposed on the part of the one imposing it or on the part of the thing on which it is imposed. On the side of the thing a name is said to be imposed from that whereby the essence of the thing the name signifies is completed; and this is the specific difference of that thing. This is what is principally signified by the name. But because essential differences are unknown to us, sometimes we use the accidents or effects in their place, as is stated in *VIII Metaph.* . . . ; and we name the thing after it. So what is taken in place of the essential difference is that from which the name is imposed on the side of the one imposing it, as for example, "lapis" is imposed from its effect which is to hurt the foot.[28]

The fundamental claim St. Thomas is making is that man is capable of discerning various necessary characteristics in the things he knows, of seeing in them the necessary principles that make a thing to be as it is and to act as it does. Where the principles are different (as they are in sensible things like plants and animals, mathematical entities like triangles and numbers, moral acts such as acting generously or unjustly), the experience needed to discover those principles is different, the definitions are different (not only in content but in the principles expressed), and the beings judged by the intellect are different. This is one of the implications of the statement that St. Thomas' thought is flexible and non-systematic. Nevertheless, in all instances the human intellect has to turn to the bodily senses if it is to discover the principles of the realities it is trying to understand; *all* of its knowledge must ultimately come from the senses.

Second, in many instances the principles are said to be indemonstrable in the more limited sense that they cannot be demonstrated within a given science. For example, optics uses as principles conclusions that are proved in geometry. Inasmuch as optics has a different subject than geometry, it has proper to it principles different from those of geometry; it makes use of propositions taken from geometry and that it (i.e. optics) is in no position to prove. Such principles are indemonstrable in optics but not in themselves. So in a given science principles may be indemonstrable without being so in the strict sense of the word. But if there is a science that uses principles that *are* ultimately indemonstrable, it will be a prime science. St. Thomas calls such a science "wisdom." And philosophy is just such a wisdom:

. . . a truth which is known through another is understood by the intellect, not at once, but by means of the reason's inquiry, and is as a *term*. This may happen in two ways: first, so that it is the last in some particular genus; secondly, so that it is the ultimate term of all human knowledge. And since things that are later knowable in relation to us are knowable first and chiefly in their nature, hence it is that that which is last with respect to all human knowledge is that which is knowable first and chiefly in its nature. And about these truths is *wisdom*, which considers the highest causes.[29]

The term "principle" has repeatedly recurred in the discussion of demonstration. When St. Thomas speaks of a principle he may have one of many points in mind; he may not be thinking of basic propositions only. Note the differences indicated in these statements:

The term principle signifies only that whence another proceeds, since anything whence something proceeds in any way we call principle.

The Greeks use the word *cause* and *principle* indifferently, when speaking of God; whereas the Latin Doctors do not use the word *cause*, but only *principle*. The reason is because *principle* is a wider term than *cause*, just as *cause* is more common than *element*. For the first term of a thing, as also the first part, is called the principle, but not the cause . . . as when we say that a point is the principle of a line, or also when we say that the first part of a line is the principle of the line.[30]

The principles of a science are the things from which the science proceeds, the first part of the subject that science considers, the origin of the science. From whence, for example, does geometry proceed? First, it proceeds from its subject, line or figure, and the first part of its subject, the point. Second, geometry proceeds from the definitions and axioms with which it starts and from which it reasons to conclusions about various conceivable figures. For St. Thomas those definitions and axioms represent primary intellectual apprehensions and judgments about continuous quantity; the geometrician imagines various configurations of points, he defines the resulting figures and tries to understand them through their properties and in the light of basic judgments about known beings—a thing cannot be said to be and not to be at the same time— and quantity—the whole is greater than the part, things equal to the same thing are equal to each other. Third, "principle" may refer to the origin of geometry in the various human capacities involved in originating geometric knowledge—senses, imagination, reason, intellect.

In a similar fashion the principles of philosophy may be set forth by examining the subject philosophy considers, the first part of its subject, its basic definitions and judgments, and the human capacities required to produce philosophic knowledge. According to St. Thomas philosophy is concerned with the being of things, and it is the act of existing that makes anything a being:

> The very act of existing is the most perfect of all, for it is compared to all things as their act; for nothing has actuality except insofar as it is. Whence, the very act of existing is the actuality of all things, even of forms themselves; wherefore it is not compared to other things as a receiver is compared to what is received, but rather as what is received is compared to the receiver. For when I speak of the being of a man or horse or anything else, the act of existing is considered as formal and received, not as that to which the act of existing belongs.[31]

For St. Thomas, as we shall see later, there is no being to receive existence; the act of existing makes the receiver to be. We may say, therefore, that being is a principle of philosophy because it is the subject from which one philosophizes; and the act of existing is a principle of philosophy, too, because it is the first part of its subject. Metaphysics or first philosophy is concerned with all beings—stones, animals, plants, men, God—as existing realities, i.e. to the extent that they exercise the act of existing; it is above all concerned with God as the cause of being in all that is. Natural philosophy (the term should not be taken as suggesting that other parts of philosophy are "supernatural" in the religious sense!) deals with being, too, but only to the extent that beings have within them principles whereby they move in one way or another, as living, growing, sensing etc. It is philosophy insofar as it concerns itself with *nature*, which St. Thomas considers to be the remote principle of motion, the constitution of a thing that makes it move as it does. Mathematical philosophy concerns itself with being insofar as it is divisible. Moral philosophy has as its subject beings to the extent that they tend or move towards their fullest maturity or happiness by acts freely exercised. Rational philosophy or logic has as its subject beings insofar as they are known, i.e. as they exercise the intentional being of knowledge; genus, predicate, proposition, demonstration are its subjects. Philosophy, therefore, has many different principles insofar as its subjects are different: the act of existing, nature, form, the good; they are, however, so many different aspects of being.

The principles of philosophy, in the sense of its basic definitions and judgments, are also different in its various parts. Definitions of such fundamental philosophic notions as essence, substance, act, form, matter, good, definition etc. are not arbitrarily set down as starting-points; they result from intellectual considerations of being in all its many facets. Nor are philosophy's primary propositions arbitrary; they are, rather, necessary, first judgments about being. Thus, the judgment usually expressed in the form "What is, is," is simply an assertion that the reality we understand exists. The philosopher does not deduce consequences *from* that proposition; rather, he makes judgments about beings in the light of that conviction.

Finally, philosophy also has principles in the sense of the human powers from which philosophic knowledge results. The philosopher has his first encounter with being, as St. Thomas understands it, when he confronts it in a sensible contact with things; being is discovered concretely in something sensible. The senses, then, are truly principles of philosophic knowledge. More proximately, however, intellect and reason originate philosophic science in the strict sense of the term. So they, too, are principles.

Now let us return to the questions with which we set out and attempt some answers. First, what does St. Thomas say philosophy is? It is scientific knowledge in which the philosopher discovers the first causes of things insofar as they are beings in some way or other. Second, how is philosophy related to other kinds of knowledge? It is not sacred doctrine or theology because it uses naturally-known principles—although the *theologian* may find it useful to use philosophical concepts in his work or to undertake philosophical work if he is to gain the theological understanding he wants. And philosophy is not opinion or doubt because it reaches conclusions that are certain. It is not geometry, astronomy, medicine etc. because its subject, being, and its principles are different. Third, what principles does philosophy use? Its subject is being, and it tries above all to understand being in virtue of the act of existing. Its basic notions and primary judgments are the work of the human intellect aided and abetted by the bodily senses and imagination. Reason enables the philosopher to draw his conclusions, whether speculative or practical, about being.

Finally, we said that we would use these three preliminary questions and the answers to them to answer this overall question: In what sense is St. Thomas' Christian philosophy *philosophic?* It is philosophic because it is a knowledge concerned with natural subjects, i.e. with existing realities; it is philosophic insofar as it uses principles available to man's natural understanding and reasoning; it is philosophic because it is directed towards natural truth and uses the tools of the philosophers to get them. It is *not* philosophic if to be so requires that such a body of knowledge be developed completely independently of the other sciences, that it *exist* as a separate discipline, that the conclusions it reaches represent the highest achievements to which man's reason can aspire. But, then, how many philosophies do remain philosophic? How many philosophies have developed outside the influence of geometry, physics, Christian faith, theology? Could Descartes, Malebranche, Spinoza, Kant, Hegel have produced their speculative insights apart from the concept of God indigenous to Judaeo-Christian belief? Yet each of these men is given credit for having provided us with new philosophic insights. The same is true of St. Thomas. His Christian philosophy also results in new knowledge. As a theologian and man of faith he simply did not comprehend or have scientific and philosophic knowledge of reality until his reason had reached its conclusions by using its own native tools. One might, as Lord Russell did, know various conclusions about numbers by mathematical reasoning and still gain new knowledge by creating a logical tool that would reveal the origin of numbers in certain logical structures of human thinking; so, too, one might have a knowledge gained by faith, of the world around us and still gain new knowledge of it by creating a new tool out of information provided by natural means and previous philosophers' experience. That is what St. Thomas did.

# CHAPTER IV

# PHILOSOPHIC KNOWLEDGE
# OF REALITY

The ancients had always believed in an animated nature. To most of them it was a work of art of beautiful suitability in which Form had not always completely subjected Matter. Others, such as the atomists, considered that nature had achieved its structure by boundless waste. None of them would have accepted the Newtonian world-machine created by God and left to run its course, the concept so dear to the eighteenth-century scientist. Even Democritus, Epicurus, or Lucretius would have shuddered before such blasphemies. In reality the ancients always based science on animism. Thales says that "All things are full of gods" and that "the magnet is proved to have a soul since it can move iron." This animism is still an essential element in the final philosophy of antiquity, Neoplatonism. The poet's "water-nymphs moving the axle of the water wheel" were real and not just an image. The ancient world did not dream of man's harnessing these supernatural powers until Christianity, by its opposition to animism, opened the door to a rational use of the forces of nature. The last obstacles to the introduction of prime-movers had fallen, when by the fourth-century A.D. the Roman Empire became officially Christian.[1]

We have seen that St. Thomas presents us with a view of philosophy as wisdom and science, and that he attaches a very precise meaning to those terms. The historical situation within which the concepts he employs developed was essentially Greek. Those concepts—science, definition, demonstration, essence, property—were derived from an experience ancient thinkers of Athens and Rome had of the world of nature. It was a world composed of natural entities; their experience of it came in direct, naive sense experience; it was a threatening world with forces in it that seemed to exceed human control and to endanger man's existence. Survival depended on appeasing the gods who embodied those forces; human activity could only persist if it proceeded rationally and treated nature as though it, too, were rational. Out of that adjustment to nature emerged the Greek theories of logos, idea, nature, abstraction, definition, demonstration etc., and the philosophies that utilized such concepts.

Now several questions at once suggest themselves. Has not the experience of contemporary man changed all of that? Is not our new concept of science an indication that we react differently to the world around us? Can a person in the twentieth century experience a natural entity or, in view of the scientific concepts we all have in some measure, must we not always experience things through the eye-glass of scientific information? Do we experience natural things or scientific objects? With our technology and scientific knowledge are we not in a position to fashion and control nature to the extent that we are no longer at its mercy? Have not elaborate modern experimental techniques and new mathematical concepts removed the need for treating the fluctuating things of nature as though they had something unchanging within them? Do we *need* the concepts of classical Greek scientific and philosophic thought today? May it not, indeed, be possible that perpetuating such concepts in the twentieth century poses a real threat to man's free political and moral life? Perhaps we have reached the point where we must candidly admit that philosophy in all its many parts must become scientific in the contemporary sense of "science" if it is to be a viable enterprise today. Indeed, it may well be true that the various sciences are now able to do all that philosophy previously claimed to do; perhaps philosophy should declare itself bankrupt. If so, the title of this chapter, "Philosophic Knowledge of Reality" is totally meaningless. Can the philosopher provide us with *any* knowledge significant to men living in the mid-twentieth century?

Well, that question need not be directed at St. Thomas alone. As modern sciences have become more varied and comprehensive, all honest and thoughtful philosophers have been compelled to ask themselves the same question in one way or another. Many have agreed that the success of scientific methods in interpreting and controlling nature have made it imperative that philosophy follow suit and cast itself in a thoroughly scientific mould. Philosophy must become positive:

> In order to understand the true value and character of Positive Philosophy, we must take a brief general view of the progressive course of the human mind, regarded as a whole; for no conception can be understood otherwise than through its history.
>
> From the study of the development of human intelligence, in all directions, and through all times, the discovery arises of a great fundamental law, to which it is necessarily subject. The law is this: that each of our leading conceptions, each branch of our knowledge, passes successively through three different theoretical conditions: the

Theological or fictitious; the Metaphysical, or abstract; and the Scientific, or positive. In other words, the human mind, by its nature, employs in its progress the three methods of philosophizing, the character of which is essentially different, and even radically opposed: viz. the theological method, the metaphysical, and the positive. Hence arise three philosophies or general systems of conceptions on the aggregate of phenomena, each of which excludes the others. The first is the necessary point of departure of the human understanding; and the third is its fixed and definite state.[2]

Once having taken this decision, however, it becomes rather difficult to uncover a distinct subject for philosophy to study, a subject distinct from that of the physicist, chemist, biologist etc. The scientific knowledge gained in physics, chemistry, biology, psychology, sociology and all their many and varied branches would, indeed, appear to exhaust all that is knowable. So the question arises: What is left for philosophy?

The answers philosophers have given in our own day have been numerous and different. Some are convinced that philosophers *do* have something distinctive to do: they are to reflect on the scientist's work. Whereas the physicist or chemist concentrates on the phenomena they discover in their laboratories, the philosopher is charged with examining what they are doing. Philosophic investigation is to concentrate on problems of scientific method, on questions raised by the validity of induction and statistical analysis, on the logical procedures involved in hypothetical reasoning. So by and large, they feel, philosophy should content itself with logical and methodological problems. Others contend that such tasks too closely resemble the work of the mathematician; the philosopher should devote his energies to the linguistic structure of scientific statements. He will, they are convinced, be doing his proper job when he explores the nature of symbols and words, tries to ascertain how they are used, determines the syntactic rules according to which one puts them together correctly to form statements, searches out the meaning of words and speculates about the meaning of meaning.

But what is it [i.e. philosophy] then? Well, certainly not a science, but nevertheless something so significant and important that it may henceforth, as before, be honored as the Queen of the Sciences. For it is nowhere written that the Queen of the Sciences must itself be a science. The great contemporary turning point is characterized by the fact that we see in philosophy not a system of cognitions, but a system of *acts;* philosophy is that activity through which the meaning of statements is revealed or determined. By means of philosophy statements are explained, by means of science they are verified. The latter is concerned with the truth of statements, the former with what they actually mean. . . . The philosophical activity of giving meaning is therefore the Alpha and Omega of all scientific knowledge. This was indeed correctly surmised when it was said that philosophy supplied both the foundation and the apex of the edifice of science. It was a mistake, however, to suppose that the foundation was made of "philosophical" statements (the statements of theory of knowledge), and crowned by a dome of philosophical statements (called metaphysics).[3]

Venturing a bit farther afield, some philosophers even try to uncover the common structure of language as such or to determine whether or not there is a universal language. They may even feel that a universal language might reveal a hidden, universal logic common to all minds and capable of revealing the world's deepest secrets. Ludwig Wittgenstein formulates such a possibility quite succinctly:

Thought is surrounded by a halo.—Its essence, logic, presents an order, in fact the a priori order of the world: that is, the order of *possibilities*, which must be common to both the world and thought. But this order, it seems, must be *utterly simple*. It is prior to all experience, must run through all experience; no empirical cloudiness or uncertainty can be allowed to affect it. . . . We are under the illusion that what is peculiar, profound, essential in our investigation, resides in its trying to grasp the incomparable essence of language.[4]

But that, he goes on to point out, is an illusion that is to be charged to philosophers who abuse ordinary language. Instead of treating language as though it plainly laid everything out before our gaze for inspection, they see something hidden in words, something demanding explanation. It is the job of the philosopher to release us from these language snares:

It was true to say that our considerations could not be scientific ones. It was not of any possible interest to us to find out empirically "that, contrary to our preconceived ideas, it is possible to think such-and-such"—whatever that may mean. (The conception of thought as a gaseous medium). And we may not advance any kind of theory. There must not be anything hypothetical in our considerations. We must do away with all *explanations*, and description alone must take its place. And this description gets its light, that is to say its purpose, from the philosophical problems. These are, of course, not empirical problems; they are solved, rather, by looking into the workings of our language, and that in such a way as to make us recognize those workings: *in despite of* an urge to misunderstand them. The problems are solved, not by giving new information, but by arranging what we have always known. Philosophy is a battle against the bewitchment of our intelligence by means of language.[5]

Study of ordinary language, then, is not preparatory to a future regularizing of language, but merely a presenting of states of affairs in word-usages meant to throw light (as so many object-lessons) on the facts of our language. Such philosophical work does not explain anything or reveal any new hidden truth.

Many philosophers, and especially a growing number of European philosophers, are opposed to this view and disagree thoroughly with the basic principle involved in thus closely associating or identifying philosophy with the work of the scientist. Scientists, they insist, deal with the *Naturwelt*, the world of things in nature; philosophers deal with the *Geisteswelt*, the world of spirit or consciousness. Thus, physics, chemistry and the other sciences concentrate on phenomena or events that can be successfully observed and measured; philosophy dedicates itself to man —not to the extent that man is a thing of nature but, rather, as the kind of reality that is capable of reacting to his world through perception, imagination, fear, love, hope etc. The philosopher's task is to examine man's conscious response to reality, not with the intention of merely tabulating and recounting human reactions as the experimental psychologist does, but of discerning the necessary structures of human consciousness —and, perhaps, the structures of reality revealed in those conscious structures.

Martin Heidegger, one of the most influential of contemporary German philosophers, contends that we must *not* philosophize in traditional Greek patterns, but we must not philosophize in the scientific manner, either! In Heidegger's reading of the history of Western thought Plato and Aristotle have bequeathed a tradition to the West that has only succeeded in forgetting Being entirely:

> We have shown at the outset (Section I) not only that the question of the meaning of Being is one that has not been attended to and one that has been inadequately formulated, but that it has become quite forgotten in spite of all our interest in "metaphysics." Greek ontology and its history—which, in their numerous filiations and distortions, determine the conceptual character of philosophy even today—prove that when Dasein understands itself or Being in general, it does so in terms of the "world," and that the ontology which has thus arisen has deteriorated to a tradition in which it gets reduced to something self-evident—merely material for re-working, as it was for Hegel. In the Middle Ages this uprooted Greek ontology became a fixed

body of doctrine. Its systematics, however, is by no means a mere joining together of traditional pieces into a single edifice. Though its basic conceptions of Being have been taken over dogmatically from the Greeks, a great deal of unpretentious work has been carried on further within these limits.[6]

Heidegger discovers the roots of this forgetfulness of Being in the meaning Plato and Aristotle found in being; they interpreted it as *physis* and *logos*, nature and reason, and thereby missed the truth and essential temporality of Being. Heidegger asserted this theme in his early work *Being and Time* (1929), and he has continued to repeat it in subsequent writings:

> In historical terms the question is: What was the nature of this bond in the crucial beginnings of Western philosophy? How was thinking understood in the beginning? That the Greek doctrine of thinking should have become a doctrine of logos, logic, gives us a hint. Indeed, we encounter an original relationship between being, *physis* and *logos*. We must merely free ourselves from the notion that originally and fundamentally *logos* and *legein* signified thought, understanding, and reason. As long as we cling to this notion and even go so far as to interpret *logos* in the light of logic as it later developed, our attempt to rediscover the beginning of Greek philosophy can lead to nothing but absurdities.[7]

The philosopher must turn away from that Platonic tradition and rediscover the true meaning of Being through an awareness of it gained from his standing immersed in Being, through a recognition that human *being* is precisely a revealing of the truth of Being. As for the contemporary scientific tradition, it is Heidegger's view that all the sciences treat reality as though it were composed of objects. At best science treats things as though various fundamental material factors were simply arranged in different patterns so as to form the things of the natural world. Philosophy, he insists, must not treat reality as though it were composed of beings (*Seiendes*), but precisely as Being (*Sein*). It must go beyond the insights and problems of science and technology, and ask: Why is there anything at all? Why is there something rather than nothing? Granted that the scientist has to take things as he finds them and try to explain them by the basic structures of physics and chemistry, the question still remains: Have we really seen the being of things as long as we have only viewed them as so many modifications of a substructure? Must we not consider their very Being (*Sein*)? The question of Being, Heidegger emphasizes, *must* be asked once more because, he is convinced, (1) the truth of the being of things will only appear when we let things be and do not merely treat them as so many transformations of an absolute, and (2) man will only find the truth of his *own* being if he lets beings be. If he does not do so he will always look upon himself, as he does upon everything else, as a part of physical nature, his actions and reactions characterized and determined by nature. Man will only be *free* and *man* if he lets himself and things *be*. So the philosopher does have something quite distinct to examine, Being (*Sein*); and his work, distinct both from that of the modern physicist as well as of the ancient philosopher, is of ultimate practical importance. Indeed, in Heidegger's view, civilization itself depends on the philosopher re-discovering Being!

> Spirit is the mobilization of the powers of the essent as such and as a whole. Where spirit prevails, the essent as such becomes always and at all times more essent. Thus the inquiry into the essent as such and as a whole, the asking of the question of being, is one of the essential and fundamental conditions of an awakening of the spirit and hence for an original world of historical being-there (*Dasein*). It is indispensable if the peril of world darkening is to be forestalled and if our nation in the center of the Western world is to take on its historical mission. Here we can explain only in these broad outlines why the asking of the question of being is in itself through and through historical, and why, accordingly, our question as to whether being will remain a mere vapor for us or become the destiny of the West is anything but an exaggeration and a rhetorical figure.[8]

Heidegger, then, came to this position while actively opposing a Western philosophical tradition that, he contends, has always treated things as *objects*, i.e. as mere correlates of a subject's experience, as definable or meaningful, as instances of universals or concretions of universals. He represents a reaction against Hegel and Nietzsche particularly. St. Thomas, too, was in reaction against Aristotle, Plato, Avicenna and Averroës; his philosophical world is as different from the Greek world of Plato and Aristotle as Heidegger's world of Being (*Sein*) is different from Hegel's. For, as will become clearer in what follows, St. Thomas' philosophical world is a universe of dynamic, contingent being and freedom. Thus fate, for example, which St. Thomas interprets to be an ordering or disposition of *secondary* causes, itself comes under the order of divine providence and is for that reason changeable; it is not the prime and supreme force the Greeks thought it to be. The actions of men only come under the "determination" of natural forces accidentally and contingently, and events that occur accidentally here below have *no* necessary natural cause. St. Thomas refutes the view that the heavenly bodies *necessarily* produce effects in men and in the things of nature:

> In the first place it is not true that, given any cause whatever, the effect must follow of necessity. For some causes are so ordered to their effects as to produce them, not of necessity, but in the majority of cases, and in the minority to fail in producing them. But that such causes do fail in the minority of cases is due to some hindering cause, and consequently the above-mentioned difficulty seems to be avoided, since the cause in question is hindered of necessity.
>
> Therefore we must say, in the second place, that everything that is a being through itself has a cause; but what is accidentally has not a cause because it is not truly a being, since it is not truly one. For that which is *white* has a cause, and likewise that which is *musical* has a cause; but that which is *white-musical* has not a cause, because it is not truly a being nor truly one. Now it is manifest that a cause which hinders the action of a cause so ordered to its effects as to produce it in the majority of cases, clashes sometimes with this cause by accident; and therefore the clashing of these two causes, inasmuch as it is accidental, has no cause. Consequently, what results from this clashing of causes is not to be reduced to a further pre-existing cause from which it follows of necessity.[9]

Rather, a thing becomes subject to divine providence to the extent that it participates in being, and then fate assumes a conditional necessity; fate will only produce an effect in nature if God wills it. In this way a threatening world ruled by fate gives way to a world dependent in the final analysis on God's intellect and will, on His free decision. And that will, acting freely in creating things by giving each being its own act of existing, is concerned with much more than the general or specific being of things; it looks to the individual precisely as such:

> We must say, however, that all things are subject to divine providence, not only in general, but even in their own individual being. This is made evident thus. For since every agent acts for an end, the ordering of effects towards that end extends as far as the causality of the first agent extends. Whence it happens that in the effect of an agent something takes place which has no reference towards the end, because the effect comes from some other cause outside the intention of the agent. But the causality of God, Who is the first agent, extends to all beings not only as to the constituent principles of the species, but also as to individualizing principles; not only of things incorruptible but of things corruptible. . . . Since, therefore, the providence

of God is nothing other than the notion of the order of things towards an end, as we have said, it necessarily follows that all things, inasmuch as they participate being, must to that extent be subject to divine providence.[10]

And those individuals are much more than mere instances of species or ideal essences: they are *beings;* each has its own distinct act of existing, an act *not* demanded by the necessity of its natural or essential structure. Individual things are *not* essences. Indeed, essences are not *beings;* they are *principles* of beings. Nor do individual things act as though they were merely individual *natures;* a nature is not a thing or a subject of action but, rather, a proximate *principle* of operation. Some natures, in virtue of their proximity to matter, bring the things of which they are principles under the determining influence of natural forces and initiate actions that are for the most part regular; other natures, in virtue of their independence of matter in some measure, release the subject's operations from those determining influences and initiate *free* actions. Man's nature is of the second variety; it is not a nature closed by matter but opened by spirit. And the individual man who possesses such a principle does not have every action of his life inscribed on his nature at birth; his life is not simply a temporal span that witnesses the enactment or realization of a series of events already stamped on his character. As an individual being with a free human nature, he inscribes his own life story on *his* nature. He must act freely and rationally, but how his freedom and rationality actually develop as principles that are distinctly and uniquely his own is for him to determine. In short: St. Thomas' world is far removed from the Greek cosmos of Plato and Aristotle.

St. Thomas would also agree with Heidegger in claiming that philosophy has a subject quite distinct from that of the sciences. There is no question about his not knowing the scientific methods and techniques with which we are so familiar today; but he was convinced that there are principles in things that lie beyond the principles that account for the physical changes we observe in them. Even without our later scientific tradition to convince him, St. Thomas still saw the need for sensible experience if we are to have knowledge; he also saw the possibility of treating sensible realities like sound and light mathematically. But beyond this he detected more in the reality of things than sensible experience and mathematical technique could grasp. The only tools he had to formulate the matter or stuff of things were the ancient physical concepts fire, earth, air, water; we have quite different tools and no longer subscribe to such crude formulations. But St. Thomas had also discovered a subject for philosophy different from and basic to the principles of the natural sciences. Philosophy provides us with conclusions about things as *existing* realities, rather than as objects, events or phenomena. Thus, for example, man is different from everything else in nature not only in consequence of different elements composing his body or of his figure being different, but because he *exists* in a distinct and unique way: knowing and choosing. For St. Thomas, philosophy has something quite distinct to consider: the *being* of things insofar as they *exist*.

Three factors would appear to have combined to bring St. Thomas to that philosophical conviction: sense-experience, philosophical experience, and his Christian belief. Before St. Thomas began to search for conclusions about the being of things formally as a metaphysician, he had, as everyone does, a long sense-experience with things. He had undoubtedly seen the sunlight reflected from the lakes and streams, witnessed the stars in their course, listened to the singing of birds, waited patiently while tiny seeds germinated, admired an obedient dog responding to its master's call, experienced human suffering and pain and, as a student, the demanding toil of learning. All of these, he was convinced, took place round about him and within him. Each was a distinct reality: the shining light distinct from the bird's singing; the flower's growing distinct from the dog's obedient trot. Indeed, each reflecting of sunlight was distinct from the next, the thrush's singing different from the lark's, and each thrush's song different from another's. They were just so many unique occurrences, and St. Thomas was there in the midst of them wondrously able to mirror their activity. He knew that he could gain some understanding of them if he had recourse to the primitive scientific explanations of his day. Sunlight, reflection, the motion of the stars, their courses, sound, germination and growth, animal behaviour and pain could have been treated as scientific facts to be explored and explained. Other scholars did just that in St. Thomas' day; a great many more do so in our own day, and they do it with far greater sophistication. The world of nature, seen through the eyes of skillfully devised physical, chemical, biological and astronomical concepts and experienced as so many complex scientific events, presents a continuing challenge to our contemporaries. And we live to enjoy the results of their magnificent insights. But the scientists' constructs and the individual instances of them that he treats as phenomena and events exist in a different way outside the confines of his laboratory. They are existing individuals in a world of nature. It was just that status that attracted St. Thomas' attention. He was aware of things as *existents,* he knew their activities as they existed in a world around him. It is not a matter of contrasting a scientific with a naive experience, but of pointing to a different factor in reality: the fact or act of existing. What most amazed St. Thomas about things was that they *existed.* So he asked: Why?

It was not difficult for St. Thomas to draw upon his predecessors' experience to understand the objects of sense-experience as *things;* Greek and Arabic science could be of some help. But the questions that intrigued him most were not physical or biological, so he naturally turned to the philosophers for answers. He was disappointed by what he found in their writings. He discovered that they, too, only gave accounts of what those things are; few came to grips with what he saw to be their basic reality: their existence. And those who did failed, in his opinion, to grasp its full dynamism or fundamental importance to the being of things. Aristotle, for example, explained the reality of the things of nature by saying that form brings being to a thing by determining matter in a suitable manner. Thus, the human form or soul organizes matter to produce a man, the form of a plant determines matter in quite a different way to fashion a plant.

> For the word "nature" is applied to what is according to nature and the natural in the same way as "art" is applied to what is artistic or a work of art. We should not say in the latter case that there is anything artistic about a thing, if it is a bed only potentially, not yet having the form of a bed; nor should we call it a work of art. The same is true of natural compounds. What is potentially flesh or bone has not yet its own "nature," and does not exist "by nature," until it receives the form specified in the definition, which we name in defining what flesh or bone is. Thus, in the second sense of "nature" it would be the shape or form (not separable except in statement) of things which have in themselves a source of motion. (The combination of the two, e.g. man, is not "nature" but "by nature" or "natural").[11]

Avicenna, on the other hand, insisted that essence (which includes both matter and form) constitutes the reality of any composite being that exists:

> The quiddity [i.e. *what* anything is] of every simple thing is itself simple. For nothing is capable of receiving its own quiddity. If there were something in it capable of receiving its own quiddity, it would not be a received quiddity that is in it. For what is received is its form, but its form is not equal to the definition. Composite things are not what they are from the form alone. For the definition of composite things is not from form alone. The definition of a thing signifies everything of which its essence is constituted; wherefore it hap-

pens that it contains matter in some way or other, and so a difference is to be noted between quiddity and form. Form is always part of the quiddity in composite things; the form of every simple thing is itself simple because there is no composition in it. But the form of composite things is not itself composed and it is not their quiddity. The composite thing is not form. Thus, because form is a part of composites and quiddity is that which is, then anything exists when a form exists in conjunction with matter. But this is beyond the intention of form. And the composition is not that intention because a composite is made of matter and form. It is the quiddity of the composite and the quiddity is this composition. Therefore form is one of the things that belong in the composition; but the quiddity is the composition itself and includes form and matter.[12]

Now according to Avicenna a quiddity or essence taken precisely in itself and as such is neither universal nor individual; it becomes universal only by existing in an intellect as known, and individual by existing in this or that substance:

An individual is anything that cannot be understood to be predicable of many things, for example the substance of this Plato to whom we are pointing. For it is impossible to think of this unless it is his only. Therefore a universal, from the very fact that it is universal and from the fact that it is something to which universality happens, is something different. Thus, from the fact it is constituted a universal, one of the aforementioned terms is indicated concerning a universal. For since a thing itself is man or horse, the intention humanity or horseness is over and beyond the intention of universality. The definition of equinity is beyond the definition of universality, and universality is not contained in the definition of equinity. For equinity has a definition that does not demand universality; it is, rather, that to which universality comes. Wherefore, equinity is nothing but equinity only; of itself it is neither many nor one, it is not something existing in these sensible properties nor in the soul. Nor is it any of these in potency or in effect in such wise that it would contain them within the essence of quiddity. It is, rather, equinity only. For unity is a property, and when it is added to equinity, equinity becomes *one* on account of that property. In like manner equinity also has over and above this many other accidents that simply befall it. Equinity is common inasmuch as many agree in its definition; but it is singular inasmuch as it is taken with designated properties and accidents. Consequently, equinity in itself is equinity only.[13] [Emphasis added.]

Quiddity or essence, then, does not demand existence of its very essence or structure. If a quiddity does exist, existence must come to it as an accident:

So if anyone asks whether the humanity that exists in Plato, inasmuch as it is humanity, is other than the one that exists in Socrates and we necessarily answer, "No," it will not be necessary to agree with him when he goes on to say: "Therefore this humanity and that one are one in number." For the negation was an absolute one and in it we understand that inasmuch as it is humanity, it is humanity *only*. But the fact that it is different from the humanity that exists in Socrates is extrinsic. And he only asked about humanity insofar as it is humanity. For when he said: "The humanity that exists in Plato, inasmuch as it is humanity," he set down the aspect *inasmuch as it is humanity;* therefore when he said: "Which exists in Plato, or which is the one that exists in Plato," he attributed to it quite a different aspect.[14] [Emphasis added.]

For Avicenna, then, existence is an extrinsic accident.

In St. Thomas' estimation every one of the philosophical explanations he found in his predecessors' writings falls far short of expressing the fulness of being. As long as the reality of things is understood to be form or essence, we only know what reality is; we still have not seen it as a *being*. Where most of the philosophers of his day were content to view the things that compose the world of nature as moving things, individual forms or essences, St. Thomas saw them as existing entities. And, he pointed out, we do not call things "beings" in virtue of their quiddity, form or essence, but because of their act of existing:

The name *thing* is imposed from the quiddity, just as the name *being* is imposed from the act of existing.[15] [Emphasis added.]

St. Thomas speaks of what is most central or vital in anything in this way:

The act of existing is what is most intimate to anything, and it is more deeply present in every thing inasmuch as it is formal with respect to everything else that exists in a thing.[16]

Without that act nothing is capable of receiving any other quality or property that might characterize a thing:

The act of existing is the most perfect of all things; for it is compared to everything as its act. Nothing has actuality except insofar as it exists; wherefore, the act of existing is itself the actuality of all else, even of the forms themselves. Consequently, it is not compared to other things as a receiver is compared to what is received, but rather as what is received is to the one receiving.[17]

Therefore, as long as reality is understood as matter, form or essence, it is only understood as a thing, only its *whatness* is known; it is still not known as a being until it is seen to exist. For St. Thomas, form is only real because it is the form of a reality that *is;* apart from its existing as a formal principle of some entity, form literally does not exist. Even the separated intellectual substances, the angels, are not just forms; in them form remains a principle requiring the actualizing of existing if they are to be:

Although there is no composition of matter and form in an angel, yet there is act and potentiality. And this can be made evident if we consider the nature of material things, which contain a twofold composition. The first is that of form and matter, from which the nature is constituted. Such a composite nature is not its own being, but being is its act. Hence the nature itself is related to its own being as potentiality to act. Therefore, if there be no matter, and given that the form itself subsists without matter, there nevertheless remains the relation of the form to its very being, as of potentiality to act. And such a composition must be understood to be in the angels.[18]

Form is not a being and cannot account for being all by itself; the same is true of matter. For St. Thomas matter is only real because it is the matter of something that *is:*

Just as *man* does not exist apart from *this man,* so *matter* does not exist apart from *this matter.*[19]

There is no matter as such in potency, no form in potency; matter and form are not two possible *entities* awaiting actualization. Matter, form and potency are real because they are principles of existing beings.

To be created is a kind of coming to be, as was shown above. Now, to be made is directed to the being of a thing. Hence *to be made* and *to be created* properly belong to whatever *being* belongs. Now being belongs properly to subsisting things, whether they be simple, as in the case of separated substances, or composite, as in the case of material substances. For being belongs to that which has being—that is, to what subsists in its own being. But forms and accidents and the like are called beings, not as if they themselves were, but because something is by them; as whiteness is called a being because its subject is white by it. Hence, according to the Philosopher, an accident is more properly said to be *of a being* than a *being.* Therefore, just as accidents and forms and other non-subsisting things are to be said to co-exist rather than to exist, so they ought to be called *con-created* rather than *created* things. But properly speaking, it is subsisting beings which are created.[20]

And there is no neutral essence, as Avicenna would have it. Essence, *what* anything is, is not a being at all except in virtue of existing in some being; and then it is only a being in the sense of constituting a *principle* of a being. And an individual being is not just an essence individualized by a full set of unique accidents. However essence is determined it remains a *principle* of being requiring an act of existing to be real. In saying these things St. Thomas is committing himself to developing a philosophical knowledge of reality that would lead him to principles beyond those discovered in the sciences, and even beyond those revealed by previous philosophical investigations. Let us see some of the consequences that result from recognizing the act of existing as most intimate, profound, and perfect in whatever is.

In St. Thomas' view it is an inescapable fact, attested to by our sense-experience of the world about us, that entities and their acts of existing are many and varied. For example, a plant exists (living) in a way that a stone does not; and *this* plant exists in a way different from *that* one, even though they belong to the same family. Like any act, the act of existing is only exercised in this or that way; for instance, a horse runs in this or that direction, with one stride or another. In short: existing, in everything that exists, requires definite determinations or modes. If a plant is to exist its act must be exercised in this or that place, through a characteristic cell-structure, with particular requirements of light, moisture and soil. It must *be* in a determinate and limited way; it is truly a *finite* thing.

This is the kind of fact St. Thomas has in mind when he says that the act of existing must be exercised according to a certain mode or determined by a certain essence.

> Everything participated is compared to the participator as its act. But whatever created form be supposed to subsist *per se* must have being by participation, for *even life*, or anything of that sort, *is a participator of being*, as Dionysius says. Now participated being is limited by the capacity of the participator; so that God alone, Who is His own being, is pure act and infinite. But in intellectual substances, there is composition of actuality and potentiality, not, indeed, of matter and form, but of form and participated being.[21]

And again,

> If being is subsisting, nothing besides this act itself is added to it. Because, even in things whose being is not subsistent, that which

is in the existing thing in addition to its being is indeed united to the thing, but is not one with the thing's being, except by accident, so far as the thing is one subject having being and that which is other than being. Thus it is clear that in Socrates, besides his substantial being, there is white, which, indeed, is other than his substantial being; for to be Socrates and to be white are not the same except by accident. If, then, being is not in a subject, there will remain no way in which that which is other than being can be united to it. Now, being, as being, cannot be diverse; but it can be diversified by something beside itself; thus, the being of a stone is other than that of a man.[22]

The term "essence" is used to indicate whatever makes a thing the kind of reality it is. Thus, for man to be man he must have flesh, blood and bone; so these are said to be of the "essence" of man. Essence determines *how* a being exercises its act; it does not determine that it *does* exercise it. Unless a man exists, this flesh, blood and bone do not exist; and if a man and a woman do not exist, humanity cannot determine that this man, their off-spring, exists. Mankind, humanity, flesh, blood and bone are not beings. Briefly stated, whereas essence endows a thing with possibilities of being and provides us with the means of knowing what that thing is, it does not give the thing its actuality nor does it give us the means of knowing whether or not it is. If essence did account for a thing's existing, then coming into being by birth and ceasing to be by death would lose their true philosophical significance. They would not be required if John Jones were to be or cease to be, and they would not be required if *we* were to know John Jones. Knowing *what* man is would suffice. But this is not so for St. Thomas; a thing is not merely in virtue of its essence, and our conviction *that* a thing is cannot be reached by merely examining *what* it is. In short: there is no reason within the essence of anything finite to account for its being, i.e. its existing. To call a thing a being does not mean that it *must* be, in the sense that its *not* being would be contradictory. One might call Mr. Jones a teacher or say that he is teaching, but there is no absolute reason why he should be a teacher or that he should be teaching. He must be a teacher only while he is teaching. And that is the result of his existing, not of his essence. With this in mind St. Thomas prefers to speak of finite things as "things *having* an act of existing," rather than as "beings." Thus, he says in one place:

A natural thing, which has been generated, is said to exist by itself and properly, as a thing having an act of existing ( *habens esse* ) and subsisting in its own act of existing.[23]

For St. Thomas *what* a thing is and the *act* by which it is are two quite distinct principles. And this conclusion leads him to several further very interesting and important convictions.

First. Finite things are *radically* contingent as regards their coming into existence. Now let us be clear about the meaning of this statement. Plants and animals come into being by generation from seeds that exist before the individual plants and animals do; as we shall see, a very real necessity—but a necessity of a definite kind—determines their coming into being in that way and their growing as they do. But that is not the point involved here. St. Thomas is not thinking of plants as plants or of animals as animals, but of plants and animals as *beings*. The kind of beings they are—finite and generated—does not demand that *any* plant exist. In their existing plants grow and produce other plants. But why does *any* plant at all exist? Insisting on the radical contingency of finite things means that there is no necessary reason within the natural structure of plants that *any* exist—always granting that when they *do* exist, they bring other plants into being. For that is, indeed, how they exist—if they do!

Second. A further consequence immediately follows from this: all finite things have to *receive* their act of existing. As we have seen, St. Thomas takes the position that without the act of existing finite being is literally nothing. And inasmuch as existing as such is not proper to any finite thing or demanded by its essence, then no finite thing can, by its own causality, confer existing *as such* on another. Every finite thing presupposes something as existing and on which it can exercise its causality; it can never produce being as such but only being of one kind or another:

> A perfect thing participating in any nature makes a likeness of itself, not by absolutely producing that nature, but by applying it to something else. For an individual man cannot be the cause of human nature absolutely, because he would then be the cause of himself; but he is the cause that human nature exists in the man begotten. And thus he presupposes in his action the determinate matter whereby he is an individual man. But just as an individual man participates in human nature, so every created being participates, so to speak, in the nature of being (*naturam essendi*); for God alone is His own being (*suum esse*), as we have said above. Therefore no created being can produce a being absolutely, except inasmuch as it causes being (*inquantum esse causat in hoc*) in some particular subject; and so it is necessary to presuppose that whereby a thing is this particular thing as prior to the action whereby it produces its like.[24]

Therefore, he concludes, every finite being must ultimately receive its act of existing from outside the order of finite being. As an *existent* a finite thing is not made by, produced from, or generated by another finite being *alone*, whatever it may be. St. Thomas expresses this quite succinctly by saying that finite beings are made from nothing, i.e. created:

> . . . what proceeds by a particular emanation is not presupposed to that emanation. Thus, in the generation of man, we must say that he does not exist before being generated, but man is made from *not-man*, and white from *not-white*. Hence if the emanation of the whole universal being from the first principle be considered, it is impossible that any being should be presupposed to this emanation. Now *nothing* is the same as *no being*. Therefore, as the generation of a man presupposes the *non-being* which is *non-man*, so creation, which is the emanation of all being, presupposes the *non-being* which is *nothing*.[25]

Third. There is no conclusive rational proof that finite things did not exist eternally. For St. Thomas the question of the ultimate production of things in being is quite different from the question of their duration. Consequently, while contending that things must receive their act of existing from another, he also insists that there is no good reason why this might not have occurred eternally. In St. Thomas' judgment, the arguments that theologians have brought forward to prove that all things are *not* eternal are just as false as the arguments philosophers (and theologians!) have advanced to prove that they *must* be eternal:

> Hence, that the world began to exist is an object of faith, but not of demonstration or science. And it is useful to consider this, lest anyone, presuming to demonstrate what is of faith, should bring forward arguments that are not cogent; for this would give unbelievers the occasion to ridicule, thinking that on such grounds we believe the things that are of faith.[26]

This was not a popular position to take in the face of the authority of some of the thinkers respected in his own day. His friend, St. Bonaventure, for example, insisted that it is a contradiction to say: "The world existed from all eternity." It is a contradiction because it is against reason and against philosophical reasoning. For if the world is eternal, then every day it exists adds to eternity; if it is eternal, it would have to have existed through an infinite number of days to reach today. And then infinity would have to grow with each succeeding day. Better to say that the world is infinite in duration during the past and that it cannot traverse that past duration so as to reach today. But what, then, of the present day? Does it not prove that the world is *not* eternal, but that it has traversed a finite number of days? The only way to remove such a dilemma, according to St. Bonaventure, is to say: "The world is *not* eternal." *Reason*, then, would seem to demand that the world began in time:

> There are, however, reasons for the opposite position (i.e. that the world cannot be eternal), and they proceed from propositions known *per se* both according to reason and philosophy. This is the first of them.
>
> It is impossible to add to infinites: this is obvious of itself (*per se*) inasmuch as everything that receives addition becomes greater. But there is nothing greater than an infinite. If, however, the world is without a beginning, it has endured infinitely. Therefore, addition cannot be made to its duration. But this is clearly false because every day one revolution (of a planet) is added to another. Therefore, etc.
>
> But if you say that the world is infinite with respect to its past, and yet actually finite as regards the present, which is *now*, and therefore discover a greater in the fact that it is finite in act, the contrary is really shown because it is to uncover a greater in the past. For this is an infallible truth: the Sun's revolutions in its orbit are infinite, if the world is eternal. Again, during one revolution of the Sun there must have been twelve revolutions of the Moon. Therefore, the Moon has revolved more than the Sun. And the Sun revolves infinitely. But this is to discover among infinites one more infinite than another, and this on the side of their being infinite. But this is impossible. Therefore, etc. . . .[27] [Emphasis added.]

A second influential contemporary of St. Thomas, Siger of Brabant, took a diametrically opposite position: reason, he taught, demands the eternity of the world. To him the finite things of nature demand a first cause, so it must be admitted that a first cause exists and is the cause of everything. But such a cause must be *eternal*, and it could not be an eternal cause unless it caused *eternally;* the first cause must, then, exercise its causality eternally. And a cause without effects is simply not a cause at all. Consequently, if reason demands that a first cause exist, it must likewise require that its effects be eternal:

> Secondly, this must be taken into account: if the whole universe of beings were at one time non-being, as some poets, theologians and certain natural philosophers would have it (as Aristotle says in XII *Metaphysics*), then potency would precede act. And if some species of being, for example the human species, began to exist when it had never actually existed before—as some think they have demonstrated

—then potency to the act of that species would precede act simply. But both of these are impossible, as is clear from the first [argument given above].

If the whole universe of beings were at one time in potency, in such a way that not one of those beings was totally in act, always actually existing and moving, then beings and the world would only be in potency and matter would pass into act by itself. But that is impossible. Wherefore Aristotle and his Commentator in XII *Metaphysics* say that for things to have been at rest through infinite time and then to be moved is to say that matter is capable of motion in itself.

That this is impossible is also clear from the second argument [given above]. Inasmuch as the prime mover and agent is always in act, and is not something first in potency and then in act, it follows that the prime mover always moves and does whatever it does without any intervening movement. And from the fact that it is always moving and, hence, acting, it follows that no species of being proceeds to act without it having proceeded beforehand, so that in the same species what was before, for example, opinions, laws and religions, returns in circular fashion. Thus lower things circulate because of the circular movement of higher ones, although memories of any of those revolutions do not last because they happened so long ago. We are saying these things in accordance with the Philosopher's view, but we do not assert them as though they were true.[28]

It is worth noting that St. Bonaventure insists that reason and philosophy support his position, and Siger claims that he is only following the arguments already formulated by Aristotle. So when St. Thomas developed his own position, which falls midway between these two extremes, he was harvesting the results of different philosophical principles and reasonings. He states:

That the world did not always exist we hold by faith alone: it cannot be proved demonstratively; which is what was said above of the mystery of the Trinity. The reason for this is that the newness of the world cannot be demonstrated from the world itself. For the principle of demonstration is the essence of a thing. Now everything, considered in its species, abstracts from here and now; which is why it is said that *universals are everywhere and always.* Hence it cannot be demonstrated that man, or the heavens, or a stone did not always exist.[29]

And directing his argument more specifically at the Averroist "demonstration" that Siger invokes, St. Thomas replies:

Nor, if the action of the first agent is eternal, does it follow that His effect is eternal, as the second argument concludes. For we have already shown in this book that God acts voluntarily in the production of things, but not in such fashion that there be some other intermediate action of His, as in us the action of the motive power intervenes between the act of the will and the effect, as we have also previously shown. On the contrary, God's act of understanding and willing is, necessarily, His act of making. Now, an effect follows from the intellect and the will according to the determination of the intellect and the command of the will. Moreover, just as the intellect determines every other condition of the thing made, so does it prescribe the time of its making; for art determines not only that this thing is to be such and such, but that it is to be at this particular time, even as a physician determines that a dose of medicine is to be drunk at such and such a particular time, so that, if his act of will was of itself sufficient to produce the effect, the effect would follow anew from his previous decision, without any new action on his part. Nothing, therefore, prevents us saying that God's action existed from all eternity, whereas its effect was not present from eternity, but existed at that time when, from all eternity, He ordained it.[30]

According to St. Thomas, then, we know that things did not always exist, i.e. that they are not eternal, *only* as a result of Revelation, "the most solid teaching of God." "Ineffectual reasonings" do not bring us to that view.

Fourth. St. Thomas draws a conclusion that may appear somewhat surprising to us today. Just as there is no conclusive reason or absolute necessity for a being that has come into being to be, so there is no reason for a being, once it has been brought into being, *not* to be, i.e. not to continue in being. Two short statements clearly indicate his mind on this matter:

The nature of creatures shows that none of them is annihilated. For, either they are immaterial, and therefore have no potentiality to not-being, or they are material, and then they continue to exist, at least in matter, which is incorruptible, since it is the subject of generation and corruption. Moreover, the annihilation of things does not pertain to the manifestation of grace, since the power and goodness of God are rather manifested by the conservation of things in being. Therefore, we must conclude by denying absolutely that anything at all will be annihilated.[31]

And again:

Although corruptible creatures were not always, yet they will endure forever according to their substance—even though it has been set down by some that all corruptible things fall into non-being in the final consummation of things.[32]

As he opposed philosophers and theologians when they tried to prove that things have had a beginning in time, St. Thomas also opposed them when they claimed that things *must* fall into non-being. Careful attention, however, should be paid to the two qualifying phrases St. Thomas uses: finite things will persist in being "according to their substance," and material things will continue "at least in matter." This is not to say that plants and animals *will* continue to exist in the form in which we experience them today, because as such they do have principles of corruption within them. They will persist, he says, at least in their matter. Nor is it to say that things *must* continue to exist in the sense that they cannot be annihilated. It is to say, rather, that there is no reason in their principles *as beings* to say that they *must* cease to be. More positively put, finite things considered in themselves as beings that subsist in their own acts of existing have every reason for continuing to be once they are.

And this brings us to a fifth and last consequence: while finite things are radically contingent, they also harbor an absolute necessity within themselves. This may appear puzzling and even contradictory at first glance, so let us see what St. Thomas says about it. In one place he asks: How can there be absolute necessity in created things? The tools he uses to fashion an answer to that question are precisely the ones we have been examining. First, in virtue of the act of existing some things have an absolute necessity to be:

> On the contrary, there are some things in the universe whose being is simply and absolutely necessary.
>
> Such is the being of things wherein there is no possibility of not-being. Now, some things are so created by God that there is in their nature a potentiality to non-being; and this results from the fact that the matter in them is in potentiality with respect to another form. On the other hand, neither immaterial things, nor things whose matter is not receptive of another form, have potentiality to non-being, so that their being is absolutely and simply necessary.[33]

Second, in addition to the act of existing, essence is also a principle of a thing's being and with it comes a certain necessity. For, as St. Thomas hastens to add, even though God freely creates and things are contingent as regards their existing, God's creative act can account for a necessity in beings as well. For *created* necessity still requires a cause of its being:

> It is because created things come into being through the divine will that they are necessarily such as God willed them to be. Now, the

fact that God is said to have produced things voluntarily, and not of necessity, does not preclude His having willed certain things to be which are of necessity and others which are contingently, so that there may be an ordered diversity in things. Therefore, nothing prevents certain things that are produced by the divine will from being necessary.[34]

Third, if we turn away from the ultimate principle of things, i.e. God, to the proximate principles that constitute the essence of a thing and to the immediate causes that affect its being, we can note a wide range of necessities in things. Let us follow St. Thomas briefly as he points a few of them out to us:

> In created things, however, there are diverse modes of necessity arising from diverse causes. For, since a thing cannot be without its essential principles, which are matter and form, whatever belongs to a thing by reason of its essential principles must have absolute necessity in all cases. Now, from these principles, so far as they are principles of existing, there arises a threefold absolute necessity in things. First, through the relation of a thing's principles to its act of being. Since matter is by its nature a being in potentiality, and since that which can be can also not be, it follows that certain things, in relation to their matter, are necessarily corruptible—animals because they are composed of contraries; fire because its matter is receptive of contraries.[35]

And examining some of the other principles and causes at work in finite things, St. Thomas gives these examples of absolute necessities:[36] men must have the elements of matter in their bodily structure, men must be capable of learning, a saw must be hard, the sense must act when moved by its proper sensible, fire must heat, bodies on earth must be influenced by the movement of the heavens, and man's will must act for an end seen to be good. The natural sciences are built on just such necessities, and in St. Thomas' thought those necessities find their proper place within the contingency of beings that have to be given an act of existing if they are to be real.

Finally, let us explore another characteristic of finite beings with St. Thomas: causality. Causality is real for St. Thomas and can best be understood—perhaps, it can *only* be understood—when things are seen to have their own act of existing. His view might be put quite succinctly in this way: causing is the way finite beings exist. Take a plant, for instance. Sunlight, moisture, the earth's minerals must act on it if it is to exist; but it must reach out for the stuff it needs to build itself, it must multiply its cells, assimilate the minerals it takes in, arrange them into stalk, leaves and flowers. That is what it is to be a plant. It must exist *causing*, i.e. making itself into a plant, once the original conditions are given. A plant is not a plant merely because it has been engendered; it is also a plant because it exists causing a plant (itself) to be. It is important for a plant to be made a plant; it is even more important for it to *be*. And it must persist in *causing*, if it is to go on being. Or take a more emotional example: the atomic bomb. People of today are not concerned because scientists have produced mathematical formulae from which possible, destructive effects might be calculated and predicted. Such causality is relatively safe because in this view the bomb is not looked upon as a *being*. We are terribly concerned, however, because bombs exist and we exist. Causality as an *existential* reality affecting our own being—not our being *men,* but our very *existing*—bothers us mightily. We have *seen* the mushroom-shaped cloud and the obliteration of whole islands. Let us hope and pray that we do not have to experience its causality before we can say: "Yes. Causality *is* real."

With such examples before us, let us try to understand causality with St. Thomas, bearing in mind his basic principle: the act of existing. What does it tell us about the causality of finite things? First, since no finite thing has its act of existing from itself, it cannot cause the act of being in its effects entirely from itself. A finite being does bring some effect into existence; it always presupposes, rather, the existence of something from which it can produce that effect. In short: its causality is never a creating, i.e. it never makes something from nothing. It is, rather, generation, transformation, or some other such causality. For example, a plant brings a leaf or another plant into being, but only by presupposing the materials it uses and the suitability of those materials for transformation into a new effect.

Second, whereas it is true that all finite beings have this in common, namely, that each brings some effect into being, still none of them causes being *as such,* but only being in this or that way. As St. Thomas says:

> All created causes communicate in one effect and that is the act of existing, even though each such cause has its own proper effect in which it is distinguished. For heat makes a warm thing to be and a builder makes a house exist. Therefore, they all agree in that they cause an act of existing, but they differ inasmuch as fire causes fire and a builder causes a house.[37]

In short: finite things cause this or that to be; they are never causes of being simply. All finite beings are, then, *secondary* causes. Such causes always presuppose that something is, i.e. they presuppose the action of a cause that does make being as such to be. Here is the way St. Thomas puts it:

> Thus, if creation is taken strictly in this way, creation can only belong to a first agent; for a secondary cause only acts through the influence of the first cause; and so every action of a second cause is on the presupposition of the acting cause.[38]

One word of caution is in order here: simply because a secondary cause presupposes a first cause does not mean that the primary cause is the *only* cause. Primary causality does not remove a true causality from secondary causes. For just as each finite being subsists in its own act of existing, so, too, is each truly a cause. It really does bring an effect into being and contributes something of itself to the effect:

> It is for the same reason that the effect tends to the likeness of the agent, and that the agent makes the effect like to itself, for the effect tends towards the end to which it is directed by the agent. The agent tends to make the patient like the agent, not only in regard to its act of being, but also in regard to causality. For instance, just as the principles by which a natural agent subsists are conferred by the agent, so are the principles by which the effect is the cause of others. Thus, an animal receives from the generating agent, at the time of its generation, the nutritive power and also the generative power. So, the effect does tend to be like the agent, not only in its species, but also in this characteristic of being the cause of others. Now things tend to the likeness of God in the same way that effects tend to the likeness of the agent, as we have shown. Therefore, things naturally tend to become like God by the fact that they are the causes of others.[39]

Consequently, St. Thomas specifically refutes those who would insist that no creature exercises any action in the production of natural effects. One of the arguments he advances is of particular interest today when we are so interested in the natural sciences. St. Thomas argues in this fashion:

> . . . if created things do not have actions to produce effects, it follows that the nature of a created thing could never be known through the effect. And in this way all the knowledge of natural science would be taken from us, for in that knowledge proofs are mainly taken from the effect.[40]

In short, if secondary causes are not real, there are *no* natural sciences.

Before summing up our findings, let us add a brief word about finality and the work of final causes. Finality and teleology have fared badly in most modern discussions of nature because they do not appear to find a proper place in the natural sciences. However, they *do* have a role to play in St. Thomas' philosophical discussion, and precisely because they are implied in the *being* of things. Much of the difficulty in understanding finality stems from two misunderstandings. First, interpreting finality and purpose as conscious decision and deliberate planning, as though each thing were looked upon as consciously and deliberately seeking some end. Second, understanding the terms "end" and "final cause" only in the most ultimate and comprehensive sense of a unique end for all things. In that view God would be considered to be the only end and He would be imagined to manipulate everything to His own plan. These are not St. Thomas' views at all. Although some beings do act with conscious design, and although God *is* the ultimate end of everything, all finality does not involve deliberate decision and God is not the only end. Here are some samples of his views on the subject:

> A thing moves or operates for an end in two ways. First, in moving itself to the end, as do man and other rational creatures; and such beings have a knowledge of their end, and of the means to the end. Second, a thing is said to move or operate for an end, as though moved or directed thereto by another, as an arrow is directed to the target by the archer, who knows the end unknown to the arrow. Hence, as the movement of the arrow towards a definite end shows clearly that it is directed by someone with knowledge, so the unvarying course of natural things which are without knowledge shows clearly that the world is governed by some reason.[41]

And again:

> . . . wherever we have order among a number of active powers, that power which is related to the universal end moves the powers which refer to particular ends. And we may observe this both in nature and in political things. For the heavens, which aim at the universal preservation of things subject to generation and corruption, move all inferior bodies, each of which aims at the preservation of its own species or of the individual. So, too, a king, who aims at the common good of the whole kingdom, by his rule moves all the governors of cities, each of whom rules over his own particular city. Now the object of the will is the good and the end in general, whereas each

power is directed to some suitable good proper to it, as sight is directed to the perception of color, and the intellect to the knowledge of truth. Therefore, the will as an agent moves all the powers of the soul to their respective acts, except the natural powers of the vegetative part, which are not subject to our choice.[42]

There are, then, many ways in which finality is exercised and there is an order of ends culminating in common ends. For St. Thomas finality is involved in the very being of all finite things, whether they are capable of knowledge and decision or not; and final cause is a principle of being in each individual being, even though there is an order of final causes that does culminate in an ultimate final cause.

St. Thomas' thinking on this subject might be illustrated by returning to our example of the plant growing. It exists, as has been stated, by living, growing, fashioning food into its own structure, and becoming more fully a plant. Thinking of this datum as a philosopher (not as a natural scientist), St. Thomas understands it as indicating that the plant exists by moving in a definite, ordered direction towards a more complete and fuller state of being. The direction is definite because the way the plant lives is in keeping with the particular kind of plant it is. Its nature determines how it will germinate, grow and assimilate food. And the path of that movement is towards being more completely a plant. This may be formulated as follows:

Since the essence of good consists in this, that something perfects another as an end, whatever is found to have the character of an end also has that of good. Now two things are essential to an end: it must be sought or desired by things which have not yet attained the end, and it must be loved by the things which share the end, and be, as it were, enjoyable to them. For it is essentially the same to tend to an end and in some sense to repose in that end. Thus by the same natural tendency a stone moves towards the center (of the world) and comes to rest there.

These two properties are found to belong to the act of being. For whatever does not yet participate in the act of being tends towards it by a certain natural appetite. In this way matter tends to form, according to the Philosopher. But everything which already has being naturally loves its being and with all its strength preserves it. Boethius accordingly says: "Divine Providence has given to the things created by it this greatest of reasons for remaining, namely, that they naturally desire to remain to the best of their ability. Therefore, you cannot in the least doubt that all beings naturally seek permanence in perduring and avoid destruction."

Existence itself, therefore, has the essential note of goodness. Just as it is impossible, then, for anything to be a being which does not have existence, so too it is necessary that every being be good by the very fact of its having existence, even though in many beings many other aspects of goodness are added over and above the act of existing.[43]

Every finite being, then, in its very existing *tends to* or *inclines* towards a more mature state of being. In short: the plant lives to make itself a plant! Every finite being, precisely because it is finite and incomplete, exists by acting so as to be more fully what it is embryonically by birth.

St. Thomas summarizes this conclusion in statements such as these: "Every agent acts for an end," and "All things naturally seek the good." We shall explore the meaning of the term "good" more fully in a later chapter when human freedom comes under examination, but in the present context it is enough to say that the good signifies the more complete state that a finite being strives to effect in its being by acting in some way or other. Not, indeed, that each one does in fact succeed in doing what is good for it; any number of factors may intervene to prevent it doing so or to deflect it from its course. It indicates, rather, that an agent as a being acts to become more complete; if it is to be an agent at all, its activity must be brought into being and given direction. Once the thing is in motion, let us say, the physicist may step in and tell us how it works. And the good has no role to play in his formulation. But a thing that moves is also a being in act, and that requires philosophic understanding.

After nearly three hundred years of philosophical discussion in which final causes have been largely replaced by mechanical causes, it is refreshing and reassuring to read the plea made for a philosophical recognition of final causes by an eminent mathematician and scientist, Alfred North Whitehead, collaborator with Bertrand Russell in the writing of *Principia Mathematica:*

It is notable that no biological science has been able to express itself apart from phraseology which is meaningless unless it refers to ideals proper to the organism in question. This aspect of the universe impressed itself on that great biologist and philosopher, Aristotle. His philosophy led to a wild over-stressing of the notion of final causes during the Christian middle ages; and thence, by a reaction, to the correlative over-stressing of the notion of "efficient causes" during the modern scientific period. One task of a sound metaphysics is to exhibit final and efficient causes in their proper relation to each other.[44]

Thus, in developing his own philosophy of organism, Whitehead places great stress on the view that reality is a process; his theory is patterned on a cell-theory of actuality, and part of his analysis constitutes a genetic-theory of the development of complex objects from primitive cell-structures. To found its own existence, the cell appropriates various elements in the universe; Whitehead calls each such appropriation a "prehension." Various prehensions bring each object into relation with all actual entities and with a selection of eternal objects, and the prehensions are integrated by the subject into a variety of categorical types. So an actual entity is a process wherein a series of prehending operations, each incomplete in itself, culminates in a completed operation called a "satisfaction;" each thing is impelled by a kind of creative urge, an urge to cause itself, and gains satisfaction as its categorical demands are met. Considered positively these prehensions are spoken of as "feelings," so that it is true to say that each subject is marked by feelings that aim to build up that subject—the subject acting as final cause of the process.

> The subject-superject is the purpose of the process originating the feelings. The feelings are inseparable from the end at which they aim; and this end is the feeler. The feelings aim at the feeler, as their final cause. The feelings are what they are in order that their subject may be what it is. Then transcendently, since the subject is what it is in virtue of its feelings, it is only by means of its feelings that the subject objectively conditions the creativity transcendent beyond itself. In our own relatively high grade of human existence, this doctrine of feelings and their subject is best illustrated by our notion of moral responsibility.[45]

It is just this integration of efficient and final causes that St. Thomas is attempting.

Finality, then, is one of the causes—alongside essence, act of existing and efficient cause—that the philosopher discovers in finite things as beings. In discovering those causes, the philosopher has to use all of his powers of knowing. It is not correct to say that he sees causes or experiences causality by using his senses alone—if, indeed, there is such a thing as a human experience involving the senses alone! All of the philosopher's powers of knowing are involved together: his senses are needed to confirm that the finite thing in question does, in fact, exist; his intellect is involved to apprehend that act of being (precisely as being) through judging; and his reason is implicated in discoursing about the dependence of a being on another being if it is to be. It is truer to say that the man, the philosopher, rather than his senses or reason, knows things as cause and effect. And inasmuch as reasoning is involved in discovering causality, it is better to speak of propositions about causality as reasoned conclusions rather than as principles—where "principle" would indicate a primary or self-evident proposition.

Now let us summarize the main conclusions reached in these brief reflections. At the outset we asked ourselves a whole series of questions that might be more briefly stated in this way: Is there a valid work for philosophy to do today when a multitude of new sciences tell us so much about ourselves and our environment? Does philosophy, conceived as a wisdom or science and employing concepts that originated in a pagan Greek matrix, have any relevance today? Does the title of this chapter "Philosophic Knowledge of Reality," have any real meaning? Well, let us see.

All the sciences consider some particular aspect of reality and try to formulate the laws of its behavior, but none of them is concerned with reality as such. Those sciences quite correctly accept what they study as given; they are concerned with learning about reality, assuming that there is something to study. St. Thomas is concerned, rather, with understanding why there is anything at all; he studies beings insofar as they *exist*. Being as be-ing is the distinct subject of his investigation. It is a subject, too, that takes us beyond the limits of particular studies of reality. St. Thomas is in search of a knowledge that is significant for *all* finite things. He is, in short, cultivating a wisdom. This does not mean that logic, psychology, semantics and the analysis of consciousness are unimportant philosophically. It implies, rather, that when their subjects are considered they will be seen in a new light: in the light of their act of being.

As regards the philosophical concepts St. Thomas inherited from Greek thought and used to understand his own world, they have all been thoroughly re-interpreted and integrated into a new philosophical complex. He is not philosophizing with a pagan's experience of the world but with a Christian's awareness of it. An uncreated universe dominated by universal species, ruled by fates and working out its destiny in necessary, recurring cycles is replaced by a freely created world of subsisting beings, each the result of a divine choice rather than an emanation from a necessary cause. And within his world the dominance of Fate is restricted to the influence of the heavenly bodies and brought under the control and guidance of a free, first cause; individual finite beings enjoy a being of their own and some of them—those that are capable of intelligent being—are free, masters of their own destiny. Finally, necessary, recurring cycles find their place taken by contingent events in linear time. The conceptual tools of Greek philosophy do their work within a completely new framework as instruments of St. Thomas' Christian philosophy.

Our own scientific concepts, i.e. the concepts of modern physics, chemistry, biology and astronomy, are undoubtedly different from the Greek and Arabic scientific concepts with which St. Thomas was familiar. To that extent we are aware of the things of nature, the heavens and our own bodily functions in a way substantially different from his. And there is no question about modern scientific developments bringing their own unique philosophical problems, problems quite unknown to St. Thomas. But the things and activities that we now formulate with new scientific concepts remain existing realities; and the fundamental questions St. Thomas raised concerning existence remain valid. Not that he has answered *all* philosophical questions about existence—as a theologian he was attracted by comparatively few such philosophical questions, as a man doing philosophical work at an earlier age he was unaware of many of the philosophical problems we face today, and as one provided with scientific tools now outmoded he was faced by many philosophical questions that do not arise today. Philosophy—and especially Christian philosophy—remains a *human* achievement, and as such it must remain incomplete at any point of time. Philosophical truth is not an eternal essence, but the result of intellectual work. And the task of understanding man and his world is an endless one.

Finally various conclusions were seen to follow upon the basic philosophical principle St. Thomas discovers in finite things: the act of existing. Let us list some of them: there is no necessary reason in any finite thing why it should exist; if it does exist, it must have received its being; in the most profound sense it is made from nothing; things are radically contingent, but having been given their being they must persist in being in some way; they harbor an absolute necessity within them; finite things are truly causes; efficient and final causality are at work in their being. These are conclusions that are true of all finite things and flow from a fundamental principle in each of them. Such conclusions do, therefore, constitute philosophical knowledge. There would, then, seem to be some justification for giving this chapter the title it bears.

So far very little has been said about man. Surely we are of some importance to the philosopher. Let us ask, then: What do St. Thomas' insights into being tell us of *human* being? Does being, viewed as primarily act, provide any philosophical knowledge of man's being, of human knowledge, or human freedom? These are questions that affect every one of us today. For not only have nuclear warfare, with its threatening physical and biological damage, and psychoanalysis, with its revelations of our hidden structures and motives, made us more and more concerned about *ourselves*, but new philosophical movements have also sprung into being to make us more self-conscious. Phenomenology and existentialism have captured the attention of serious thinkers in the wake of a growing concern for man's survival *as man* in the face of science and technology, and of a deepening conviction about the uniqueness of human reality inspired by religious experience. Traditional philosophy has been pictured as either disregarding man or construing him as merely one more natural entity; existential philosophers, on the contrary, have emphasized that man is not an object as trees and stones are, that he is free and transcends the determinations of nature, that his being should be interpreted as a unique, personal existence (*Existenz*) quite unlike the existence (*esse*) of things.

Now we have just seen St. Thomas insisting on the fundamental reality of existence. Is there a hidden snare awaiting us here? Does St. Thomas' emphasis on the act of existing as fundamental to all finite being really mean that he is reducing human reality to the status of every other being? Does his doctrine of existing (*esse*) threaten man's free, personal being (man as *Existenz*)? Let us try to answer these questions by turning to the significance which St. Thomas' doctrine of being holds for man.

# CHAPTER V

# *HUMAN BEING*

"Curiosity exists in animals, too. Many animals are exceedingly curious."

"But they do not have *ju-jus* [talisman]?" asked the judge. "No."

"So it isn't the same kind of curiosity. They haven't asked the same questions."

"That is true," said Sir Peter. "The metaphysical mind is peculiar to man. The animal doesn't have it."

"Can one be quite sure of it though? Has no animal ever shown signs of that type of curiosity, even at its most rudimentary level?"

"I don't think so," said Sir Peter. "This is rather outside my sphere, but on the face of it. . . . The animal watches, observes, waits to see what this or that will do, or become, but . . . that's all. If the object disappears, his curiosity disappears with it. Never this . . . this refusal, this struggle against the silence of things. For the fact is that the animal's curiosity has remained purely functional: it does not really apply to the thing as such, but only to its relationship with himself; the animal always remains part of things—part of nature, in every fiber. He never detaches himself from things in order to know or understand them from outside. In a word," concluded Sir Peter, "the animal is incapable of abstract thinking. There indeed we may have . . . a network of connections . . . a specific network given to man, and man alone."

Nobody having any more questions to put, the judge thanked the professor and allowed him to stand down.[1]

At the end of the last chapter this question came up for consideration: Do St. Thomas' conclusions about finite beings as existing entities have any significance for *human* being? It must be recognized at once that this is not a frivolous question. Most of our contemporaries are convinced that man's great need today is for practical solutions to his problems, not theoretical observations about being. Thus in *The Secular City* Harvey Cox designates practicality and the pragmatic spirit as fundamental traits resulting from the urbanization and secularization that mark the lives of men in twentieth-century cities:

To say that technopolitan man is pragmatic means that he is a kind of modern ascetic. He disciplines himself to give up certain things. He approaches problems by isolating them from irrelevant considerations, by bringing to bear the knowledge of different specialists, and by getting ready to grapple with a new series of problems when these have been provisionally solved. Life for him is a set of problems, not an unfathomable mystery. He brackets off the things that cannot be dealt with and deals with those that can. He wastes little time thinking about "ultimate" or "religious" questions. And he can live with highly provisional solutions.

He sees the world not so much as an awesome enigma, evoking a sense of hushed reverence, [but] as a series of complex and interrelated projects requiring the application of competence. He does not ask religious questions because he fully believes he can handle this world without them.[2]

To men imbued with such a spirit the metaphysical properties of beings—existing, essence, finality, causality—seem to be abstract in the extreme, even though St. Thomas' intention was that they be understood as most concrete! In addition, thoughtful voices have been raised to insist that traditional metaphysics actually poses a serious threat to man's true being. For does not wisdom, in the very effort it makes to discover the first and most universal causes of things, seem to be working directly at cross-purposes with what is most important to human beings, their individuality, their personal lives in a unique point of space and time? Indeed, the metaphysician's task of trying to understand the common properties of being is interpreted by some of our contemporaries as nothing more than an effort to treat human beings as though they were identical with any other thing in the world of nature. Thus, in Jean-Paul Sartre's view the fundamental fallacy to be avoided in reflecting on human reality is the error of confusing the *pour-soi* with the *en-soi*, "man" with "thing;" our constant temptation is to shirk responsibility by taking refuge in the anonymity of a fixed reality.

The ultimate meaning of determinism is to establish within us an unbroken continuity of existence in itself. The motive conceived as a psychic fact—i.e., as a full and given reality—is, in the deterministic view, articulated without any break with the decision and the act, both of which are equally conceived as psychic givens. The in-itself has got hold of all these "data;" the motive provokes the acts as the physical cause its effect; everything is real, everything is full. Thus the refusal of freedom can be conceived only as an attempt to apprehend oneself as being-in-itself; it amounts to the same thing. Human reality may be defined as a being such that in its being its freedom is at stake because human reality perpetually tries to refuse to recognize its freedom. Psychologically in each one of us this amounts to trying to take the causes and motives as *things*. We try to confer permanence upon them. We attempt to hide from ourselves that their nature and their weight depend each moment on the meaning which I give to them; we take them for constants. This amounts to considering the meaning which I gave them just now or yesterday—which is irremediable because it is past—and extrapolating from it a character fixed still in the present. I attempt to persuade myself that the cause *is* as it was. Thus it would pass whole and untouched from my past consciousness to my present consciousness. It would inhabit my conciousness. This amounts to trying to give an essence to the for-itself.[3]

Metaphysical thinking, then, would seem to be a real danger and a useless luxury at a time when man is most in need of understanding himself and of formulating practical plans and workable solutions to his myriad problems. Many of our contemporaries would unhesitatingly recommend that we leave theoretical wisdom and metaphysics alone and get on with the practical task of living.

Strangely enough, however, a strong plea has been made in recent years for a revival of metaphysics, for centering our thinking about man and the problems of life precisely on the study of being. And the plea has come from a most unexpected quarter, the psychiatrist. To some psychiatrists the study of being does *not* endanger man, nor does its supposed abstractness threaten either their own experimental methods or practical therapies. Indeed, the plea has been justified on the grounds that a proper understanding of being would make the psychiatrist's work even *more* dependent on observation than less dependent on it. In his book entitled *Existence: A New Dimension in Psychiatry and Psychology*, Rollo May describes the work of a group of psychiatrists in Germany and the United States, and publishes several articles in translation to illustrate what they are doing. All the members of this group were trained as psychiatrists in the techniques of Sigmund Freud and Carl Jung, but progressively they came to feel that a deeper and, at the same time, more comprehensive penetration of man's mind and personality must be made. As Rollo May states:

. . . many psychiatrists and psychologists in Europe and others in this country have been asking themselves disquieting questions, and others are aware of gnawing doubts which arise from the same half-suppressed and unasked questions.

Can we be sure, one such question goes, that we are seeing the patient as he really is, knowing him in his own reality; or are we seeing merely a projection of our own theories *about* him? . . . the crucial question is always the bridge between the system and the patient—how can we be certain that our system, admirable and beautifully wrought as it may be in principle, has anything whatever to do with this specific Mr. Jones, a living, immediate reality sitting opposite us in the consulting room?

Another such gnawing question is: How can we know whether we are seeing the patient in his real world, the world in which he "lives and moves and has his being," and which is for him unique, concrete, and different from our general theories of culture? In all probability we have never participated in his world and do not know it directly; yet we must know it and to some extent must be able to exist in it if we are to have any chance of knowing him.

Such questions were the motivations of psychiatrists and psychologists in Europe who later comprised the *Daseinsanalyse,* or existential-analytic, movement. The "existential research orientation in psychiatry," writes Ludwig Binswanger, its chief spokesman, "arose from dissatisfaction with the prevailing efforts to gain scientific understanding in psychiatry." [4]

These scholars, then, have come to believe that man must be seen as a whole and viewed as closely integrated into the world he inhabits. Such a line of thinking has led them to accept a closer partnership with the metaphysician precisely in trying to do their scientific and therapeutic work as psychiatrists! Eugen Kahn describes the alliance between ontology and therapy in this way:

Existential analy*tics, Dasein*sanaly*tik,* has nothing at all to do with therapeutic practice, with practical intentions and purposes. As the fundamental ontology of Martin Heidegger, it asks "only" for the Being of all being . . . for the mode of existence of man and his belonging to Being. Even there where existential analy*tics* is modified and restricted to Ludwig Binswanger's existential analy*sis* as a merely anthropological method of research, it is nothing else but phenomenological examination and elucidation of essence of the healthy and sick human existence. Boss discusses the necessity "of a definite *Weltanschauung* or metaphysics without which he (the physician) would not want to help at all." He calls this the doctor's "Faith" based on the desire to open to our patients the way to their being fully human. Boss does not leave us in any doubt about his *Weltanschauung* or metaphysics, or if one wants to call it so: his faith. It is grounded in Heidegger's teaching. It is as though he were backing up Freud's psychoanalytic technique with the theory offered in Heidegger's ontology. [5]

During the nineteenth century, they reasoned, the psychologist as a scientist quite properly proclaimed his independence of the metaphysics of the day. But it has become clear in fairly recent years that in casting off what was expressly recognized as metaphysical thinking in the early days of experimental science, a new and oftentimes unrecognized metaphysic had been substituted for the old. Science always has its presuppositions, and it is important for the psychiatrist to know just what they are, lest those assumptions unwittingly intrude themselves between himself and the patient he is trying to cure. Careful investigation has convinced this group of scholars that on at least three points an unobserved metaphysic has, indeed, come to interfere with their treatment of patients: first, a view of man that alienates him from the world he inhabits; second, an interpretation of human sensation that results from such a view of man and divorces human response from the sensible things of the world; third, a progressive fragmentation of man attendant upon the specialization of the various sciences.

The contributors to Rollo May's volume trace the roots of these three positions back to the philosophical speculation of René Descartes and the classical philosophers of the seventeenth and eighteenth centuries, especially John Locke and David Hume. The foundations of the new sciences and, indeed, the very possibility of the human mind attaining truth were at stake in Descartes' meditations. Our capacity for knowing the truth, he was convinced, must be established on a base that could not be challenged; it must be a foundation capable of justifying itself. To Descartes' mind merely logical thinking or the evidence of the senses hardly measured up to such demands. For the senses can, and indeed very often do, deceive us; we have no really solid guarantee that in logical argument we are not merely consistently wrong and perpetually deceived.

> The Meditation of yesterday filled my mind with so many doubts that it is no longer in my power to forget them. And yet I do not see in what manner I can resolve them; and, just as if I had all of a sudden fallen into very deep water, I am so disconcerted that I can neither make certain of setting my feet on the bottom, nor can I swim and so support myself on the surface. I shall nevertheless make an effort and follow anew the same path as that on which I yesterday entered, i.e. I shall proceed by setting aside all that in which the least doubt could be supposed to exist, just as if I had discovered that it was absolutely false; and I shall ever follow in this road until I have met with something which is certain, or at least, if I can do nothing else, until I have learned for certain that there is nothing in the world that is certain. Archimedes, in order that he might draw the terrestrial globe out of its place, and transport it elsewhere, demanded

only that one point should be fixed and immoveable; in the same way I shall have the right to conceive high hopes if I am happy enough to discover one thing only which is certain and indubitable.

I suppose, then, that all the things that I see are false; I persuade myself that nothing has ever existed of all that my fallacious memory represents to me. I consider that I possess no senses; I imagine that body, figure, extension, movement and place are but the fictions of my mind. What, then, can be esteemed as true? Perhaps nothing at all, unless there is nothing in the world that is certain.[6]

We can be absolutely certain of only one thing, he said: thought itself. Thought appears to be self-authenticating in the sense that the very effort to deny it proves its reality. Here at last, Descartes was sure, philosophical speculation would seem to have reached bed-rock; we can be sure without any possible question that thinking is real even though things are not:

But immediately afterwards I noticed that whilst I thus wished to think that all things were false, it was absolutely essential that the "I" who thought this should be somewhat; and remarking that this truth, "*I think, therefore, I am*," was so certain and so assured that all the most extravagant suppositions brought forward by the sceptics were incapable of shaking it, I came to the conclusion that I could receive it without scruple as the first principle of the Philosophy for which I was seeking.[7]

The mind, in other words, is capable of drawing a completely convincing evidence from itself; the mind is certain of the ideas it finds in its own thinking and arrives at truth by methodical examination of those ideas. As Malebranche was to put it shortly afterwards: our knowledge would be the same whether the world existed or not:

Let us suppose, Aristes, that God were to annihilate all the beings He created except you and me, your body and mine. . . . Let us suppose, moreover, that God impresses on our brain all the same traces, or rather that he produce in our minds all the same ideas we have there today. Supposing that were so, Aristes, in what world would we pass our days? Would it not be in an intelligible world? Now take care, we are and live in that world, even though the body that we animate lives in another and walks in another world. That is the world we contemplate, admire and feel. But the world at which we look, the one we consider when we turn our heads in every direction, is only matter that is invisible in itself and that has none of the beauties we admire and feel when we look upon them. For, I beg you, reflect on this well. Nothingness has no properties. Thus, if the

world were destroyed, it would have no beauty. Now upon the sup-
position that the world were destroyed and that God nevertheless
produced the same traces on our brain, or rather that He presented
our mind with the same ideas that are produced there when the objects are present, we would see the same beauties. Therefore the
beauties we see are not material beauties but, rather, intelligible
beauties rendered sensible in virtue of the laws governing the union
of soul and body, since the supposed annihilation of matter does not
imply the annihilation of the beauties we see when we look upon the
objects that surround us.[8]

Now what did this philosophical conviction about the primary evidence
of thought lead Descartes to conclude about man? Three conclusions
followed rather quickly. First, Descartes was able to say with certainty
*that* we exist, inasmuch as thinking necessarily implies the subject who
thinks. Second, he could say *what* we are: thinking things.

And then, examining that which I was, I saw that I could conceive
that I had no body, and that there was no world nor place where I
might be; but yet that I could not for all that conceive that I was
not. On the contrary, I saw from the very fact that I thought of
doubting the truth of other things, it very evidently and certainly
followed that I was; . . . From that I knew that I was a substance
the whole essence or nature of which is to think, and that for its
existence there is no need of any place, nor does it depend on any
material thing; so that this "me," that is to say, the soul by which
I am what I am, is entirely distinct from body, and is even more easy
to know than is the latter; and even if body were not, the soul would
not cease to be what it is.[9]

Now it should be noted that for Descartes such a statement about our
being did not merely state a fact, i.e. that man is a thing that does, in
fact, think; it is, rather, a definition expressing our essence, i.e. that man
is by nature thought! Third, his original insight led him to a further conclusion about our relations with the world of things. Trees, stones, animals,
the planets have figures and dimensions, they move either in place or from
place to place; thoughts about them do *not* have such characteristics.
Consequently, unless some necessary relationship can be established
between thoughts and things, i.e. unless something in the definition of
thought and body demands a necessary connection between the two, they
must be said to constitute two quite distinct orders of reality.

And first of all, because I know that all which I apprehend clearly
and distinctly can be created by God as I apprehend them, it suffices

that I am able to apprehend one thing apart from another clearly and distinctly in order to be certain that the one is different from the other, since they may be made to exist in separation at least by the omnipotence of God; and it does not signify by what power this separation is made in order to compel me to judge them to be different; and, therefore, just because I know certainly that I exist, and that meanwhile I do not remark that any other thing necessarily pertains to my nature or essence, excepting that I am a thinking thing, I rightly conclude that my essence consists solely in the fact that I am a thinking thing (or a substance whose whole essence or nature is to think). And although possibly (or rather, certainly, as I shall say in a moment) I possess a body with which I am very intimately conjoined; yet because, on the one side, I have a clear and distinct idea of myself inasmuch as I am only a thinking and unextended thing, and as, on the other, I possess a distinct idea of body, inasmuch as it is only an extended and unthinking thing, it is certain that this I (that is to say, my soul by which I am what I am) is entirely and absolutely distinct from my body, and can exist without it.[10]

In short: man and his thoughts stand over against the natural, physical world of moving things—even over against his own body as an extended thing! Man is a spectator in a physical world; he is not in it or of it.

The story is the same when we come to consider sensation. Descartes is convinced that sensation is merely a state of consciousness, a "confused thinking." [11] Sensations are the affections (things that "affect" us) which the mind originates within itself when motions are introduced into the body and transmitted by the nerves to the brain. Having established that mind is a substance distinct from body and that nothing should be attributed to it except thoughts, Descartes is careful to distinguish between the actions of the mind and its passions. Actions originate directly within the mind and are the many desires we experience; passions originate in the mind, too, but they are not solely from the mind alone. Some passions are perceptions of our acts of desire or imagination; others are perceptions of changes wrought in the body by other bodies. The latter perceptions or sensations are not produced in the mind by the motion of sensible things but originate with the mind and represent the changes taking place in the body.

I distinguish all the objects of our knowledge either into things or the affections of things, or as eternal truths having no existence outside our thought. Of the things we consider as real, the most general are *substance, duration, order, number* and possibly such other similar matters as range through all the classes of real things. I do not however observe more than two ultimate classes of real things—the one is intellectual things, or those of the intelligence, that is, pertaining to the mind, or to thinking substance, the other is material things, or that pertaining to extended substance, i.e. to body. Perception, volition and every mode of knowing and willing, pertain to thinking substance; while to extended substance pertain magnitude or extension in length, breadth and depth, figure, movement, situation, divisibility into parts themselves divisible, and such like. Besides these, there are, however, certain things which we experience in ourselves and which should be attributed neither to mind nor body alone, but to the close union that exists between the body and mind as I shall later on explain in the right place. Such are the appetites of hunger, thirst etc., and also the emotions or passions of the mind which do not subsist in mind or thought alone, as the emotions of anger, joy, sadness, love etc.; and, finally, all the sensations such as pain, pleasure, light and colour, sounds, odours, tastes, heat, hardness, and all other tactile qualities.[12]

Now inasmuch as sensations are *passions* of the mind, they require some *active* power correlative to them. Such an active power, according to Descartes, cannot belong to mind but only to body. We must admit, then, that there are bodies. But inasmuch as sensations are *thoughts,* they cannot share in the active properties of body. In short: we do not perceive things as they exist, but as they are represented to us in our thoughts. They are confusedly represented in sensation, more clearly and distinctly represented in the necessary thoughts we have about the properties of extension that constitute the essence of body. There can be certitude about the size, figure and dimensions of bodies because such properties necessarily belong to bodies; there cannot be certainty regarding their color, taste or odor because they are not necessarily demanded by the nature of body. We can only be sure of our perceptions of them.

This active faculty cannot exist in me (inasmuch as I am a thing that thinks) seeing that it does not presuppose thought, and also that some of those ideas are often produced in me without my contributing in any way to the same, and often even against my will; it is thus necessarily the case that the faculty resides in some substance different from me in which all the reality which is objectively in the ideas that are produced by this faculty is formally or eminently contained, as I remarked before. And this substance is either a body, that is, a corporeal substance in which there is contained formally (and really) all that which is objectively (and by representation) in those ideas, or it is God Himself, or some other creature more noble than body in which that same is contained eminently. But, since God is no deceiver, it is very manifest that He does not communicate to me these ideas immediately and by Himself, nor yet by the intervention of some creature in which their reality is not formally, but only eminently, contained. For since He has given me no faculty to recognize that this is the case, but, on the other hand, a very great inclination to believe (that they are sent to me or) that they are conveyed to me by corporeal objects, I do not see how He could be defended from the accusation of deceit if these ideas were produced by causes other than corporeal objects. Hence we must allow that corporeal things exist. However, they are perhaps not exactly what we perceive by the senses, since this comprehension by the senses is in many instances very obscure and confused; but we must at least admit that all things which I conceive in them clearly and distinctly, that is to say, all things which, speaking generally, are comprehended in the object of pure mathematics, are truly to be recognized as external objects.[13]

Inasmuch as we are minds, we cannot be certain of the sensible properties of things but only of their mathematical characteristics. And we are only certain of those properties because we can deduce them from the ideas of figure and number, not in virtue of learning them from the things of the external world. We are, indeed, spectators, not participants.

On this score the account of sensation given by Locke and Hume is little different in its results, even though they approach the subject more empirically than Descartes did and examine the senses from the side of body rather than mind. Both agree that the proper philosophical method is an approach to reality through the testimony of the senses. Locke presents his position in this way:

Though the qualities that affect our senses are, in the things themselves, so united and blended that there is no sensation, no distance between them; yet it is plain the ideas they produce in the mind enter by the senses simple and unmixed. For though the sight and touch often take in from the same object, at the same time, different ideas—as a man sees at once motion and color, the hand feels softness and warmth in the same piece of wax—yet the simple ideas thus united in the same subject are as perfectly distinct as those that come in by different senses; the coldness and hardness which a man feels in a piece of ice being as distinct ideas in the mind as the smell and whiteness of a lily, or as the taste of sugar and smell of a rose: and there is nothing can be plainer to a man than the clear and distinct perception he has of these simple ideas; which, being each in itself uncompounded, contains in it nothing but one uniform appearance or conception in the mind and is not distinguishable into different ideas.

These simple ideas, the materials of all our knowledge, are suggested and furnished to the mind only by those two ways above mentioned, viz. sensation and reflection. When the understanding is once
stored with these simple ideas, it has the power to repeat, compare
and unite them, even to an almost infinite variety, and so can make
at pleasure new complex ideas. But it is not in the power of the most
exalted wit or enlarged understanding, by any quickness or variety
of thought, to invent or frame one new simple idea in the mind not
taken in by the ways before mentioned . . .[14]

Hume in turn would have us put aside abstract philosophical thinking
and abstruse metaphysics; in their place he would recommend that we
follow the example of the geographer or astronomer in experimentally
plotting the outlines of the human mind.

But may we not hope, that philosophy, if cultivated with care, and
encouraged by the attention of the public, may carry its researches
still farther, and discover, at least in some degree, the secret springs
and principles, by which the human mind is actuated in its operations? Astronomers had long contented themselves with proving,
from the phenomena, the true motions, order and magnitude of the
heavenly bodies. Till a philosopher, at last, arose, who seems, from
the happiest reasoning, to have also determined the laws and forces,
by which the revolutions of the planets are governed and directed.
The like has been performed with regard to other parts of nature.
And there is no reason to despair of equal success in our inquiries
concerning the mental powers and economy, if prosecuted with equal
capacity and caution.[15]

However, even though both Locke and Hume insist that the senses and
sensation, rather than mind and thought, must be our starting points in
understanding human knowledge, sensation still does not give us a knowledge of things in the natural world. According to Locke we are aware
in sensation of impulses brought about in the nerves of the body and
transmitted to the brain.

If, then, external objects be not united to our minds when they produce ideas therein, and yet we perceive these original qualities in
such of them as singly fall under our senses, it is evident that some
motion must be thence continued by our nerves or animal spirits by
some parts of our bodies to the brain or the seat of sensation, there
to produce in our minds the particular ideas we have.[16]

The ideas thereby produced are the *objects* of perception, thought or understanding.

I must here, in the entrance, beg pardon of my reader for the frequent use of the word "idea" which he will find in the following treatise. It being the term which, I think, serves best to stand for whatever is the *object* of the understanding when a man thinks.[17]

In short: we understand *ideas*, not the physical things of the world of nature.

Moreover, qualities normally deemed sensible—tastes, colors, odors—are really so many modifications effected in the senses of the perceiver.

After the same manner that the ideas of these original qualities are produced in us, we may conceive that the ideas of secondary qualities are also produced, viz. by the operation of insensible particles on our senses. For it being manifest that there are bodies, and good store of bodies, each whereof are so small that we cannot by any of our senses discover either their bulk, figure or motion (as is evident in the particles of the air and water, and others extremely smaller than those, perhaps as much smaller than the particles of air or water as the particles of air or water are smaller than peas or hailstones): let us suppose at present that the different motions and figures, bulk and number, of such particles, affecting the several organs of our senses, produce in us these different sensations which we have from the colors and smells of bodies, v.g. that a violet, by the impulse of such insensible particles of matter of peculiar figures and bulks, and in different degrees and modifications of their motions, causes the ideas of the blue color and sweet scent of that flower to be produced in our minds; it being no more impossible to conceive that God should annex such ideas to such motions, with which they have no similitude, than that He should annex the idea of pain to the motion of a piece of steel dividing our flesh, with which the idea hath no semblance.

What I have said concerning colors and smells may be understood also of tastes and sounds, and other the like sensible qualities; which, whatever reality we by mistake attribute to them, are in truth nothing in the objects themselves, but powers to produce various sensations in us, and depend on those primary qualities, viz. bulk, figure, texture and motion of its parts.[18]

We are aware, then, of changes in the subject, and we can only be sure of what things in the natural world are by a kind of inference. We have to remain ignorant of the thing's substance—indeed, it is, to use Locke's phrase, an "I-know-not-what" that we infer is in things.[19] Hume has pushed this position one step further. For while agreeing, as we have seen, that we have to construct our knowledge from impressions and ideas, he has insisted that sensations are atomic, isolated data of consciousness. In their own way they are Descartes' distinct ideas in a new garb. There is no reason for them to be inter-connected except the pattern effected in the subject by a repetition of similar stimuli.

> Suppose a person, though endowed with the strongest faculties of reason and reflection, to be brought on a sudden into this world; he would, indeed, immediately observe a continual succession of objects, and one event following another; but he would not be able to discover anything farther. He would not, at first, by any reasoning, be able to reach the idea of cause and effect; since the particular powers, by which all natural operations are performed, never appear to the senses, nor is it reasonable to conclude, merely because one event, in one instance, precedes another, that therefore the one is the cause, the other the effect. Their conjunction may be arbitrary and casual. There may be no reason to infer the existence of one from the appearance of the other. And in a word, such a person, without more experience, could never employ his conjecture or reasoning concerning any matter of fact, or be assured of anything beyond what was immediately present to his memory and senses.[20]

Necessary connection between any two events can only be the result of repeated experiences of similar successions of events.

> It appears, then, that this idea of a necessary connection among events arises from a number of similar instances which occur of the constant conjunction of these events; nor can that idea ever be suggested by any one of these instances, surveyed in all possible lights and positions. But there is nothing in a number of instances, different from every single instance, which is supposed to be exactly similar; except only, that after a repetition of similar instances, the mind is carried by habit, upon the appearance of one event, to expect its usual attendant, and to believe that it will exist. This connection, therefore, which we *feel* in the mind, this customary transition of the imagination from one object to its usual attendant, is the sentiment or impression from which we form the idea of power or necessary connection.[21]

When we say, therefore, that one object is connected with another, we mean only that they have acquired a connection in our thoughts and give rise to an inference whereby they become proofs of each other's existence; we do not mean to state anything of the relations between the things themselves. In short: even in sensation, where we might expect men to have some access to the world about them, they find themselves cut off from the world and forced to devise reasons that will tell them a little of what it is like. But can they ever be sure, apart from God's benign presence, that their own creations are not imposing a meaning on the things they experience? If that presence should fade, would men ever be certain of the world confronting them?

This fragmentation of experience has left its mark on the sciences and effected a subsequent fragmentation of man by the sciences. For if the data provided by sensation has no intrinsic reason for holding together, then the scientist's genius is required to formulate it and give it some kind of unity or pattern. As Kant has demonstrated so clearly in his first *Critique*, reason must provide the key ideas of totality in accordance with which scientific understanding can proceed to organize the data provided by sensible intuition into meaningful scientific objects.

If we consider in its whole range the knowledge obtained for us by the understanding, we find that what is peculiarly distinctive of reason in its attitude to this body of knowledge, is that it prescribes and seeks to achieve its *systematisation*, that is, to exhibit the connection of its parts in conformity with a single principle. This unity of reason always presupposes an idea, namely, that of the form of a whole of knowledge—a whole which is prior to the determinate knowledge of the parts and which contains the conditions that determine *a priori* for every part its position and relation to the other parts. This idea accordingly postulates a complete unity in the knowledge obtained by the understanding, by which this knowledge is to be not a mere contingent aggregate, but a system connected according to necessary laws. . . . These concepts of reason are not derived from nature; on the contrary, we interrogate nature in accordance with these ideas, and consider our knowledge defective so long as it is not adequate to them.[22]

Objects, however, remain phenomenal and our knowledge of them never provides us with any information about things in the natural world. Moreover, the physicist may interpret his data in one way, the chemist in another, the economist and biologist in still different ways. For each of these sciences men become something different as they fit into different patterns of organization; the only unity they preserve is the transcendental unity of a thinking subject. Ernst Cassirer, writing of the "autonomous sciences" of the nineteenth century in his *Essay on Man* describes the situation in this way:

The principal aim of all these theories was to prove the unity and homogeneity of human nature. But if we examine the explanations which these theories were designed to give, the unity of human nature appears extremely doubtful. Every philosopher believes he has found the main-spring and master-faculty—*l'idée maitresse*, as it was called by Taine. But as to the character of this master-faculty all the explanations differ widely from, and contradict, one another. Each individual thinker gives us his own picture of human nature. All these philosophers are determined empiricists: they would show us the facts and nothing but the facts. But their interpretation of the empirical evidence contains from the very outset an arbitrary assumption—and this arbitrariness becomes more and more obvious as the theory proceeds and takes on a more elaborate and sophisticated aspect. Nietzsche proclaims the will to power, Freud signalizes the sexual instinct, Marx enthrones the economic instinct. Each theory becomes a Procrustean bed on which the empirical facts are stretched to fit a preconceived pattern. . . . Theologians, scientists, politicians, sociologists, biologists, psychologists, ethnologists, economists all approached the problem from their own viewpoints. To combine or unify all these particular aspects and perspectives was impossible.[23]

We have succeeded in divorcing what we have called thought or consciousness from the natural world of things; we have conceived man as a subject consciously reflecting about a world he can only know as an object; we have fitted him out with atomic information that he has to piece together but of which he can never be sure that the reconstruction is valid—unless it happens to work!—; and we have destroyed his unity by progressive fragmentation. Now can St. Thomas' insights into being and existing help us here? Well, Descartes' metaphysical insight apparently set these changes in motion, so let us see if St. Thomas' views offer any hope of understanding man as a unified being in intimate relationship with his world.

To speak of man as a *human being* is just too deceptively simple. St. Thomas himself usually speaks of man simply as *homo*, man; if we designate him "human being" it is with a view to discovering Aquinas' understanding of man in the light of the profound significance he has discovered in the reality of being. Being, he has told us, is to be encountered or discovered concretely in something sensible; anything is a being when it subsists.

The sense of sight, as being altogether material, cannot be raised up to anything immaterial. But our intellect, or the angelic intellect, inasmuch as it is elevated above matter in its own nature, can be

raised up above its own nature to a higher level by grace. An indication of this is that sight cannot in any way know in abstraction what
it knows concretely; for in no way can it perceive a nature except as
this one particular nature; whereas our intellect is able to consider
in abstraction what it knows in concretion. For although it knows
things which have a form residing in matter, still it resolves the composite into both elements, and considers the form separately by
itself. Likewise, also, the intellect of an angel, although it naturally
knows the being concreted in any nature, still it is able to separate
that being by its intellect; since it knows that the thing itself is one
thing, and its being is another. Since therefore a created intellect is
naturally capable of apprehending the concreted form and the concreted being in abstraction, by way of a certain resolution, it can by
grace be raised up to know separate subsisting substance and separate subsisting being.[24]

Consequently, if we are to discover man, we must encounter him *sensibly*
as he exists. Moreover, St. Thomas has told us that we learn about being
by induction, memory, reason and intellect. So all of these activities likewise have to be trained on man if we are to know him as a human being.
We must not simply read off a series of characteristics that we might
deduce from the nature of being and attribute them to man. Being reveals
itself in many, many ways in a variety of entities; knowing man as a
being still leaves us with the mystery: what kind of a being is he? How
does he exist? What characteristics must we associate with man as a
being? To answer these questions we need a philosophy of being, but
we also need a philosophy of human being. And if human being works out
its meaning in a material world of time and change, then we need more
than a capacity for deduction if we are to learn of man. We have to experience him in a material situation, we have to call upon the memory
of the race in traditional lore, anthropology and social studies. Nor should
we neglect the study of the artifacts he produces and has produced, for
the symbols of painting, poetry, music and religion can reveal man to us
just as truly as the scientific symbols he fashions can teach us about him.
Let us start at the beginning, then, and ask: Why do we call man a being?
Why, above all, do we call him a distinct kind of being, a *human* being?

Well, in keeping with his conviction that a thing's actions reveal its
being, St. Thomas calls man a being because his actions show that he
exists—he is a *subject* of action and existing, he is not an accident of some
other subject.

Of no thing whatever can a perfect knowledge be obtained unless
its operation is known, because the measure and quality of a thing's

power is judged from the manner and type of its operation, and its power, in turn, manifests its nature; for a thing's natural aptitude for operation follows upon its actual possession of a certain kind of nature.[25]

Now if man's operations are examined, it becomes clear that he does many of the things other physical things do: he acts and reacts chemically; he assimilates food and organizes it into arms, legs, eyes and ears; he reacts consciously to light, heat and odors; he builds houses and the most amazing scientific instruments; he is jealous or friendly; he acts justly or dishonestly; he decides the kind of life he will lead and the kind of person he will be; he paints, composes music, builds cities, and worships in any number of ways. Man is, in short, a center of activity and causality. He is a being. He has to receive his being by generation and lose it by death. While he has his being he strives to better it, to grow into a more mature state of manhood. In short: man exhibits all the marks we usually consult to discover whether or not something is a being.

Moreover, as St. Thomas has pointed out, all beings act and interact one upon the other so as to act as causes of becoming.

Every effect depends on its cause, so far as it is its cause. But we must observe that an agent may be the cause of the becoming of its effect, but not of its *being*. This may be seen both in artificial and in natural things. For the builder causes the house in its *becoming*, but he is not the direct cause of its being. For it is clear that the *being* of the house is a result of its form, which consists in the putting together and arrangement of the materials, and which results from the natural qualities of certain things. Thus a cook prepares the food by applying the natural activity of fire; and in the same way a builder constructs a house by making use of cement, stones and wood, which are able to be put together in a certain order and to conserve it. Therein the *being* of the house depends on the nature of these materials, just as its *becoming* depends on the action of the builder. The same principle applies to natural things. For if an agent is not the cause of a form as such, neither will it be directly the cause of its *being* which results from that form; but it will be the cause of the effect only in its *becoming*.[26]

The sunlight and moisture of the soil act on the plant, the plant acts on the earth's minerals, its flowers act on the birds and insects, and so on. Man is not one whit different. He is a *part* of the natural physical world in which he finds himself—indeed, St. Thomas refers[27] with approval to Aristotle's statement "Man is begotten by man and by the sun as well," and accords the heavenly bodies a causal role in the generation of inferior bodies even though they differ in species from them.

> There is acquired from birth, however, in the body of the child a certain disposition both from the power of the heavenly bodies and from inferior causes, which are the semen and the matter of the one conceived; and by it the soul is in some sense made prone to choose something inasmuch as the choice of the rational soul is inclined by the passions, which are in the sense appetite, a bodily power dependent upon the dispositions of the body. But no necessity in choosing is thereby introduced into it, since it is within the power of the rational soul to admit or to repress the passions which arise.[28]

The physical world enters into him physically and consciously, and he effects physical and chemical changes in it—both voluntarily and involuntarily. Other human beings, too, acting not merely as physical entities but as distinctly *human* beings, affect him and he affects them. He loves some, deplores others; he makes friends and enemies; he brings mental and emotional comfort to some, heartfelt anguish to others; he learns from his teachers and influences the lives of his friends and children. In short: man is a part of a great natural world around him and shares the inter-personal world of moral and artistic experience with others of his kind. He does not exist as a spectator but as a participant.

St. Thomas also tells us that every being, precisely because it is a being, is *one* and acts as a unity.

> One does not add any reality to *being*, but is only the negation of division; for *one* means undivided *being*. This is the very reason why *one* is convertible with *being*. For every being is either simple or composite. But what is simple is undivided, both actually and potentially; whereas what is composite has not being while its parts are divided, but after they make up and compose it. Hence it is that everything guards its unity as it guards its being.[29]

And inasmuch as each thing acts in accordance with the actual being it possesses,[30] then a being that is *one, acts* as a unity. Every being is *a* being, not in the sense of being numerically one so that it can be counted and numbered—*one* man, *two* men, *three* men—, but in the sense that when it acts all of its parts act together to perform the action as a whole. For example, we say that a flower or leaf grows when actually it is the whole plant, with its whole complicated organism, that grows and produces the flower or leaf. St. Thomas always insists that actions are the accomplishments of the *whole* substance, of the whole being held together, as it were, by the being's one act of existing.

Actions are of subjects (*suppositorum*) and totalities (*totorum*), and not, properly speaking, of parts and forms or potencies; for a hand is not properly said to strike a blow, but man does so with his hand, nor is heat properly said to warm, but fire does so through heat.[31]

A man, too, is a being and acts as a unity. As with the plant, so too with man. Philosophers have often spoken as though our ear hears someone's voice or our hand shakes another's hand. But St. Thomas warns us that this is not, strictly speaking, so; a *human being* hears a sound and the one making the analysis singles out one of the organs, the ear, to designate the special relationship to sound. But a physical ear or even the complex mechanism of ear, nerves etc., hears nothing; at best it might vibrate a bit with the motion of the air. So, too, with the hand and its supposed ability to shake another hand—truly a most unsatisfying handshake without a human being at either end! Indeed, one is tempted to ask: is the real significance of the handshake to be found in the physical clasping of hands or in the inter-personal insight occasioned by two human beings entering into communion with each other? In short: for St. Thomas, man is viewed as a being, acts as a whole, and it is only by way of abstraction or as a convenient shorthand that we say: the eye sees color, the intellect judges a thing to be or not.

Now what is the source of unity in man? We have one clue in the act of existing. We have said that all the parts composing a thing *are* and are *one* because they are held in existence by *an* act of existing. For St. Thomas, the existing proper to man is the act of understanding, so if we are to find the source of unity in man it is in this direction that we have to look. As St. Thomas says in one of his early works: "*Intellectus est principale.*" [32] What, then, does he mean by "understanding?" It has several meanings:

> . . . we are said to understand something in three ways. First, as we understand by means of the intellect which is the power from which such an operation proceeds; hence, both the intellect itself is said to understand, and also the intellect's act of understanding becomes our act of understanding. Second, we understand by means of an intelligible species; of course, we are not said to understand by it, in the sense that it understands, but because the intellective power is actually perfected by it, as the visual power is by the species of color. Third, we understand as by an intermediary through the knowing of which we come to the knowledge of something else.[33]

Understanding, then, is the act of the intellect, and in simple terms it is the act of accepting or seeing something as true. Thus, the act whereby we note a necessary property in things such that they can be defined and distinguished from otherwise similar things is called an act of understanding. For example: if one were to discover that some things are capable of reproducing themselves whereas others were not, he would have some understanding of what living meant. Or if a person were to know that some people were interested in his welfare and actively promoted it, he would begin to understand friendship. In short: seeing those necessary properties in things or human acts that can be formulated in definition is to understand them. This is one meaning of understanding.

St. Thomas also associates a further activity with understanding: the act of judging.

> The human intellect must of necessity understand by composition and division. For since the intellect passes from potentiality to act, it has a likeness to generable things, which do not attain to perfection all at once but acquire it by degrees. In the same way, the human intellect does not acquire perfect knowledge of a thing by the first apprehension; but it first apprehends something of the thing, such as its quiddity, which is the first and proper object of the intellect; and then it understands the properties, accidents and various dispositions affecting the essence. Thus it necessarily relates one thing with another by composition or division.[34]

In a sense judging completes the intellect's apprehension of a thing. By its initial act the intellect only sees *what* the thing is; by the act of judging it assents or dissents to existence, and thereby apprehends the thing's act of existing. Similarly, if the intellect is engaged in the practical understanding of a human act that has still to be brought into existence, rather than the theoretical or speculative understanding of a thing already in existence, its work is not complete until it judges. It must first understand what the action is, but then to complete its *practical* understanding of the action it must go on to judge whether or not it should be performed—and, above all, whether or not it is an act that an individual person should perform in a given set of entirely unique spatio-temporal conditions.

> Some knowledge is speculative only, some is practical only, some is partly speculative and partly practical. In proof whereof it must be observed that knowledge can be called speculative in three ways: first, in relation to the things known, which are not operable by the knower; such is the knowledge of man about natural or divine things. Secondly, as regards the manner of knowing—as, for instance, if a builder were to consider a house by defining and dividing, and con-

sidering what belongs to it in general; for this is to consider operable things in a speculative manner, and not as they are operable;
for *operable* means the application of form to matter, and not the
resolution of the composite into its universal formal principles.
Thirdly, as regards the end; *for the practical intellect differs from the
speculative by its end*, as the Philosopher says. For the practical intellect is ordered to the end of operation; whereas the end of the
speculative intellect is the consideration of truth. Hence, if a builder
were to consider how a house can be made, but without ordering this
to the end of operation, but only towards knowledge, this would be
only a speculative consideration as regards the end, although it concerns an operable thing.[35]

So when one judges that a plant is alive or an animal is dead, or that
he should not cheat the person with whom he is doing business, he is
exercising acts of understanding. In such acts one either sees an identity
in existence of what he understands plant and living thing to be, or he
sees that bringing an act of cheating into existence is not good for him
because it will not help him to become the man he should be. To understand, then, is to judge.

St. Thomas is also convinced that every time a person judges he implicitly uses various primary judgments and that it is also the work of
understanding to make those judgments and to acquire the habit of
applying them.

> . . . man's act of reasoning, since it is a kind of movement, proceeds
> from the understanding of certain things (namely, those which are
> naturally known without any investigation on the part of reason) as
> from an immovable principle; it also terminates in the understanding,
> inasmuch as, by means of those naturally known principles, we judge
> of those things which we have discovered by reasoning. Now, it is
> clear that, as the speculative reason reasons about speculative mat-
> ters, so the practical reason reasons about practical matters. There-
> fore we must be naturally endowed with not only speculative princi-
> ples, but also practical principles. Now the first speculative principles
> bestowed on us by nature do not belong to a special power, but to a
> special habit, which is called the *understanding of principles*, as the
> Philosopher explains. Hence, the first principles, bestowed on us by
> nature, do not belong to a special power, but to a special natural
> habit, which we call *synderesis*. Whence *synderesis* is said to incline
> to good, and to murmur at evil, inasmuch as through first principles
> we proceed to discover and judge of what we have discovered.[36]

Such principles or starting points for making judgments are "bestowed
on us by nature" in the sense that men are endowed by nature at birth

with intellects that operate according to the rules represented by the first principles. Thus, any simple judgments about the plant and its being alive or dead presuppose, first, that what the plant is and what a living thing is remain identical in the judgment; and second, that every such judgment is about existence, i.e. it assumes the primary judgment that "What is, is." And the same is true in the case of judgments about the course of action one should take. They, too, assume a primary practical judgment or rule of practical thinking: one is to do what is good and not do what is evil. For a thing is considered to be an agent because it acts, and every act is performed because it brings some good or perfection to the agent. In this sense a good is a principle for an agent. In the case of man, who acts with understanding, the precise good eliciting his action is of his own determining, but every practical judgment is aimed at some good or at some action or end deemed good. The primary *practical* judgment: "Good is to be done, evil avoided," is the principle that expresses this universal concern of practical thinking for the good. In this sense, then, all judgments about the realities we experience and the actions we are to do are based on primary judgments about being and good. Understanding, therefore, is the act by which we grasp principles: metaphysical principles of being, moral principles of acting, and logical principles of thinking.

All of these meanings of "understanding" refer, in one way or another, to the *beginnings* of knowledge, both speculative and practical: definitions, judgments and principles. But St. Thomas is ever-mindful that *human* understanding has a precise and uniquely human character; it has to grow from seeds of knowledge just as all generable things must do. The analogy of principles as seeds repeatedly recurs in his analysis of human understanding. Thus in his work *On Truth* St. Thomas says:

> Hence it is that human nature, in so far as it comes in contact with the angelic nature, must both in speculative and practical matters know truth without investigation. And this knowledge must be the principle of all the knowledge which follows, whether speculative or practical, since principles must be more stable and certain. Therefore, this knowledge must be in man naturally, since it is a kind of seed plot containing in germ all the knowledge which follows, and since there pre-exist in all natures certain natural seeds of the activities and effects which follow. Furthermore, this knowledge must be habitual so that it will be ready for use when needed.
>
> Thus, just as there is a natural habit of the human soul through which it knows principles of the speculative sciences, which we call understanding of principles, so, too, there is in the soul a natural habit of first principles of action, which are the universal principles

of the natural law. This habit pertains to synderesis. This habit exists in no other power than reason, unless, perhaps, we make understanding a power distinct from reason. But we have shown the opposite above.[37]

And the same is true of speculative understanding. The distinguishing characteristic of *human* understanding is that it is discursive. Beginning with the seeds of principles and definitions, man has to build up his understanding of things gradually by reasoning from what he knows to new truths, new conclusions. Thus, St. Thomas speaks of reason as though it were the intellect in motion—the intellect rests in the stable knowledge of principles, moves through discursive reasoning, and comes to rest again in the understanding of the truth of a conclusion. Reason is not a power distinct from intellect, it is really the intellect "moving" discursively. To speak of man as a rational being, then, does not mean that he has a reason distinct from his intellect; it means, rather, that he is the kind of intellectual being that understands *discursively* and partially, not immediately and totally.

Reason and intellect in man cannot be distinct powers. We shall understand this clearly if we consider their respective acts. For to understand is to apprehend intelligible truth absolutely, and to reason is to advance from one thing understood to another, so as to know an intelligible truth. And therefore the angels, who possess a perfect knowledge of intelligible truth according to the mode of their nature, have no need to advance from one thing to another; they rather apprehend the truth of things absolutely and without discursiveness, as Dionysius says. But man arrives at the knowledge of intelligible truth by advancing from one thing to another; and therefore he is called *rational*. Reasoning, therefore, is compared to the understanding as movement is to rest, or acquisition to possession; of which one belongs to the perfect, the other to the imperfect. And since movement always proceeds from something immoveable, and ends in something at rest, hence it is that human reasoning, in the order of inquiry and discovery, proceeds from certain things absolutely understood—namely, the first principles; and, again, in the order of judgment returns by analysis to first principles in the light of which it examines what it has found.[38]

Thus, man has to grow in understanding, and that growth is expressed in the scientific conclusions and moral laws he formulates. He has to start with the fragmentary bits of information he is able to gather through his senses—information that is both speculative and practical, information about color and sound as well as of pleasure and pain—and then gradually build it up into more comprehensive understanding. His typical way of understanding, then, is rational.

Exercising the act of understanding indicates, according to St. Thomas, that man is capable of acting in an order that transcends matter and the conditions of time and place; understanding is a sign of immateriality.

> We must conclude, therefore, that the material things known must needs exist in the knower, not materially, but rather immaterially. The reason for this is that the act of knowledge extends to things outside the knower; for we know even the things that are outside us. Now by matter the form of a thing is determined to some one thing. Therefore, it is clear that knowledge is in inverse ratio to materiality. Consequently, things that are not receptive of forms, save materially, have no power of knowledge whatever—such as plants, as the Philosopher says. But the more immaterially a being receives the form of the thing known, the more perfect is its knowledge. Therefore the intellect, which abstracts the species not only from matter, but also from the individuating conditions of matter, knows more perfectly than the senses, which receive the form of the thing known, without matter indeed, but subject to material conditions. Moreover, among the senses themselves, sight has the most perfect knowledge, because it is the least material, as we have remarked above. So, too, among intellects, the more perfect is the more immaterial.[39]

Now what does this mean? Well, let us return to our example of the plant living and the person cheating. The plant, as we have seen, exists by living and growing, but always in conditions limited in time and place. But when a person comes to understand what plant is and to judge whether certain plants are alive or dead, he has a knowledge of plant and its behavior that is not confined to this or that plant or to a definite set of environmental conditions. He understands plant and not this or that plant only. Plant, in being understood, has become universal, capable of being seen in many different individual plants; understanding enables things to exist in a new way, beyond the limiting conditions of matter. Instead of exercising a physical being in sensible matter, it takes on the *intentional being* of understanding. So, too, with understanding at work deciding that one should not cheat in a particular business transaction. In this case what is understood is not what some *thing* like a plant is; an act of cheating is not a thing and does not exist because of natural birth or physical action but in virtue of a human decision. In that decision a person has to determine whether or not bringing an act of cheating into being is good for him or not. After repeated experiences of that kind we come to see what cheating is and to the conviction that it is the kind of act that should not be brought into being because it does not help us grow as men. This whole activity is the work of understanding, and once again it is an operation in an immaterial or spiritual order. The fitness of such an act as cheating, the good or benefit it will bring, the decision—all of these are not physical or material acts. In short: for St. Thomas acts of understanding such as these indicate that man is more than *this* flesh and bone (i.e. *this* material entity), or even than flesh and bone (i.e. *some* material thing). He is *immaterial*, too. His *proper* way of being is not to live and sense (although he must do so), but to understand.

That is why St. Thomas speaks of man as the lowest of the intelligences or as an intellectual substance. He says:

> As a matter of fact, human souls hold the lowest rank in relation to the other intellectual substances, because, as we said above, at the start of their existence they receive a knowledge of divine providence, wherein they know it only in a general sort of way. But the soul must be brought to a perfect knowledge of this order, in regard to individual details, by starting from the things themselves in which the order of divine providence has already been established in detail. So, the soul had to have bodily organs by which it might draw knowledge from corporeal things.[40]

By this St. Thomas means: first, man is a substance, i.e. a being capable of his *own* act of existing; he is not an accidental manifestation of matter nor a mode of divine being. Second, the proper and distinctive way in which man does exist is *understanding*. He is, then, an understanding being, i.e. an intellectual substance. However, our analysis of understanding as defining, judging, accepting principles and reasoning has shown that *human* understanding differs radically from *angelic* understanding. Men have to start all of their understanding by making sensible contact with the sensible world into which they came by birth; they have to grow and persist through a long period of repeated sense experiences before they do define, judge and reason. Sensation, induction, memory, imagination and reasoning all indicate to St. Thomas that men only come to understand as they develop and grow—unlike other intellectual substances, the angels, that do *not* require such discursive steps in their understanding. Man is, therefore, a peculiar kind of intellectual substance, one who requires the complex organism of a living and sensing body precisely so that he can *be* intellectual. He has no innate knowledge and no capacity for coming to perfect knowledge all at once. This is the way St. Thomas describes man's condition:

. . . there is a similarity between the distinction and order of spiritual substances and the distinction and order of corporeal substances. The highest bodies have in their nature a potentiality which is fully perfected by the form; whereas in the lower bodies the potentiality of matter is not entirely perfected by the form, but receives now one form, now another, from some agent. In like fashion also the lower intellectual substances—that is to say, human souls—have a power of understanding which is not naturally complete, but is successively completed in them by their drawing intelligible species from things. But in the higher spiritual substances—that is, the angels—the power of understanding is naturally perfected by intelligible species, in so far as they have such species connatural to them, so as to understand all things which they can know naturally. The same is evident from the manner of being (*essendi*) of such substances. The lower spiritual substances, that is souls, have their act of existing in kinship with the body (*esse affine corpori*)in so far as they are the forms of bodies; and consequently from their very mode of being it is necessary for them to attain their intelligible perfection from bodies and through bodies. For otherwise such substances would be joined to bodies in vain.[41]

Man is, then, an intellectual substance, but he is the kind of intellectual substance that needs a body *to be* intellectual and that is, as a result, joined to a body as its form. This means, to St. Thomas, that just as there is in a plant some proximate principle to organize the minerals and moisture that are common to many kinds of plants into the specific roots, stems, and leaves of a rose as distinct from an apple tree—a principle that he calls "form" or "soul"—so too, is man's intellect present in his body as form. He is an incarnate spirit. In order to be actually an intellectual substance, his intellectual soul has to organize the materials to which it gives *human* being into hands, ears, nerves, brain etc., i.e. into an organized *human* body. Food, drink, minerals, air and light can be organized into many different kinds of bodies, but the intellectual soul presides over the organization of materials in such a way that they can assist in acts of knowing. The intellectual substance or human soul acts, then, as the form of a body, giving it its act of existing and its specific determination as *human*.

St. Thomas expresses this most succinctly by saying that the human soul is an intellectual substance that communicates its act of existing (by which it subsists) to the matter of the body so that *one* being results (in which the act of existing of the whole composite is also the act of existing of the soul).

For one thing to be another's substantial form, two requirements must be met. First, the form must be the principle of the substantial being of the thing whose form it is; I speak not of the productive but of the formal principle whereby a thing exists and is called a *being*. The second requirement then follows from this, namely, that the form and the matter be joined together in the unity of one act of being; which is not true of the union of the efficient cause with that to which it gives being. And this single act of being is that in which the composite substance subsists: a thing one in being and made up of matter and form. Now, as we have shown, the fact that an intellectual substance is subsistent does not stand in the way of its being the formal principle of the being of the matter, as communicating its own being to the matter. For it is not unfitting that the composite and its form should subsist in the same act of being, since the composite exists only by the form, and neither of them subsists apart from the other.[42]

One conclusion that St. Thomas draws from this view of the soul as intellectual substance—a conclusion that clearly states his own position on the much-debated question of the soul's immortality—is that the human soul persists in its own act of existing when the body is destroyed. It does not exist as a complete substance inasmuch as its perfection requires the body; but it does have its own act of existing which it communicates to the body. Thus, the basic reason that the human soul is immortal for St. Thomas is not that it is intellectual and, hence, immaterial but, rather, that it has its own act of existing!

We must assert that the intellectual principle we call the human soul is incorruptible. For a thing may be corrupted in two ways—in itself and accidentally. Now it is impossible for any subsistent being to be generated or corrupted accidentally, that is by the generation or corruption of something else. For generation and corruption belong to a thing in the same way that being (*sicut et esse*) belongs to it, which is acquired by generation and lost by corruption. Therefore, whatever has being (*esse*) in itself cannot be generated or corrupted except in itself; while things which do not subsist, such as accidents and material forms, acquire being or lose it through the generation or corruption of composites.[43]

We return, therefore, to the very same doctrine with which we began: the act of existing accounts for the unity of man as a human being and, because there is no reason for such a being not to persist in being once it has been given existence, the doctrine of being and existing also explains the immortality of the human soul.

Now what does this view of man imply as regards the problems with which we began—man's alienation from his world, the character of sensation, human fragmentation? Let us first see what St. Thomas' doctrine of being tells us about man's knowledge. Ultimately the act of existing is the reason that things are intelligible because, as we have seen, without that act a thing is not a being at all. Things are intelligible, then, insofar as they *are*. Man, on the other hand, is an intellectual substance, and that means that he *is*, that he is an understanding *being* precisely insofar as he grasps the being of things. In short: apart from man's understanding the being of things, he is not an intelligence, he is not man—and there is *no* understanding! We might, indeed, paraphrase Martin Heidegger's phrase here with somewhat different intent and say: man's being is revealed as the being of an intellectual substance when he lets things be.

This general position has several important consequences. First, it means that, for St. Thomas, the being of things is the cause and source of man's being actually intelligent. You cannot divorce understanding from the being of man and the being of things. In St. Thomas' view understanding—Descartes would call it thought or consciousness—is not and cannot be a first evidence or first datum with which to philosophize. Either the act of existing is allowed to act as a primary principle, i.e. as a first starting-point, or there is no understanding. Moreover, in St. Thomas' approach there is no world of thought as something set over against being and as somehow distinct from it. Knowing is a way of being, and as a finite being knowing, too, must be caused. It cannot be primary in the order of being. Human knowing, then, is only intelligible in virtue of the being of things. And man is able to know *himself* only because the being of things is the principle from which his understanding derives. We know ourselves secondarily in knowing things.

> . . . a thing is known according as it is in act. Now the ultimate perfection of the intellect consists in its own operation. For this is not an act tending to something else in which lies the perfection of the work accomplished, as building is the perfection of the thing built; but it remains in the agent as its perfection and act, as is said in *Metaph.* IX. Therefore, the first thing of the intellect that is understood is its own act of understanding. This occurs in different ways with different intellects. . . . And there is yet another, namely, the human intellect, which is not its own act of understanding, nor is its own essence the first object of its act of understanding for this object is the nature of a material thing. And therefore that which is first known by the human intellect is an object of this kind, and that which is known secondarily is the act by which that object is known; and through the act the intellect itself is known, whose perfection is the act itself of understanding.[44]

We do know ourselves, then, but only secondarily in knowing things. The world of things very truly makes it possible for us to know ourselves. And, in marked contrast with Locke's view, in knowing things it is *not* the impressions they make on us that we know. St. Thomas is very clear in stating that impressions on the senses, images in imagination and concepts in understanding are *not* objects of knowing but necessary *means* the human being has to use to know its proper object, a thing in the material world. Impressions and concepts are only known secondarily.

> Some have asserted that our intellectual powers know only the impressions made on them; as, for example, that sense is cognizant only of the impressions made on its own organ. According to this theory, the intellect understands only its own impressions, namely, the intelligible species which it has received. This is, however, manifestly false for two reasons. First, because the things we understand are also the objects of science. Therefore, if what we understand is merely the intelligible species in the soul, it would follow that every science would be concerned, not with things outside the soul, but only with the intelligible species within the soul; just as, according to the teaching of the Platonists, all the sciences are about Ideas, which they held to be that which is actually understood. Secondly, it is untrue, because it would lead to the opinion of the ancients who maintained that *whatever seems, is true*, and that consequently contradictories are true simultaneously. For if a power knows only its own impressions, it can judge only of them. Now a thing *seems* according to the impression made on the cognitive power. Consequently, the cognitive power will always judge of its own impressions as such; and so every judgment will be true. For instance, if taste perceived only its own impression, when anyone with a healthy taste perceives that honey is sweet, he would judge truly, and if anyone with a corrupt taste perceives that honey is bitter, this would be equally true; for each would judge according to the impression on his taste. Thus, every opinion, in fact, every sort of apprehension would be equally true.
>
> Therefore, it must be said that the intelligible species is related to the intellect as that by which it understands.[45]

Not only does man properly exist as man when he knows, but when he knows he *is* what he knows—not, indeed, that he is petrified in knowing a stone, for to *be* petrified is to be a stone, not a knower. Man's being as *knower* is determined by the same essential determinations as the stone's being is determined as a *physically* existing thing. We have to think about a stone with the same necessary determinations of thought that the stone must respect if it is going to be a stone. It must be hard and we have to think of it as being hard. In short: the very being of things in the natural world—their being in the sense of essence, what they are—enters into man's very being as knower. Man, for St. Thomas, is not alienated from his world; he is *in* it, affecting it by his being and being affected by its being.

Second, man's consciousness is not estranged from his body. Understanding, for St. Thomas, does not exist as in a separate realm, somehow or other tucked away in the body and merely reflective of what goes on in the body. As we have seen, St. Thomas speaks of understanding "existing in kinship with the body;" it exists in the whole body and in every part as form, giving all the parts their being. Every activity of that body is a human activity precisely in virtue of the soul's giving it being. Thus, sensation is not an act or passion of the body or physical sense-organ alone, but of the composite. The whole *being* senses. Indeed, so intimate is the union of intellectual principle and body that St. Thomas always stresses that knowledge starts from sensible contact with things and returns to things in sensible contact. This is just as true of the human intellect's speculative operation of knowing as it is of its practical activity, whether artistic or moral. Men have a real need to experience physical pleasure and pain if they are going to grow morally; the mature moral being is as dependent on physical experience as is the mature scientist. Thus, the prudent man has to have a vast experience and long memory if he is to make the correct practical decision in a given situation—and his bodily appetites have to be well disciplined, too.

Third, sensation is not an isolated impression in some part of the body; it is a way of *knowing* and, consequently, involves far more than the purely physical being of two interacting bodies. A finger is, indeed, a complex physico-chemical organism, but it *senses* and, in the case of a *human* finger, it senses knowingly and experiences pain rationally. For without the informing presence of an intellective soul, there is *no* human body—as St. Thomas says, a hand cut off from the body is not properly a human hand any more than a corpse is properly a human body. Operations are performed by the *whole* substance; the eye does not see color, nor does the ear hear sound. A *man* sees a colored thing when his eye is affected by that thing's distinct ability to reflect light. And as that color is more than just color—it being the color of a rose, the sky, another human being—, so, too, is his seeing more than the mere work of an eye. A man sees that color with sense, memory, reason and understanding. And after a long experience in which all his senses and knowing-powers cooperate, he interprets those data as flower, sky or man.

Fourth, while it is true to say that a man is a *thing*, it is not true to speak of him as a thing of nature, i.e. as though his whole being were

determined for him by nature and the physical things around him. St.
Thomas attributes a very precise meaning to "thing" and it means quite
different things in a variety of contexts.

> . . . some predicates may be said to add to being inasmuch as they
> express a mode of being not expressed by the term *being*. This hap-
> pens in two ways.
>
> First, the mode expressed is a certain special manner of being; for
> there are different grades of being according to which we speak
> when we speak of different levels of existence, and according to
> these grades different things are classified. Consequently, *substance*
> does not add a difference to being by signifying some reality added
> to it, but *substance* simply expresses a special manner of existing,
> namely, as a being in itself. The same is true of the other classes of
> existents.
>
> Second, some are said to add to being because the mode they ex-
> press is one that is common, and consequent upon every being. This
> mode can be taken in two ways: first, insofar as it follows upon
> every being considered in itself; second, insofar as it follows upon
> every being considered in relation to another. In the first, the term
> is used in two ways, because it expresses something in the being
> either affirmatively or negatively. We can, however, find nothing that
> can be predicated of every being affirmatively and, at the same time
> absolutely, with the exception of its essence by which the thing is
> said to be. To express this the term *thing* is used; for, according to
> Avicenna, thing differs from being because being gets its name from
> to-be, but thing expresses the quiddity or essence of the being.[46]

To call a human being a "thing," then, is simply to say that it is a finite
being, one principle of whose finitude is called "essence." It is a direct
outgrowth of the doctrine of being we have seen developed by St.
Thomas: every being has a principle determining its *way* of being, and
another principle giving it an act of being. "Thing" does not indicate that
a being *is* an essence nor that it *acts* as an essence; it signifies only that
it *has* an essence. It *is* a being. Man is not an essence but a being, a
*human* being. And "thing" tells us nothing whatsoever about the character or properties of the essence. A being might be a *free* being like
man, or a thoroughly determined being like a stone and still be called a
"thing." Thus, when a man acts as a man, he has to act rationally, sensibly, freely and socially; but the use he makes of his reason or sense,
the kind of sciences he develops, the arts he creates, the type of society
he fashions are for *him* to decide. They are not decided for him by the
forces of nature. "Thing" and "free" are not opposed; if man must be free
to be truly man, then, in St. Thomas' language it is his essence to be free.

St. Thomas would refuse to restrict the meaning of "thing" to physical, material things, just as he would refuse to set reason against freedom. Indeed, he would probably be amazed at Sartre's confrontation of human nature and human freedom. Man's nature is to be free, to determine the ends he will pursue, the kind of person he will be; he is free to develop himself historically in time and to grow into the individual nature he wants his to be. That is precisely what it means for *man* to have a nature, the nature of an *intelligent* agent; it is not what it means for a tree to have a nature, the nature of a *natural* agent. If one is intent on knowing the kind of essence signified by "thing," he should refer to the being's act of existing. A man has an act of existing (*esse*), but it does not make him a thing of nature. It is, therefore, an essentialist perversion to overlook the act of existing when speaking of man as a "thing;" it is an existentialist perversion to overlook differences in acts of existing. He *is* a "thing," but he is nonetheless *free*. Taking the act of existing as a principle, St. Thomas is convinced that man is a *substance*. He is, however, a substance of a particular kind. He is an intellectual or rational substance, and it is with this notion of man before his eyes that St. Thomas calls him a "person."

> Although this name *person* may not belong to God as regards the origin of the term, nevertheless it most excellently belongs to God in its objective meaning. For as famous men were represented in comedies and tragedies, the name *person* was given to signify those who held high dignity. Hence, those who held high rank in the church came to be called *persons.* Hence, some define person as a *hypostasis distinct by reason of dignity.* And because subsistence in a rational nature is of high dignity, therefore every individual of a rational nature is called a *person.*[47]

A man, then, is not a thing of determined physical nature incapable of acting otherwise than as dictated by necessary causes; he is a thing whose nature is intellectual or rational, a thing that subsists in such a nature, a thing capable of rationally initiating and directing his *own* actions. He is a person—in virtue of his act of existing.

Fifth, fragmentation enters our discussion of man, his knowledge, and his being when we look upon human knowledge as abstractive and confined to knowing *what* things are. When we do that we forget or overlook the priority St. Thomas attaches to the act of existing and his subsequent conviction that human knowledge is completed in judgment—wherein *existing* is apprehended—rather than in definition. It is true that the *human* intellect has to attain its object by abstracting from sensible things; it is true, too, that St. Thomas makes the essence of a sensible thing the proper object of the human intellect. But the human intellect does not abstract just to have the satisfaction of dealing with abstractions; it does so in order that *man* may have the means of understanding *things*. The essence of a sensible thing *is* the intellect's proper object, but there is no such essence actually intelligible to man without all the individual idiosyncracies proper to an individual existent. Nor is there a human intellect existing all by itself, ready and able to grasp such an essence. Intellect, essence, concept are just so many abstractions, and as such they are only useful means for understanding how one knows. In the same way it is useful for the scientist to study abstractions like heat, atom, sodium, triangle, worker, owner, paralytic etc. As a scientist he has to deal with them in that way. But he has to bear in mind above all that essence is not the deepest reality in things as *beings;* those scientists who are concerned with human beings in any way have to remember that in dealing with man they have not reached his roots by discovering, even in abstraction, the various properties he possesses. Beyond essence is the act of existing. Not only does it give reality to the abstractions, but it also makes them *one*, it makes them exist as one of a whole unified complex of properties, each of which might be *considered* by itself, i.e. abstractly. Whereas a substance is a thing and is defined by essence, it is a being in virtue of its act of existing. Viewed from the standpoint of essence, man is an animal or worker, a scientist, worshipper or consumer. And each of these is quite distinct in definition: to be an animal is not to be a scientist; what a worshipper is is not what a consumer is. But one being, *this man,* may be animal-worker-scientist-worshipper-consumer. Distinct in essence, these are *identical* in existing. Indeed, it is the *only* way they can be identical, i.e. in being the same *being*. Actually, it is the only way they *are* at all. Bearing in mind the fundamental role of the act of existing the man called "scientist" realizes that he has not adequately considered man until he returns to his senses, whence he had his first contact with this "consumer" as a being; he knows that this "consumer" is only truly real as a being having existence when he is seen to be *this man,* i.e. a person subsisting in this body among other beings.

Finally, a point we will just touch upon here and explore at greater length later—man's being is not only with other things or even with other men as merely physical entities. He also exists socially with other human beings precisely as human persons. We have seen that, in addition to knowledge gained by grasping *what* things are, St. Thomas also teaches that man as intellectual substance has moral and artistic knowledge. We gain a very real, although not speculative, knowledge when we act morally and artistically; we learn something about ourselves, other men and, indeed, about man himself when we cheat or act fairly and honestly. Love and friendship tell us a great many things about ourselves and about those round about us, things that mere sense experience and speculative understanding can never succeed in revealing. Above all the experience of our ability to make free, practical decisions, i.e. our awareness of acting morally, opens up facets of man's reality at which we have still not looked.

Does St. Thomas' philosophy of being have anything to tell us about a human being's freedom? We shall search for an answer to that question in our next chapter.

# CHAPTER VI

## MAN'S BEING FREE

For what is freedom? That one has the will to assume responsibility for oneself. That one maintains the distance which separates us. That one becomes more indifferent to difficulties, hardships, privation, even to life itself. That one is prepared to sacrifice human beings for one's cause, not excluding oneself. Freedom means that the manly instincts which delight in war and victory dominate over other instincts, for example, over those of "pleasure." The human being who has *become free*—and how much more the *spirit* who has become free—spits on the contemptible type of well-being dreamed of by shopkeepers, Christians, cows, females, Englishmen, and other democrats. The free man is a *warrior*.[1]

Jean-Paul Sartre gives a very personal and dramatic account of human reality and its freedom in his play *The Flies*. His presentation takes the form of a challenging exchange between the god Zeus and Orestes, the hero of freedom. Zeus has just reminded Orestes that he made him and everything else in the world, that everything is ruled by his justice, that everything is good because he made it, and that he (Orestes) should return to his saner self and submit. Orestes replies:

Yesterday when I was with Electra, I felt one with Nature, the nature of your making. It sang the praises of the Good—*your* good— in siren tones and lavished estimations. . . . Suddenly out of the blue freedom crashed down on me and swept me off my feet. Nature sprang back, my youth went with the wind, and I knew myself alone, utterly alone in the midst of this well-meaning little universe of yours. I was like a man who lost his shadow. And there was nothing left in heaven, no Right or Wrong, nor anyone to give me orders.

Zeus: . . . Remember, Orestes, you once were of my flock, you fed in my pastures among my sheep. Your vaunted freedom isolates you from the fold; it means exile.

Orestes: Yes, exile.

Zeus: . . . The disease you're suffering from is inhuman, foreign to my nature, foreign to yourself. Come back.

Orestes: Foreign to myself—I know it. Outside nature, against nature, without excuse, beyond remedy, except what remedy I find within myself. But I shall not return under your Law. I am doomed to have no other law but mine. Nor shall I come back to Nature, the Nature you found Good; in it are a thousand beaten paths all leading to you—but I shall blaze my own trail. For I, Zeus, am a man, and every man must find his own way. Nature abhors man, and you, god of gods, abhor mankind.[2]

In these moving lines Sartre gives us his interpretation of the dreadful paradox of human freedom, a paradox that has perplexed and challenged philosophers throughout the ages. They have formulated the paradox in a variety of ways and given many different solutions. Is man free at all? Or does he only think that he is free because he does not properly or clearly understand himself? Perhaps, like Orestes before freedom smote him, man is so thoroughly one with Nature that his every action is, in reality, but an act of Nature working through him. Fichte suggests this possibility:

Bestow consciousness on a tree, and let it grow, spread out its branches, and bring forth leaves and buds, blossoms and fruits, after its kind, without hindrance or obstruction—it will perceive no limitation to its existence in being only a tree, a tree of this particular species, and this particular individual of the species; it will feel itself perfectly *free*, because, in all those manifestations, it will do nothing but what its nature requires; and it will desire to do nothing else, because it can desire only what that nature requires. But let its growth be hindered by unfavorable weather, want of nourishment, or other causes, and it will feel itself *limited and restrained*, because an impulse which actually belongs to its nature is not satisfied. Bind its free-waving boughs to a wall, force foreign branches on it by ingrafting, and it will feel itself *compelled* to one course of action; its branches will grow, but not in the direction they would have taken if left to themselves; it will produce fruits, but not those which belong to its original nature. In immediate consciousness, I appear to myself as free; by reflection on the whole of Nature, I discover that freedom is absolutely impossible; the former must be subordinate to the latter, for it can be explained only by means of it.[3]

Or, if Nature is understood to be identical with the divine substance, then human freedom is revealed as God's action within us. Thus, Spinoza looks upon the paradox as he looks upon the problem of being. Are there beings? No. There is only the being of God; if our intellects were properly corrected, they would see that we are Substance, not substances. Are we free? Yes—but only with the freedom of God, for only God is free from compulsion by anything else. The paradox, then, is this: how can we be free in virtue of God's freedom?

God acts merely according to his own laws, and is compelled by no one.

*Proof.*—That infinite things must follow from the mere necessity of divine nature, or what is the same thing, by the mere laws of divine nature, we have just shown (Prop. 16), and (Prop. 15) we have shown that nothing can be conceived without God, but that everything exists in God. Therefore nothing outside God can exist by which he could be determined or compelled in his actions; and therefore God acts merely according to the laws of his nature, and is compelled by no one. *Q. E. D.*

Corollary I.—Hence it follows that no cause can be given except the perfection of God's nature which extrinsically or intrinsically incites him to action.

Corollary II.—Hence it follows that God alone is a free cause. For God alone exists from the mere necessity of his own nature (Prop. 11, and Coroll. I, Prop. 14), and by the mere necessity of his nature he acts (prev. Prop.). And therefore (Def. 7) he is the only free cause. *Q. E. D.*[4]

But then the further question arises: if man is merely moved by Nature or God, is *he* free at all? For how can he be free and still be a part of nature, when all of the workings of nature are governed by necessary physical laws? If he *is* free, is it because in some way or other man escapes those laws? If he is free from the determinations of physical laws, what of the influence of motives, inclinations, emotional circumstances? Are we to purchase freedom at the price of claiming that a free action is totally uncaused? It would seem that we are here entering very dangerous territory; defending that view would compel us to give evidence of a single human act that lacked necessary connection with antecedents. Surely, it would be a most abstract human act! The paradox, then, might have to be formulated in this way: how can an act remain free while it is at the same time caused by and necessarily connected with antecedent determinations?

It is universally allowed that nothing exists without a cause of its existence, and that chance, when strictly examined, is a mere nega-

tive word, and means not any real power which has anywhere a being in nature. But it is pretended that some causes are necessary,
some not necessary. Here then is the advantage of definitions. Let
anyone *define* a cause, without comprehending, as a part of the
definition, a *necessary connection* with its effect; and let him show
distinctly the origin of the idea, expressed by the definition; and I
shall readily give up the whole controversy. But if the foregoing
explication of the matter be received, this must be absolutely im-
practicable. Had not objects a regular conjunction with each other,
we should never have entertained any notion of cause and effect;
and this regular conjunction produces that inference of the understanding, which is the only connection, that we can have any comprehension of. Whoever attempts a definition of cause, exclusive of
these circumstances, will be obliged either to employ unintelligible
terms or such as are synonymous to the term which he endeavours
to define. And if the definition above mentioned be admitted, liberty,
when opposed to necessity, not to constraint, is the same thing with
chance, which is universally allowed to have no existence.[5]

There is no disputing the fact, according to Hume, that we do have a
power to act or not to act according to the determinations of the will;
only violence, constraint or chains could prevent that. The real problem
is, rather, this one: are we free to will or not to will in the face of the
will's necessary connection with a whole host of antecedent conditions?
Are we free in escaping all causal determinations? If such an escape is
a factual impossibility, are we free in willing what the will is ultimately
determined to will?

Fichte has remarked that all efforts to believe that liberty is identified
with necessity while intellectually satisfying, still leave the human heart
uneasy:

> Why must my heart grieve over, and be torn by, that which so per-
> fectly satisfies my understanding? Since nothing in Nature contra-
> dicts itself, is man alone a contradiction? Or perhaps not man in
> general, but only myself and those who resemble me? Had I but re-
> mained amid the pleasant delusions that surround me, satisfied with
> the immediate consciousness of my existence, and had never raised
> those questions concerning its foundations! But if the answer—which
> has caused me this misery—be true, then I *must* of necessity have
> raised these questions: or, rather, the thinking nature within me—
> and not I myself—raised them. I was destined to this misery, and it
> is in vain that I mourn the lost innocence of soul which can never
> return.[6]

Perhaps, then, we can only solve the riddle of freedom, if we re-examine man's relations with nature; perhaps man enjoys a transcendence that has hitherto gone unnoticed and unexplored. Would he not be free if he stood above all physical and psychological determinations, enjoying membership in a realm of being wherein he is autonomous or self-legislating? For as an agent capable of acting in the practical order under the inspiration of purely intelligible motives, men would effectively escape the determining influence of all inclinations and passions. That was the possibility to which Kant dedicated his critical ingenuity. Freedom, he reasoned, is only possible if an agent acts in a noumenal order ruled by laws that do not find a place in the phenomenal order of space-time realities. The laws of physics are ample proof that human reason does, in fact, operate in the realm of sensible phenomena; is there any proof that it also functions practically in a noumenal order? Yes. In addition to experiences of things that *are*, we also experience "things" that *ought* to be. But if we try to find an ultimate explanation for things that are, it will be found in the idea of a world to which they all belong and in which all are necessarily inter-related; similarly, if we want to find an ultimate explanation of our experience of "oughts," we will find it in the idea of freedom that makes all such experiences possible. Freedom, then, is the ultimate condition of moral experience.

The *Will* is a kind of causality belonging to living beings in so far as they are rational, and *freedom* would be this property of such causality that it can be efficient, independently on foreign causes *determining* it; just as *physical necessity* is the property that the causality of all irrational beings has of being determined to activity by the influence of foreign causes.

The preceding definition of freedom is *negative*, and therefore unfruitful for the discovery of its essence; but it leads to a *positive* conception which is so much the more full and fruitful. Since the conception of causality involves that of laws, according to which, by something that we call cause, something else, namely, the effect, must be produced; hence, although freedom is not a property of the will depending on physical laws, yet it is not for that reason lawless; on the contrary, it must be a causality according to immutable laws, but of a peculiar kind; otherwise a free will would be an absurdity. Physical necessity is a heteronomy of the efficient causes, for every effect is possible only according to this law—that something else determines the efficient cause to exert its causality. What else then can freedom of the will be but an autonomy, that is, the property of the will to be a law to itself? [7]

Negatively, then, freedom may be considered to be merely an escape from *outside* determination; positively, it must appear as an *inner* determination, i.e. as autonomy. If our "oughts" come to us from a world of sensible entities, a human nature, inclinations and passions, our autonomy is jeopardized; if they come to us from a revealed code of behavior, the Ten Commandments, say, our freedom is also threatened inasmuch as we are not acting autonomously, i.e. we are not giving *ourselves* laws. Laws of freedom, then, must come from man's own practical reason alone.

What, then, of God and His laws? Must not divine law, precisely because it is *God's* law, be foreign to man? Must it not stand as a threat to human freedom? How, for example, can a man be a *free* being while he remains a *Christian?* It would appear that the only way to be human and free would be to escape the alienating influence of Christianity as well as the constraints of physical nature. That, certainly, was Friedrich Nietzsche's conviction!

> . . . Dionysus versus "the Crucified One:" there you have the contrast. It is not martyrdom that constitutes the difference—only here it has two different senses. Life itself, its eternal fruitfulness and recurrence, involves agony, destruction, the will to annihilation. In the other case, suffering—"the Crucified One as the Innocent One"—is considered an objection to this life, as the formula of its condemnation. Clearly, the problem is that of the meaning of suffering: whether a Christian meaning or a tragic meaning. In the first case, it is supposed to be the path to a sacred existence; in the second case, *existence is considered sacred enough* to justify even a tremendous amount of suffering. The tragic man affirms even the harshest suffering: he is sufficiently strong, rich and deifying for this; the Christian negates even the happiest life on earth: he is sufficiently weak, poor, and disinherited to suffer from life in any form. The God on the cross is a curse on life, a pointer to seek redemption from it; Dionysus cut to pieces is a *promise* of life: it is eternally reborn and comes back from destruction.[8]

God, nature, human freedom: can they be reconciled? Orestes' revolt against Zeus represents Sartre's dramatic expression of an answer; his theoretical reply is given in his major philosophical work *Being and Nothingness* wherein he develops a philosophy of being that owes many of its basic insights to Descartes, one of the early heroes of the new freedom.

> Doubt reaches all propositions that affirm anything outside our thought, that is to say, I can put all existents into brackets, I fully exercise my liberty when, being empty and nothing myself, I make

everything that exists nothing. Doubt is a breach of contract with
being; through it man has a permanent capacity for "ungluing" himself from the existing universe and contemplating it all at once as a
pure series of phantasms. In this sense, doubt is the most magnificent
affirmation of the reign of man: the hypothesis of the evil genius, in
fact, clearly indicates that man can escape every deceit and trap;
there is an order of truth because man is free; and even if that order
did not exist, it would suffice that man is free to guarantee there
would never be a reign of error. For since man is a pure negation,
a pure suspension of judgment, he can, provided he stays immobile
as one who holds his breath, withdraw at every instant from a false
and faked nature; he can even withdraw from every trace of nature
in himself: from memory, imagination, his own body. He can even
withdraw from time itself and take refuge in the eternity of the
moment; nothing is greater proof that man is not a being of "nature." [9]

Indeed, Sartre's conception of man as freedom is in many ways the twentieth-century counterpart of the estranged man we examined in our last
chapter. In Sartre's language man or human reality is "being-for-itself,"
and he describes it variously as "consciousness-self," as a Nothingness that
reveals Being, as freedom. Human reality is the kind of being that is more
properly a *to-be*, a deliberate projection into the future, rather than a
being that *is*. No essence or nature lies beneath man's existence; he has
no reason for existing. The great cloud to a clear understanding of man
and being is, according to Sartre, the prejudice of "creationism:"

A clear view of the phenomenon of being has often been obscured
by a very common prejudice which we shall call "creationism."
Since people supposed that God had given being to the world,
being always appeared tainted with a certain passivity. But a creation *ex nihilo* cannot explain the coming to pass of being; for if
being is conceived in a subjectivity, even a divine subjectivity, it
remains a mode of intra-subjective being. Such subjectivity cannot
have even the representation of an objectivity, and consequently it
cannot even be affected with the will to create the objective. Furthermore being, if it is suddenly placed outside the subjective by
the fulguration of which Leibniz speaks, can only affirm itself as distinct from and opposed to its creator; otherwise it dissolves in him.
The theory of perpetual creation, by removing from being what the
Germans call *Selbständigkeit*, makes it disappear in the divine subjectivity. If being exists as over against God, it is its own support;
it does not preserve the least trace of divine creation. In a word, even
if it had been created, being-in-itself would be *inexplicable* in terms

of creation; for it assumes its being beyond the creation. This is equivalent to saying that being is uncreated.[10]

Distinct from human being and constituting the reality of being-in-itself are the things of nature. They lack consciousness, they are not created, and they are neither possible nor necessary. They simply *are*.

Finally—this will be our third characteristic—being-in-itself *is*. This means that being can neither be derived from the possible nor reduced to the necessary. Necessity concerns the connection between ideal propositions but not that of existents. An existing phenomenon can never be derived from another existent qua existent. This is what we shall call the *contingency* of being-in-itself. But neither can being-in-itself be derived from a *possibility*. The possible is a structure of the *for-itself;* that is, it belongs to the other region of being. Being-in-itself is never either possible or impossible. It *is*. This is what consciousness expresses in anthropomorphic terms by saying that being is superfluous (*de trop*)—that is, that consciousness absolutely cannot derive being from anything, either from another being, or from a possibility, or from a necessary law. Uncreated, without reason for being, without any connection with another being, being-in-itself is *de trop* for eternity.[11]

In Sartre's view all previous efforts to understand human freedom have been doomed to failure in advance because these two orders of being have been confused. Determinists have interpreted human acts as though they occurred in the world of nature, where there is no freedom. Greater success could have been expected if a real effort had been made to understand the conditions of any action:

It is strange that philosophers have been able to argue endlessly about determinism and free-will, to cite examples in favor of one or the other thesis without even attempting to make explicit the structures contained in the very idea of *action*. The concept of an act contains, in fact, numerous subordinate notions which we shall have to organize and arrange in a hierarchy: to act is to modify the *shape* of the world; it is to arrange means in view of an end; it is to produce an organized instrumental complex such that by a series of concatenations and connections the modifications effected on one of the links causes modifications throughout the whole series and finally produces an anticipated result. But this is not what is important here. We should observe first that an action is on principle *intentional*.[12]

If this approach is taken to freedom, it will become clear that an action depends on some being, a for-itself or human reality, discerning a *lack* in the world, and a determination or decision to act. But discerning a *lack* is only possible for a being that is capable of introducing a *nothingness* into being. Every being-in-itself, precisely because it simply *is*, is only capable of producing a being that is; only the human reality is able to insert a nothingness into being for the very reason that it is a nothingness. As a consciousness-self it can suspend all that was or is, and as a being whose being is more properly *to-be* it can project its own possibilities into a future moment. The human reality is the only being whose very being is to create its *own* being! Action, then, depends on there being an agent that can detect a lack, project a possibility that does not now exist, bestow the character of means upon things that are otherwise indifferent, and realize a new end or value. In short: action is only possible if there is a *free* being that is a consciousness-self. Human reality is just such a freedom.

> Cause, act, and end constitute a *continuum*, a *plenum*. These abortive attempts to stifle freedom under the weight of being (they collapse with the sudden upsurge of anguish before freedom) show sufficiently that freedom in its foundation coincides with the nothingness which is at the heart of man. Human reality is free because it is *not enough*. It is free because it is perpetually wrenched away from itself and because it has been separated by a nothingness from what it is and from what it will be. It is free, finally, because its present being is itself a nothingness in the form of the "reflection-reflecting." Man is free because he is not himself but presence to himself. The being which is what it is cannot be free. Freedom is precisely the nothingness which is made-to-be at the heart of man and which forces human-reality to *make itself* instead of to be. As we have seen, for human reality, to be is *to choose* oneself; nothing comes to it either from the outside or from within which it can receive or accept. Without any help whatsoever, it is entirely abandoned to the intolerable necessity of making itself be—down to the last detail. Thus freedom is not a being, it is *the being* of man—i.e. his nothingness of being.[13]

As for God, it would be very nice, as Sartre remarks in one place, if He existed because then our existence would be much more secure and comfortable—although *not* more human! [14] For we would have values for which to live and laws to guide us. But granting God's existence involves serious contradictions.

First of all, it contradicts human liberty. If God exists and is a Creator, then man either depends on God or he does not. If he does, then he cannot be free—his own subjectivity must somehow remain wrapped in the divine subjectivity, his essence must be determined by God's; if he does not, then he is free, he has his own being, but he does not *need* God.

But there is an error here analogous to that which we pointed out earlier in connection with Leibniz although it is put at the other end of existence. For Leibniz we are free since our acts derive from our essence. Yet the single fact that our essence has not been chosen by us shows that all this freedom in particulars actually covers over a total slavery. God chose Adam's essence. Conversely if it is the closing of the account which gives our life its meaning and its value, then it is of little importance that all the acts of which the web of our life is made have been free; the very meaning of them escapes us if we do not ourselves choose the moment at which the account will be closed. This has been clearly perceived by the free-thinking author of the anecdote echoed in the work of Diderot. Two brothers appeared at the divine tribunal on the Day of Judgment. The first said to God: "Why did you make me die so young?" And God said: "In order to save you." Then the brother in turn asked: "Why did you make me die so old?" If death is not the free determination of our being, it cannot *complete* our life. If one minute more or less may perhaps change everything and if this minute is added to or removed from my account, then even admitting that I am free to use my life, the meaning of my life escapes me. Now the Christian death comes from God. He chooses our hour.[15]

A birth and death over which God presides would remove all meaning from human life and liberty. Liberty is only intelligible if there is *no* God.

Second, God's existence involves a contradiction within itself. God has been thought of traditionally as a totality of being, a being so perfect as to need no cause of His being (He is cause of Himself—*causa sui*). Now totality and *causa sui* are self-contradictory. How can God include all being if, to do so requires that He be both being-for-itself and being-in-itself? Being-for-itself is more properly a nothingness; it must assert a lack of being if it is to be a revelation of being. If God is to be perfect being, He must be an identity of Being and Non-Being. And how can God be a cause of Himself? He cannot at once be contingent and necessary. The only solution is to deny God's existence as self-contradictory.

If we wish to conceive of a synthetic organization such that the for-itself is inseparable from the in-itself and conversely such that the in-itself is indissolubly bound to the for-itself, we must conceive of this synthesis in such a way that the in-itself would receive its existence from the nihilation which caused there to be consciousness of it. What does this mean if not that the indissoluble totality of in-itself and for-itself is conceivable only in the form of a being which is its own "self-cause?" It is this being and no other which could be valid absolutely as that olon of which we spoke earlier. And if we can raise the question of the being of the for-itself articulated in the in-itself, it is because we define ourselves a priori by means of a pre-ontological comprehension of the *ens causa sui*. Of course this *ens causa sui* is *impossible*, and the concept of it, as we have seen, includes a contradiction. Nevertheless the fact remains that since we raise the question of the being of the olon by adopting the point of view of the *ens causa sui*, it is from this point of view that we must set about examining the credentials of this olon. Has it not appeared due to the mere fact of the upsurge of the for-itself, and is not the for-itself originally a project of being its own self-cause? Thus we begin to grasp the nature of total reality.[16]

God's existence, then, would only prove a threat to human reality by imposing an essence, values and laws on us; the impossibility of His existing secures a thoroughly human life for man. Man is left to himself, he stands alone in the whole universe, he is condemned to be free and to make his own way without laws to guide him. He must simply choose and, thereby, make himself what he wants to be. As Orestes comments,

"Human life begins on the far side of despair." [17]

Now what does St. Thomas have to say about the mystery of man's being free? We have already seen that his philosophy of being is a necessary guide to our understanding of man. Man is an intellectual substance, and his body makes it possible for him to be intelligent, i.e. to understand. He is an active participant in his world; his world enters into his very being. Does this mean, then, that man is not free because he is a part of physical nature? Is he free with his own freedom or only with God's freedom? Is he only free to do what he must do? Is he autonomous? Is he free in opposition to both nature and God? Is he doomed to have no other law than that of his own making? Must he turn away from paths that lead to God, if he is to preserve his humanity and freedom? Let us go back to St. Thomas' understanding of being as primarily act and see if he has anything to say about these questions.

In various discussions of being throughout his works, St. Thomas repeatedly refers to three dimensions he observes: beings exist, and to exist is to subsist, to tend and to rest. Just what does this mean? Well, in not-

ing that each being subsists, he means that it stands on its own feet, so
to speak.

> According to the philosopher, substance is twofold. In one sense, it
> means the *quiddity of a thing*, signified by the definition, and thus
> we say that the definition signifies the substance of a thing; in which
> sense substance is called by the Greeks οὐσία, which we may call
> *essence*. In another sense, substance means a *subject* or *suppositum*
> which subsists in the genus of substance. To this, taken in a general
> sense, can be applied a name expressive of an intention; and thus it
> is called the *suppositum*. It is also called by three names signifying
> a reality—that is, a *thing of nature, subsistence* and *hypostasis*, ac-
> cording to a threefold consideration of the substance thus named.
> For, as it exists in itself and not in another, it is called *subsistence;*
> for we say that those things subsist which exist in themselves, and
> not in another. As it underlies some common nature, it is called a
> *thing of nature;* as, for instance, this particular man is a reality of a
> human nature. As it underlies the accidents, it is called hypostasis
> or substance. What these three names signify in common in the
> whole genus of substance, this name *person* signifies in the genus of
> rational substance.[18]

A finite being must receive its act of being, as we have seen, and it must
receive it by an act of creation from nothingness. But once a thing is
created, it exists by standing on its own and exercising its *own* act of
existing. To be created is not merely to be moved, so that everything the
thing does is due to the first cause. In St. Thomas' view, to be created
means to be given an act whereby the thing exists *in itself* and truly
originates acts by itself; it subsists and has a unique being of its own
which no other being can have. Substance in St. Thomas' thought is, then,
at poles apart from Spinoza's concept of it. A man is a substance, he subsists, he has a capacity for acts that are his own; he is a particular kind
of substance, a rational substance or *person*. He has characteristics and
acts that are uniquely his own.

> Although universal and particular exist in every genus, nevertheless,
> in a certain special way the individual belongs to the genus of sub-
> stance. For substance is individuated through itself, whereas the ac-
> cidents are individuated by the subject, which is the substance. For
> this particular whiteness is called *this* because it exists in this par-
> ticular subject. And so it is reasonable that the individuals of the
> genus substance should have a special name of their own; for they
> are called *hypostases* or first substances.

Further still, in a more special and perfect way, the particular and
the individual are found in rational substances, which have dominion
over their own actions, and which are not only made to act, as are
others, but act of themselves; for actions belong to singulars. Therefore, individuals of a rational nature even have a special name among
other substances; and this name is *person*.[19]

Thus, in the example to which we have referred so often before, a plant
is a being, it exists by performing its own living activities, its leaves and
flowers are uniquely its own, it exercises its own individual causality,
which no other plant—even of the same species—can exercise. Unless that
individual plant performs its own acts, it will not live; no other plant can
grow for it! And, says St. Thomas, man is a subsistent being "in a more
special and perfect way." The reason he gives is that men have dominion
over their own acts and are not merely made to act. As an incarnate
spiritual being, man exists in a unique way and he subsists in a unique
way; not only does he initiate actions, but he does so through free, rational choice. He is master of his own destiny and solely responsible for
it. All beings, then, in a very real sense originate their own acts.

However, every finite thing is limited and incomplete not only by its
nature (a thing can only *be* as a plant *is* or as a dog *is*), but also in the
sense that it never is all that it can be.

For everything that is an imperfect member of any species desires to
attain the perfection of its species. For instance, a man who has an
opinion regarding something, that is, an imperfect knowledge of the
thing, is thereby aroused to desire knowledge of the thing.[20]

The seedling, for instance, is a plant and not a cat; a baby is a *human*
being and not a monkey. But neither the seedling nor the baby is fully
what it can be; each has to grow into its full being as a member of its
own particular species. This is the dimension of existing St. Thomas has
in mind when he speaks of existing as *tending;* to exist is to reach forward
for the being that will complete the finite, limited being that a thing has
from nature, i.e. from birth.

Since the essence of good consists in this, that something perfects
another as an end, whatever is found to have the character of an end
also has that of good. Now two things are essential to an end: it must
be desired by things which have not yet attained the end, and it must
be loved by the things which share the end, and be, as it were, enjoyable to them. For it is essentially the same to tend to an end and
in some way to repose in that end. . . . These two properties are
found to belong to the act of being. For whatever does not yet

participate in the act of being tends towards it by a certain natural appetite. In this way matter tends to form, according to the Philosopher. But everything which already has being naturally loves its being and with all its strength preserves it.[21]

For St. Thomas a finite being exists striving to preserve its being and working to complete itself in its own way by reaching out for the things that can make it more complete in its being. It may try to perfect itself by merely exercising its powers so that they are better able to act, and then it finds its growth in the acting itself. Or it may perfect itself through an operation that is productive of something else.

Moreover, every action and movement are for the sake of some perfection. Even if the action itself be the end, it is clear that it is a secondary perfection of the agent. But, if the action be a changing of external matter, it is obvious that the mover intends to bring about some perfection in the thing that is moved. Even the thing that is moved also tends towards this, if it be a case of natural movement. Now we call what is perfect a good. So, every action and movement are for the sake of a good.[22]

A geometrician, for example, is inspired to puzzle out the properties of figures so that he may eventually acquire a facility in thinking about them; a builder is motivated to build so that a house may exist; a dog is driven to find food so that it may continue to be and grow. And, as St. Thomas is careful to point out, one thing is perfective of another in virtue of its *own* act of being and not merely in virtue of *what* it is.

The true and the good must therefore add to the concept of being, a relationship of that which perfects. But in any being there are two aspects to be considered, the formal character of its species and the act of being by which it subsists in that species. And so a being can be perfective in two ways. (1) It can be so just according to its specific character. In this way the intellect is perfected by a being, for it perceives the formal character of the being. But the being is still not in it according to its natural existence. It is this mode of perfecting which the true adds to being. . . . (2) A being is perfective of another not only according to its specific character but also according to the existence which it has in reality. In this fashion the good is perfective; for the good is in things, as the Philosopher says. Inasmuch as one being by reason of its act of existing is such as to perfect and complete another, it stands to that other as end. And hence it is that all who rightly define *good* put in its notion something about its status as an end.[23]

A harpist does not become a better harpist by merely knowing what playing the harp means but, rather, by actually exercising acts of playing the
harp; the dog is not nourished by merely seeing the food, but by the very
being of the actual food. Tending, therefore, is in the direction of the act
of existing of the thing that perfects; in desire and love a person goes out
to the very being of the one he loves or the thing he desires.

Now, as we have seen, the *way* in which anything exists is determined
by *what* it is; its striving for perfection is similarly determined and so,
too, is the suitability of the thing that completes it.

Now the good that is proper to a thing may be received in many
ways. One way depends on what is appropriate to the essential character of the individual. It is thus that an animal seeks his good, when
he desires the food whereby he may be kept in existence. A second
way depends on what is appropriate to the species. It is in this way
that an animal desires his proper good, inasmuch as he desires the
procreation of offspring and the nourishment of the same, or the per-
formance of any other work that is for the preservation or protection
of individuals belonging to his species.[24]

Thus, for example, a plant finds its food in one kind of being because it
is a plant, a man finds it in a different kind of food. What is befitting,
then, is measured by the kind of thing that is struggling to complete itself
in one way or another. St. Thomas formulates this in philosophical language by saying that each being exists in a manner determined by its
essence and finds its more mature state of being or perfection in the good
of some being befitting or suited to it, the good being that towards which
anything tends.

Although goodness and being are the same really, nevertheless,
since they differ in thought, they are not predicated of a thing absolutely in the same way. For since being properly signifies that something actually is, and actuality properly correlates to potentiality, a
thing is, in consequence, said absolutely to have being according as
it is primarily distinguished from that which is only in potentiality;
and this is precisely each thing's substantial being. Hence it is by its
substantial being that everything is said to have being absolutely;
but by any further actuality it is said to have being relatively. Thus
to be white signifies being relatively, for to be white does not take
a thing out of absolutely potential being, since it is added to a thing
that actually has being. But goodness expresses perfection, which is
something desirable, and hence it expresses something final. Hence,
that which has ultimate perfection is said to be absolutely good, but
that which has not the ultimate perfection it ought to have (al-

though, insofar as it is at all actual, it has some perfection) is not said to be perfect absolutely nor good absolutely, but only relatively. In this way, therefore, viewed in its first (i.e. substantial) being, a thing is said to be absolutely, and to be good relatively (i.e. insofar as it has being); but viewed in its complete actuality a thing is said to be relatively, and to be good absolutely.[25]

The capacity of a being to be perfective of another and, hence, to be desired by it is precisely what St. Thomas has in mind in statements that he repeatedly makes about action and human action: "Every agent acts for a good,"[26] "The good is what all things seek,"[27] "The end is the principle of the practical order."[28] He means that a being is an agent because it is moved to act by a good that will bring it to a more complete state of being; that beings are good because they can perfect other beings, i.e. make them better, and thereby move other things to seek them; that the principle or starting-point in the order of action and production is the good or end that sets the operation in motion—or brings the operation into being! In short: each finite thing exists striving for its good.

As for the third dimension St. Thomas detects in existing, namely, rest, he means that in every striving there is a moment of satisfaction when the thing's desire rests in the enjoyment of the good it has been seeking.

Besides, that toward which a thing tends, while it is beyond the thing, and in which it rests, when it is possessed, is the end for the thing. Now, if anything lacks a proper perfection, it is moved toward it, insofar as lies within its capacity, but if it possesses it the thing rests in it. Therefore, the end of each thing is its perfection. Now, the perfection of anything is its good. So, each thing is ordered to a good as an end.[29]

This does not mean that a being attains its final growth all at once. It means, rather, that in gaining a good, in which it finds its need satisfied for the moment, it has a certain satisfaction, it achieves a measure of completion or perfection, and then moves on to a further good. Thus, for example, a young man may be inspired to grow intellectually by studying geometry. He cannot become a geometrician all at once; his desire is, rather, satisfied with each step he takes. Each Euclidean theorem he masters leads him nearer to his goal; and even though he knows that his final goal still eludes him, he gains a real satisfaction from learning each new theorem. It is as though he experiences an inchoative and incomplete taste of his final intellectual joy at each step. In this way the terms "perfection" and "end" take on a somewhat different meaning for St. Thomas.

They do not *necessarily* signify ultimate completeness or last end, even though they sometimes do have that meaning. They also refer to intermediary states of being wherein one perfection or end may be subordinated to a further perfection or end. So an end may truly inspire a thing to act and still not be a final (i.e. ultimate) end. In the case of the student-geometrician, he has all the equipment needed to be a human being and, in the knowledge of axioms, principles and definitions, he has all that is required to be a geometrician. But as he makes his way, each bit of new knowledge gained is a good that brings its own satisfaction with it; it is a limited, proximate or subordinate end. His final end is the knowledge of the skilled geometrician. So a thing may be perfect in the sense of having all the parts needed for it to be, but it may still be imperfect in not actually being all that it can be. And as it becomes more and more what it can be, it is more and more perfect without being totally completed. In this way a thing may exist striving for its perfection but still rest in the proximate goods or ends it attains. To exist, then, is to rest, to gain satisfaction, to enjoy as well as to strive or tend.

St. Thomas uses the term "appetite" to designate being's tending to the good, the root-meaning of the word being simply "to seek for" something. He describes it in this fashion:

> Now every appetite is only of something good. The reason for this is that the appetite is nothing else than the inclination of a being desirous of a thing towards that thing. Now every inclination is to something like and suitable to the thing inclined. Since, therefore, everything inasmuch as it is being and substance, is a good, it must needs be that every inclination is to something good.[30]

Now inasmuch as "every inclination is to something like and suitable to the thing inclined," then inclinations and appetites will vary as the being of the thing varies. On this basis St. Thomas distinguishes between natural, sensitive and intellective inclinations.

> To make this evident, we must observe that some inclination follows every form: for example, fire, by its form, is inclined to rise, and to generate its like. Now the form is found to have a more perfect existence in those things which participate in knowledge than in those which lack knowledge. For in those which lack knowledge, the form is found to determine each thing only to its own being—that is, to the being which is natural to each. Now this natural form is followed by a natural inclination which is called the natural appetite. But in those things which have knowledge, each one is determined to its own natural being by its natural form, but in such a manner that it

is nevertheless receptive of the species of other things. For example, sense receives the species of all sensible things, and the intellect, of all intelligible things; so that the soul of man is, in a way, all things by sense and intellect.[31]

Thus, fire, plants and inanimate bodies are incapable of knowledge and, consequently, the only good to which they incline is the good of their natural forms; the plant acts to become more perfectly what it is in virtue of its nature, minerals act physically and chemically as causes in accordance with their natural structures. Such things, says St. Thomas, are moved by natural appetite. Animals, on the other hand, are moved by what they sense to be good or bad in the things around them: the lamb is moved to flee by sensing a wolf, the dog is moved by the smell of food, sniffing some food and rejecting it, sniffing other food and accepting it.

> . . . we must observe that some things act without judgment, as a stone moves downward; and in like manner all things which lack knowledge. And some act from judgment, but not a free judgment, as brute animals. For the sheep, seeing the wolf, judges it to be a thing to be shunned, from a natural and not a free judgment, because it judges, not from deliberation, but from natural instinct. And the same thing is to be said of any judgment in brute animals. But man acts from judgment, because by his apprehensive power he judges that something should be avoided or sought. But because this judgment, in the case of some particular act, is not from a natural instinct, but from some act of comparison in the reason, therefore he acts from free judgment and retains the power of being inclined to various things.[32]

The animal has instinct as a kind of judgment in sensible matters, and it enables the animal to determine what is good for it and what is not. As St. Thomas sees it, the brute animal finds its good in something sensibly perceived as good. It is moved by sensitive appetite.

Man, on the other hand, is moved by intellective appetite or will.

> The will is a power distinct from sense appetite. It should be noted in this connection that rational appetite is distinguished from that of sense in just the same way as sensitive appetite is distinguished from that of nature—because of a more perfect way of tending. . . . a rational nature, being closest to God, not merely, like inanimate things, has an inclination to something, end, like a sentient nature, a mover of this inclination determined as it were extrinsically, but further so has its inclination within its own power that it does not necessarily incline to anything appetible which is apprehended, but

can incline or not incline. And so its inclination is not determined
for it by anything else but by itself. This belongs to it inasmuch as
it does not use a bodily organ; and so, getting farther away from the
nature of what is moved, it approaches that of what moves and acts.
It can come about that something determines for itself its inclination
to an end only if it knows the end and the bearing of the end upon
the means to it. But this belongs to reason alone. Thus such an appetite, which is not determined of necessity by something else, follows the apprehension of reason. Hence, rational appetite, called will,
is a power distinct from sense appetite.[33]

This does not mean that he is moved *solely* by intellective appetite because as we saw in our last chapter, man is not *simply* an intellective
substance but, rather, the kind of intellectual substance that needs the
senses and an organized physical body precisely so that it can *be* an intellectual substance. He has a body and senses—and in this he resembles
the brute animals—but he also creates sciences, arts, moral codes and
religions. These, as works of reason, are his *unique* works, but they still
depend on the use of his body and senses. St. Thomas calls man an *intellectual* substance so as to designate the way he properly and distinctively acts. So, too, is he said to seek his good by intellective appetite in
order to point out how he properly tends to his good as man. True, he
does have a physical body and may fall as a stone does; and he lives and
grows much as a plant does. He is moved, then, in a way by natural
appetite. Indeed, in a more profound sense, consequent upon his intellective form or rational soul there is a natural appetite in man that naturally
and necessarily inclines him to seek such rational goods as knowledge and
virtue. But in addition to inclinations that follow natural forms, man also
resembles brute animals in pursuing good things revealed to him by his
bodily senses. Thus, he experiences pleasant things, he is aroused by fear
of dangerous situations and he is hungry even as the brute animals are.
So he is moved by sensitive appetite. St. Thomas points out, however,
that the natural judgments of the brute animal's instinct are somewhat
different in men because they are *rational:*

> Now we must observe that as to sensible forms there is no difference
> between man and other animals; for they are similarly immuted by
> external sensibles. But there is a difference as to the above inten-
> tions: for other animals perceive these intentions only by some sort
> of natural instinct, while man perceives them also by means of a
> certain comparison. Therefore, the power which in other animals is
> called the *natural estimative* in man is called the *cogitative,* which
> by some sort of comparison discovers these intentions. Therefore it

is also called the *particular reason*, to which medical men assign a
particular organ, namely, the middle part of the head; for it compares individual intentions, just as the intellectual reason compares
universal intentions.[34]

So man does have these various appetites, but it is precisely so that he
can become an intellectual substance; the desire to become an actual intellectual substance is uniquely man's. To that desire all other appetites
are subordinated. Being an intellectual substance, then, man has a distinct
appetite, a *rational* appetite. Now exactly what is distinctive about such
an appetite?

Well, first let us see a little more clearly what St. Thomas means by
"*intellective* appetite."

> Other things, again, have an inclination toward good but with a
> knowledge whereby they perceive the nature of goodness. This be-
> longs to the intellect. Things so inclined are most perfectly inclined
> toward what is good; not, indeed, as if they were guided by another
> toward the good, like things devoid of knowledge, nor as if they were
> guided only toward some particular good, as things that have only
> sensitive knowledge, but as inclined toward the universal good itself.
> Such inclination is termed will.[35]

There we have it: as an intellectual substance man is naturally inclined
to, i.e. spontaneously desirous of, a good befitting his being—the *universal*
good. The parallel between intellect and will is particularly striking and
instructive. The human intellect, as we have seen, makes it possible for
man to know something universal and common; for example, what a living thing, animal, or man is. He has a capacity for discovering general
causes in things—as he does in physics and biology—or even more fundamental causes, as he does in philosophy. And when he comes to judge
any particular thing presented to him by his senses, he does so in virtue
of the general knowledge his intellect gives him. A man is an intellect in
*this* organic body, and he knows individual things as they incorporate
universal, essential principles in their structures; similarly, he desires
or loves individual sensible things to the extent that they incorporate
universal principles of goodness in their being. He knows things as being
and loves them as good. Man can strive for such universal goods as
knowledge and virtue, and he can love individual entities insofar as
they help him gain those ends. Politically, he can be moved by causes
like Patriotism, Liberty, Self-determination; morally, he can be motivated
by Pleasure, Duty, Service-to-humanity; artistically, he can produce
works inspired by Nature, ideal geometric or physical form, pure abstrac-

tion. All of these are general goods, and in each instance man's appetite is moved by what he understands the nature of the good to be. He judges the acts he should perform and the things he should produce in the light of these general notions of goodness.

Suppose, for example, that a community decides that its survival depends on more trade. Noting the role that capital, equipment and resources play in gaining that end, it will create the political, economic and social institutions needed to provide them; it may decide that private property in a very special sense is sacrosanct, or that national survival depends on social ownership. Whatever their decision in these more precise matters may be, men will always make them as judgments about a general good and in the light of a universal good. Briefly, man understands everything in virtue of what he considers being and truth to be, and he desires everything in virtue of what he understands the nature of goodness to be. In this sense "universal," "general" or "common" do not imply that he has to know *all* good things before he can have any desire, for then he would never desire anything. It means, rather, that as an intellectual substance he can gain some understanding of the nature of goodness and is naturally and necessarily moved by that good. Thus, St. Thomas says that the will *must* desire man's being, the well-being of his body, the perfecting of his intellect and will by knowledge and virtue. It must, in short, seek man's fulness or happiness. In this the will acts precisely as a nature, necessarily inclining to its end. That is why he contends that the first judgment in the practical order is a judgment about the good: The good is to be done, evil is to be avoided. That is the first step in following St. Thomas' understanding of human freedom. Now let us follow him in the second step.

As we saw in the last chapter, the human intellect does have the nature of a sensible thing as its proper object, but it can only come into contact with that object through sensation and abstraction. Human intellect and intelligible nature do not exist as such confronting each other; *this man* exists and *this sensible thing* exists. Put in another context, the human intellect has to give its assent to first principles, but in fact it finds itself confronted by particular, contingent propositions that do not have any clear and immediate relationship to any first principle. The intellect only gives its assent to such propositions when a necessary connection has been established with judgments to which it does have to assent. The same is true of the human will as of an intellective appetite.

The will does not desire of necessity whatsoever it desires. In order to make this evident we must observe that, just as the intellect naturally and of necessity adheres to first principles, so the will adheres to the last end, as we have said already. Now there are some intelligible things which have no necessary connection with first principles, e.g. contingent propositions, the denial of which does not involve a denial of first principles. And to such the intellect does not assent of necessity. But there are some propositions which have a necessary connection with first principles, namely, demonstrable conclusions, a denial of which involves a denial of first principles. And to these the intellect assents of necessity, when once it is aware (by demonstration) of the necessary connection of these conclusions with the principles; but it does not assent of necessity until through the demonstration it recognizes the necessity of such a connection.

It is the same with the will. For there are certain particular goods which have not a necessary connection with happiness, because without them a man can be happy; and to such the will does not adhere of necessity.[36]

The will must, then, desire whatever is presented to it as the good of man; but as an appetite that craves things sensibly through the senses of the body, the will finds itself confronted by *particular* goods that may not clearly have a necessary relationship to man's universal good. It may not be clear that man cannot be happy without them. To these the will does *not* necessarily incline or adhere. It does so only after the judgment has been made that this particular good is a means to man's good and must, therefore, be sought. That judgment is made by practical reason, according to St. Thomas, and becomes the matter of a choice; the ultimate choice of what is to be done in a given situation is a combined act of practical reason and will.

Now it is evident that, in a sense, reason precedes the will and directs its act, namely, insofar as the will tends to its object according to the order of reason; for the apprehensive power presents to the appetite its object. Accordingly, that act whereby the will tends to something proposed to it as being good, through being ordained to the end by the reason, is materially an act of will, but formally an act of the reason. Now in such matters, the substance of the act is as the matter in comparison to the order imposed by the higher power. Therefore, choice is substantially not an act of the reason but of the will; for choice is accomplished in a certain movement of the soul towards the good which is chosen. Consequently, it is evidently an act of the appetitive power.[37]

Practical reason is not a power distinct from speculative reason but, rather, reason as it turns its attention to a work that is to be made or to an act to be performed. Its proper work as reason is a syllogism or demonstration, but inasmuch as it has to do with something practical, its reasoning culminates in a practical conclusion. That conclusion becomes a matter for choice by the will.

> As we have already stated, choice follows the decision or judgment which is, as it were, the conclusion of a practical syllogism. Hence, that which is the conclusion of a practical syllogism is the matter of choice.[38]

Thus, a person may or may not be happy enjoying some particular good or other; it may not clearly appear to be a means to happiness nor an intermediary end leading to his final end. As such, it cannot move his will. Only when reason has judged that such a good does have a necessary relation to man's good as such, that it is man's good existing here and now, that *this* good is *the* good for the moment, is the will moved by it. And the judgment is a *free* judgment.

> . . . man acts from judgment, because by his apprehensive power he judges that something should be avoided or sought. But because this judgment, in the case of some particular act, is not from a natural instinct, but from some act of comparison in the reason, therefore he acts from free judgment and retains the power of being inclined to various things. For reason in contingent matters may follow opposite courses, as we see in dialectical syllogisms and rhetorical arguments. Now particular operations are contingent, and therefore in such matters the judgment of reason may follow opposite courses, and is not determined to one. And in that man is rational, it is necessary that he have free choice.[39]

In a certain sense man enjoys a kind of liberty even as regards the good of man itself. For even though the will does necessarily desire that he exist, live and understand—for these constitute man's good as a human intellectual substance—he still has to determine for himself just what these are. The human will is only moved by a good that is understood, so man has to gain some understanding of what he is and what his happiness consists in before the will is moved. In contrast to a merely natural agent, man is an intellectual agent and determines his own end in a sense by reaching a knowledge of what he is and what is good for him.

> Again, an intelligent agent acts for the sake of an end, in the sense that it determines the end for itself. On the other hand, an agent

that acts from a natural impulse, though acting for an end, as we showed in the preceding chapter, does not determine the end for itself, since it does not know the meaning of an end, but, rather, is moved toward an end determined for it by another being. Now the intelligent agent determines the end for itself only by considering the rational character of the good, for an object of the intellect is only motivating by virtue of the rational meaning of the good, which is the object of the will.[40]

The will is above all free as regards particular ends or goods, i.e. as regards its actually willing those things that are good for man here and now in a determined set of circumstances. Here the desire of the will is directed toward many things that *might* be good for man in some way or other, but that are not determinately good for him in the sense that he could not be happy without them. An individual person at a given point in time must decide that this thing—be it this apple, this game, this scientific conclusion, this work of art—is good for man. And that deciding, says St. Thomas, is a free act.

The proper act of free choice is election, for we say that we have a free choice because we can take one thing while refusing another; and this is to elect. Therefore we must consider the nature of free choice by considering the nature of election. Now two things occur in election: one on the part of the cognitive power, the other on the part of the appetitive power. On the part of the cognitive power, counsel is required, by which we judge one thing to be preferred to another; on the part of the appetitive power, it is required that the appetite should accept the judgment of counsel.[41]

As regards particular objects of desire, then, man is free because he has to take counsel and elect the good that he will actually pursue. Finally, man is free in another sense: he can will either to will or not to will. And the basic reason for this is that an individual act of willing is itself a particular good precisely because it is an individual moment of existing. Consequently, it, too, is subject to election.

Man does not choose of necessity. And this is because that which is possible not to be, is not of necessity. Now the reason why it is possible not to choose, or to choose, may be gathered from a twofold power in man. For man can will and not will, act and not act; and again, he can will this or that, and do this or that. The reason for this is to be found in the very power of the reason. For the will can tend to whatever the reason can apprehend as good. Now the reason can apprehend as good not only this, viz. *to will* or *to act,* but also this, viz. *not to will* and *not to act.*[42]

Man is, then, an intelligent agent free to determine the character of the good he will seek, free to elect the particular goods he will desire, and free to will or not to will.

Now an act of free choice is a most complicated affair. Just as man's act of sensing involves his whole being as knower (sense, memory, reason and intellect), and as his cognitive life as scientist involves, in addition to memory and reason, all the information his senses can provide, so also does his choosing to do this or that involve his whole appetitive life. For free choice is thoroughly human; it is a prerogative of neither the brute animal nor the angel. It is man's alone. Thus, for example, the pleasant flavor he enjoys through his sense of taste and that he recalls so vividly from past experience, is a very real factor in the choice he will make. As a human being his choice is not the work of a disembodied reason—whatever such a monstrosity would be! But in a special way it is the work of intellective appetite, an appetite moved by a good presented by reason and intellect. It is not as though man's will were a kind of blind drive that only occasionally came under the influence of his intellect. His is an intellective appetite that moves towards its object as his intellect presents it. In a free choice there is a reciprocal dependence of reason on will and of will on reason.

> The will moves the intellect as to the exercise of its act, since even the true itself, which is the perfection of the intellect, is included in the universal good as a particular good. But as to the determination of the act, which the act derives from the object, the intellect moves the will; for the good itself is apprehended under a special aspect as contained in the universal true. It is therefore evident that the same is not mover and moved in the same respect.[43]

The person who has to make a choice is confronted by a particular, contingent good; practical reason has to take counsel about that thing. One may have to decide, for example, whether or not to take a dose of medicine that is unpleasant to the taste but good for his health. If it is the practical judgment after counsel that the dose should be taken, it is presented to his will as *the* good here and now—he sees that the wellbeing of his body at this moment consists in taking the dose of medicine. Of course it will still require the discipline of courage on the side of the will to follow that decision! In this sense, from the side of the object and the judgment about its goodness, reason has a kind of primacy or priority in determining the will by informing it that, in the judgment of reason, *this* good is *the* good for the moment. Yet reason itself is a power requiring to be "set in motion" so that it *will* take counsel. Reason is prompted to the act of judging (which is *its* good) by the will, precisely so that the will can choose and incline to this particular thing as good.

> The higher powers of the soul, because immaterial, are capable of reflecting upon themselves. Both the intellect and the will, therefore, reflect upon themselves, upon each other, upon the essence of the soul, and upon all its powers. The intellect understands itself and the will and the essence of the soul and all the soul's powers. Similarly the will wills that it will, that the intellect understand, that the soul be, and so of the other powers. Now when one power is brought to bear upon another, it is referred to that other according to what is proper to itself. When the intellect understands that the will is willing, it receives within itself the intelligible character of willing. When the will is brought to bear upon the other powers of the soul, it is directed to them as things to which motion and operation belong, and it inclines each to its own operation. Thus the will moves in the manner of an efficient cause not only external things but also the very powers of the soul.[44]

The will moves as an efficient cause and is concerned with the being and act both of powers and things.

Thus, even in speculative matters such as the reasonings involved in the geometrician's pursuit of truth, the intellect is moved by the will. For, as St. Thomas remarks, any truth gained by the intellect is a perfection and, hence, a particular good. It comes, then, under the dominance of the will; the will moves the geometrician to speculate so that the intellect may be satisfied. One might say that the intellect loves the truth and searches for it, but it is always at the will's prodding. And the conclusions reached by the geometrician's proofs are strict and rigid effects of careful reasoning; but they are conclusions that *satisfy* the intellect and permit it to enjoy its objects. Similarly, laws of justice in the social order may be strict and unpleasant, but they may be demanded by the situation and express a real love of man. Opposing a law inspired by love to a law of truth or justice is not in the spirit of St. Thomas. All love, if it is properly human, must be informed by reason and understanding; a love divorced from them and acting impetuously or in disorderly fashion is not human. And human reason can come to quite different conclusions about the nature of the good, and love can pursue vastly different presentations of beloved objects in different times and places. Bringing human love under reason does not, therefore, condemn it to conformity or drabness. But whenever reason does think about the good and work to discover what is good in a given situation, it is moved to do so by the will. For then reason is seeking its own satisfaction, namely, the truth of a particular, given, practical situation, and practical reason is moved to take counsel by the will. As St. Thomas says in one place, the will wills to be counselled so that it can act as will, i.e. so that it can love.

> When the acts of two powers are ordered to one another, in each of them there is something belonging to the other power; and consequently each act can be denominated from either power. Now it is evident that the act of the reason giving direction as to the means, and the act of the will tending to these means according to the reason's direction, are ordered to one another. Consequently, there is to be found something of the reason, viz. order, in the act of the will which is choice; and in counsel, which is an act of reason, something is found of the will, both as matter (since counsel is of what man wills to do), and as motive (because it is from willing the end that man is moved to take counsel in regard to the means).[45]

In this sense the choice belongs substantially to the will, and the will preserves a very real dominion over its own act even while being informed by the reason.

Now, strictly speaking, counsel and choice are never concerned with man's ultimate happiness or good. As St. Thomas remarks,[46] if there can be counsel about the ultimate end, it is only as long as some doubt remains about the nature of the end; and where such doubt exists, the end is still not fixed and is more truly a means than an end. But when the character of happiness or the ultimate good *is* determined, counsel and choice are required concerning the means that should be taken to gain the end.

> The end is the principle in practical matters, because the nature of the means is taken from the end. Now the principle cannot be called in question, but must be presupposed in every inquiry. Since, therefore, counsel is an inquiry, it is not of the end, but only of the means to the end. Nevertheless, it may happen that what is the end in regard to some things is ordained to something else; just as also what is the principle of one demonstration is the conclusion of another. Consequently, that which is looked upon as the end in one inquiry may be looked upon as the means in another, and thus it will become an object of counsel.[47]

As regards the end in this sense the will must, for example, seek to pre-serve the being and identity of the person, and reason will only take counsel about the means of doing so. Counsel and choice are limited to the means one must follow to enjoy that end or, to put it in other terms, to deciding which particular goods may serve as intermediary ends lead-ing to that final end. Free choice, then, only extends to the means to happiness and not to happiness itself.

Many factors can influence that choice, sometimes even to the point of destroying its freedom. For a man's will must be informed by reason, and it is quite possible that through extremely violent passions of anger or lust, for instance, it is impossible for reason to act and make its judgment fairly and objectively. St. Thomas says that such a person acts much as an irrational animal acts; he acts without reason and, hence, without choice.

As we have stated above, the passion of the sensitive appetite moves the will insofar as the will is moved by its object—inasmuch as, namely, through being disposed in such and such a way by a passion, a man judges something to be fitting and good, which he would not judge thus were it not for the passion. Now this in-fluence of passion on man occurs in two ways. First, so that his reason is wholly bound, so that he has not the use of reason: as happens in those who, through violent anger or concupiscence, become mad or insane, just as they may from some other bodily disorder; for such passions do not take place without some change in the body. And of such men the same is to be said as of irrational animals, which follow of necessity the impulse of their passions; for in them there is neither movement of reason, nor, conse-quently, of will.[48]

And even though the movement of passion and sense-appetite is not so strong as to overcome reason completely, it may still influence the reason and, hence, the will in its choice. The will of an angry man may make one choice, the will of a placid person another; food may be deemed good by a person who is healthy, bad by one who is ill. In short: dispositions of the sensible appetites may very definitely affect the decision reason makes. Practical reason may also be influenced by a variety of factors more indigenous to reason than to the body and its appetites: the moral experiences one has had in the past, the general moral judgments one has reached—whether or not stealing is bad, whether killing another person is forbidden or not, what one thinks man is. All of these may in-fluence the decision. Indeed, the very ability to bring one's whole moral life to bear on a given situation so as to make a decision at all will affect the choice. Man is, indeed, capable of acts of free choice, but any number of physical, psychological, moral and social factors may and do intrude themselves to diminish or destroy that freedom. He remains free to the extent that his reason remains capable of making its decisions and of directing his will to seek what he understands to be good for man.

In this sense it is true to say that, while man is free, he can grow in freedom. At birth he is free, but only inchoatively; he has all that is required to be and act freely, but must grow and develop if he is to be free in the fullest sense. He has to develop what St. Thomas often describes as a second nature, a complement of virtues. According to St. Thomas habits are needed whenever powers are directed to many things indeterminately, and good habits are virtues.

> Virtue denotes a certain perfection of a power. Now a thing's perfection is considered chiefly in relation to its end. But the end of power is act. Therefore power is said to be perfect according as it is determined to its act. Now there are some powers which of themselves are determined to their acts, for instance, the active natural powers. And therefore these natural powers are in themselves called virtues. But the rational powers, which are proper to man, are not determined to one particular action, but are inclined indifferently to many; but they are determined to acts by means of habits, as is clear from what we have said above. Therefore, human virtues are habits.[49]

Thus, for example, in human knowing man's reason is directed toward many different kinds of objects; a person can know physical bodies, plants, animals and the stars. But if reason is not disciplined, it will not be able to know any of them well nor to think about any of them easily. We need a disciplined reason if we are to think correctly—indeed, we need disciplined senses and imagination, too! The same is true of the body's appetites: they, too, are directed towards many things—food, wine, other human beings. If they are to act as the sense-appetites of an intellectual substance, they have to be brought under reason and ordered to the good of man. Pleasures of the body (food, drink, sex) must not be sought or enjoyed in isolation from the intellect and pursued for their own sake; they must, rather, be brought within the order of the whole man. As St. Thomas remarks in one place, even games that seem to be pointless must be brought within the general hierarchy of things good for man; they have to be enjoyed as providing relaxation for the body so that the intellect can pursue its studies more easily!

Now, all practical sciences, arts, and powers are objects of love because they are means to something else, for their purpose is not knowledge but operation. But the speculative sciences are lovable for their own sake, since their end is knowledge itself. Nor do we find any action in human affairs, except speculative thought, that is not directed to some other end. Even sports activities, which appear to be carried on without any purpose, have a proper end, namely, so that after our minds have been somewhat relaxed through them we may be then better able to do serious jobs. Otherwise, if sport were an end in itself, the proper thing to do would be to play all the time, but that is not appropriate.[50]

All the appetites, sensitive and intellective, have to be perfected by moral virtues so that they desire their proper good with due order to the whole. It should be noted that in St. Thomas' mind appetites are made more perfect as appetites when disciplined by virtue; they are not denied or obliterated, but enabled to be more completely *human* appetites.

Practical reason, too, has to learn to make its judgments in accordance with right appetite; it has to be perfected by a virtue that is absolutely central to the moral life (i.e. to man's free acting), the virtue of prudence. The depth of the chasm separating Kant's view of freedom and the moral life from that of St. Thomas can best be judged by the attitude each takes to prudence. For Kant, prudence is fundamentally self-interested, gain-seeking, compromising (in the pejorative sense), a concession to lower sensual inclinations; prudence is always concerned with happiness, all of whose elements are, in Kant's view, empirical and, hence, incapable of yielding a valid moral imperative.

Let the question be, for example: May I when in distress make a promise with the intention not to keep it? I readily distinguish here between the two significations which the question may have: whether it is prudent or whether it is right to make a false promise. The former may undoubtedly often be the case. I see clearly indeed that it is not enough to extricate myself from a present difficulty by means of this subterfuge, but it must be well considered whether there may not hereafter spring from this lie much greater inconvenience than that from which I now free myself, and as, with all my supposed cunning, the consequences cannot be so easily foreseen but that credit once lost may be much more injurious to me than any mischief which I seek to avoid at present, it should be considered whether it would not be more prudent to act herein according to a universal maxim, and to make it a habit to promise nothing except with the intention of keeping it. But it is soon clear to me that such a maxim will still only be based on the fear of consequences. Now it is a wholly different thing to be truthful from duty, and to be so from apprehension of injurious consequences.[51]

St. Thomas' view of prudence, indeed his whole understanding of the moral life, is quite different. One of the principles that recurs most frequently in his examination is this one: "It is intrinsic to the very formal structure of human virtue that it make man's acts *good*." A habit that would accustom a person to doing actions that might have a limited, private value that would divert him from his final end so that he was not a good man, would not be a virtue at all. So in the case of prudence much more is at stake than the person's private good; prudence intends an end common to the whole of human life. There is a prudence that intends a particular good as, for example, a limited prudence in warfare may mark a person as a prudent general. But *human* prudence strictly and simply concerns itself with man's whole well-being (*ad totum bene vivere*).

> According to the Philosopher (*Ethics* VI, 8) some have held that prudence does not extend to the common good but only to the good of the individual, and this because they thought that man is not bound to seek other than his own good. But this opinion is opposed to charity, which *seeketh not her own* (I *Cor.* XIII, 5): wherefore the Apostle says of himself (*Ibid.* X, 33): *Not seeking that which is profitable to myself, but to many, that they may be saved*. Moreover, it is contrary to right reason, which judges the common good of the individual.
>
> Accordingly, since it belongs to prudence rightly to counsel, judge, and command concerning the means of obtaining a due end, it is evident that prudence regards not only the private good of the individual, but also the common good of the multitude.[52]

Indeed, St. Thomas remarks, a person who seeks the common good of the multitude also strives for his own good as a consequence.[53] For one's own proper good is impossible unless the good of the family, city or country is realized; a man is part of a household or a civil community and has to judge his own good in the light of prudent judgments about the good of the whole community. Prudence, then, is not a selfish virtue—whatever that anomaly might be!

Prudence does counsel and judge the act appropriate to a given situation, and these two functions belong properly to practical reason. But, as distinct from the virtue of art, prudence does not make its judgments in dissociation from a right and disciplined appetite. Art, according to

St. Thomas, disregards appetite and only makes it possible for a person to make a good work; prudence, on the other hand, presupposes the appetite's rectitude.

> *Now in human acts ends are what principles are in speculative matters*, as is stated in *Ethics* VII. Consequently, it is requisite for prudence, which is right reason about things to be done, that man be well disposed with regard to ends; and this depends on the rectitude of his appetite. Therefore, for prudence there is need of moral virtue, which rectifies the appetite. On the other hand, the good of things made by art is not the good of man's appetite, but the good of artificial things themselves, and hence art does not presuppose rectitude of the appetite.[54]

Prudence, then, is not a native cunning intent only on gaining some advantage; it is a virtue aiding practical reason to make a correct judgment about the act suited to a given situation and has to be abetted by disciplined appetites.

> Prudence is a virtue most necessary for human life. For a good life consists in good deeds. Now in order to do good deeds, it matters not only what a man does, but also how he does it; in other words, it matters that he do it from right choice and not merely from impulse or passion. Now since choice is about means to ends, rectitude of choice requires two things, namely, the due end, and that which is suitably ordained to that due end. Now man is suitably directed to his due end by a virtue which perfects the soul in the appetitive part, the object of which is the good and the end. But to that which is suitably ordained to the due end man needs to be rightly disposed by a habit in his reason, because counsel and choice, which are about means ordained to the end, are acts of the reason. Consequently, an intellectual virtue is needed in the reason, to perfect the reason and make it suitably affected towards means ordained to the end; and this virtue is prudence. Consequently prudence is a virtue necessary for a good life.[55]

Not only is it a virtue perfecting practical reason but, precisely because it is dependent on the other moral virtues, it has the formal character of the other moral virtues as well and is even numbered among them. Practical reason, then, is guided from within by prudence and the other moral virtues; it is not selfish.

Apart from the virtue that resides within it, practical reason also has to be guided from without; if a correct free decision is to be made, it must also be directed by law to what is good for man. Unlike speculative reason, practical reason has to make its judgments about individual, contingent things and actions. They are infinite in number and variety, most complex in structure. Conclusions of practical reasoning, then, require the guidance of more general premises just as scientific conclusions have to be reduced to more universal propositions.

> Just as, in external acts, we may consider the work and the work done, for instance, the work of building and the house built, so in the acts of reason, we may consider the act itself of reason, i.e. to understand and to reason, and something produced by its act. With regard to the speculative reason, this is first of all the definition; secondly, the proposition; thirdly, the syllogism or argument. And since the practical reason also makes use of the syllogism in operable matters, as we have stated above and as the Philosopher teaches, hence we find in the practical reason something that holds the same position in regard to operations as, in the speculative reason, the proposition holds in regard to conclusions. Such universal propositions of the practical reason that are directed to operations have the nature of law.[56]

In St. Thomas' view, law is a product of reason and is concerned with the order that should exist in human actions as man searches for happiness. Law formulates an order to a good; it states what is the common good of man and whatever is for his common good. He defines law in this way:

> Thus, from the four preceding articles, the definition of law may be gathered. Law is nothing else than an ordinance of reason for the common good, promulgated by him who has the care of the community.[57]

True to his own fundamental philosophical principle, St. Thomas is well aware that practical reason is concerned with a thing or action that will exist and be involved in a great many orders of reality and goodness; the human act that should be brought into being may be ordered to the individual person's good as father of a household, business man, citizen, human being and, perhaps, Christian. Determining what he should do will require the assistance of many virtues and a variety of laws. In the broadest possible terms, St. Thomas distinguishes four general kinds of law: eternal, natural, human and divine. He compares eternal and natural law in this way:

> As we have stated above, law, being a rule and a measure, can be in a person in two ways: in one way, as in him that rules and measures; in another way, as in that which is ruled and measured,

since a thing is ruled and measured insofar as it partakes of the rule or measure. Therefore, since all things subject to divine providence are ruled and measured by the eternal law, as was stated above, it is evident that all things partake in some way in the eternal law, insofar as, namely, from its being imprinted on them, they derive their respective inclinations to their proper acts and ends. Now among all others, the rational creature is subject to divine providence in a more excellent way, insofar as it itself partakes of a share of providence, by being provident both for itself and for others. Therefore, it has a share of the eternal reason, whereby it has a natural inclination to its proper act and end; and this participation of the eternal law in the rational creature is called the natural law.[58]

Now man is provident for himself and for others precisely in prudence, so that prudence is his share in the divine providence. As St. Thomas states at the very outset of his treatment of man's return to God through his human acts, man is like God in being lord of his own acts:

Since, as Damascene states (*De Fide Orthod.* II), man is said to be made to God's image, insofar as the image implies *an intelligent being endowed with free-will and self-movement:* now that we have treated of the exemplar, i.e. God, and of those things which come forth from the power of God in accordance with His will; it remains for us to treat of His image, i.e. man, inasmuch as he too is the principle of his actions, as having free-will and control of his actions.[59]

And the natural inclination to good, which we have discussed above and which prudence has to determine for itself in a particular situation, is man's share in the eternal law. That inclination, however, functions differently in irrational and rational beings, even as nature functions differently in the two orders.

As Boethius says, and the Philosopher also, the term *nature* is used in a manifold sense. For sometimes it stands for the intrinsic principle in movable things. In this sense, nature is either matter or the material form, as is stated in *Physics* II. In another sense, nature stands for any substance, or even any being. And in this sense, that is said to be natural to a thing which befits it according to its substance; and this is what is in a thing essentially. Now whatever does not belong to a thing essentially is reduced to something which belongs to that thing essentially, as to its principle. This is evident in regard to the intellect, for the principles of intellectual knowledge are naturally known. In like manner, the principle of voluntary movement must be something naturally willed.[60]

Here St. Thomas deliberately contrasts the natural movement of physical bodies, that are moved by intrinsic material and formal principles to
ends thereby determined and by means fixed by nature, with the natural
inclinations of intellect and will that are moved by their objects, being
as true or good. Laws of nature, governing physical bodies, and natural
laws, governing rational substances, are not the same and do not govern
in the same way; in neither case is there any question of violence. To
think of law as opposed to nature is not in line with St. Thomas' thinking.

Speculative reason judges spontaneously; the same thing cannot be
affirmed and denied. Practical reason judges spontaneously; good is to
be done and promoted, and evil is to be avoided. All the other precepts
of the natural law are based on this latter judgment. As St. Thomas says:

> All the things which practical reason naturally apprehends as
> man's good belong to the precepts of the natural law under the
> form of things to be done or avoided.[61]

The first common principles, then, are the results of spontaneous practical judgments and are self-evident. It is vital, however, to have a correct
understanding of St. Thomas' mind when he speaks of the self-evidence
of such precepts. For although some precepts of natural law may be
self-evident *in themselves,* they are not always so *to us.* As rational beings
we have to learn them and for various reasons we may not always understand them in the same way.

> As was stated above, the precepts of the natural law are to the
> practical reason what the first principles of demonstration are to
> the speculative reason, because both are self-evident principles.
> Now a thing is said to be self-evident in two ways: first, in itself;
> secondly, in relation to us. Any proposition is said to be self-evident
> in itself, if its predicate is contained in the notion of the subject;
> even though it may happen that to one who does not know the
> definition of the subject, such a proposition is not self-evident. For
> instance, this proposition, *Man is a rational being,* is in its very
> nature self-evident, since he who says *man,* says *a rational being;*
> and yet to one who does not know what a man is, this proposition
> is not self-evident. Hence it is that, as Boethius says, certain axioms
> or propositions are universally self-evident to all, as *Every whole is
> greater than its part,* and *Things equal to one and the same are
> equal to one another.* But some propositions are self-evident only
> to the wise, who understand the meaning of the terms of such
> propositions.[62]

And if we bear in mind that practical reason, as distinct from reason seeking speculative knowledge in the sciences, has the different and very difficult task of judging the contingent and individual, it should not be surprising that its understanding of the natural law is not the same in all men.

> . . . as regards the common principles whether of speculative or practical reason, truth or rectitude is the same for all, and is equally known by all. But as to the proper conclusions of the speculative reason, the truth is the same for all, but it is not equally known to all. Thus it is true for all that the three angles of a triangle are together equal to two right angles, although it is not known to all. But as to the proper conclusions of the practical reason, neither is the truth or rectitude the same for all, nor, where it is the same, is it equally known by all. Thus it is right and true for all to act according to reason, and from this principle it follows, as a proper conclusion, that goods entrusted to another should be restored to their owner. Now this is true for the majority of cases. But it may happen in a particular case that it would be injurious, and therefore unreasonable, to restore goods held in trust; for instance, if they are claimed for the purpose of fighting against one's country. And this principle will be found to fail the more, according as we descend further towards the particular, e.g. if one were to say that goods held in trust should be restored with such and such a guarantee, or in such and such a way; because the greater the number of conditions added, the greater the number of ways in which the principle may fail, so that it be not right to restore or not to restore.
>
> Consequently, we may say that the natural law, as to the first common principles, is the same for all, both as to rectitude and as to knowledge. But as to certain more particular aspects, which are conclusions, as it were, of those common principles, it is the same for all in the majority of cases, both as to rectitude and as to knowledge; and yet in some few cases it may fail, both as to rectitude, by reason of certain obstacles (just as natures subject to generation and corruption fail in some few cases because of some obstacle), and as to knowledge, since in some the reason is perverted by passion or evil habit, or an evil disposition of nature. Thus at one time theft, although it is expressly contrary to the natural law, was not considered wrong among the Germans, as Julius Caesar relates.[63]

Practical reason has to determine just what does belong to man and, hence, to man's natural goodness; it has to discover exactly what is demanded for his happiness. Once it becomes clear that something is necessarily involved in human happiness, the precept commanding it is recognized as a precept of natural law. In some sense, then, natural law may change.

A change in the natural law may be understood in two ways. First, by way of addition. In this sense, nothing hinders the natural law from being changed, since many things for the benefit of human life have been added over and above the natural law, both by the divine law and by human laws.

Secondly, a change in the natural law may be understood by way of subtraction, so that what previously was according to the natural law, ceases to be so. In this sense, the natural law is altogether unchangeable in its first principles. But in its secondary principles, which, as we have said, are certain detailed proximate conclusions drawn from the first principles, the natural law is not changed so that what it prescribes be not right in most cases. But it may be changed in some particular cases of rare occurrence, through some special causes hindering the observance of such precepts, as was stated above.[64]

Natural law, therefore, provides practical reason with various objective principles to guide it in judging individual situations. More proximately reason is guided by purely human laws, for even the equipment provided individuals by nature is not sufficient for them to lead good lives. They require the help and example of other persons as well as the discipline of laws.

. . . man has a natural aptitude for virtue; but the perfection of virtue must be acquired by man by means of some kind of training. Thus we observe that a man is helped by diligence in his necessities, for instance, in food and clothing. Certain beginnings of these he has from nature, for instance, his reason and his hands; but he has not the full complement, as other animals have, to whom nature has given sufficiency of clothing and food. Now it is difficult to see how man could suffice for himself in the matter of this training, since the perfection of virtue consists chiefly in withdrawing man from undue pleasure, to which above all man is inclined, and especially the young, who are more capable of being trained. Consequently a man needs to receive this training from another, whereby to arrive at the perfection of virtue. And as to those young people who are inclined to acts of virtue by their good natural disposition, or by custom, or rather by the gift of God, paternal training suffices, which is by admonitions. But since some are found to be dissolute and prone to vice, and not easily amenable to words,

it was necessary for such to be restrained by force and fear. . . .
Now this kind of training, which compels through fear of punishment, is the discipline of laws.[65]

Such human laws are remote specifications of more general precepts of
natural law; like conclusions drawn from scientific principles through
long experience, such human laws are the results of life's experience
proving to reason that certain acts are beneficial to human life. They
retain some of the authority of natural law. Other human laws are more
thoroughly human and resemble, according to St. Thomas, the specifications and determinations a craftsman or artist gives to a model or art-
form when he adapts it to his own needs. For example, natural law may
dictate that one must not kill, and that an evil-doer must be punished, but
the manner and extent of punishment still has to be determined. Thus,
capital punishment or life imprisonment would be determinations of
natural law rather than conclusions even remotely drawn from it. Such
human laws would have no force beyond that of purely human laws.

Consequently, whether law be eternal, natural, or human, it tells
us what is good for man to do. Sometimes it guides practical reason in
more or less general terms through directives that are more closely akin
to general moral principles; at other times (as in human laws) it does
so through rules that are more detailed and proximate to the actual
conditions within which a man is trying to do what is right. In short:
law acts as an extrinsic guide to a person who has to make a free choice,
i.e. when he acts as a moral being. All such laws are laws of freedom.

Well, with that brief sketch of a few of the main elements in St.
Thomas' view of man's free being before us, let us return to the questions
with which we started. Does St. Thomas' view of being as primarily act
reveal anything of man's being free? Yes, it does. Just as St. Thomas'
view of being held a very real significance for the understanding of man's
nature, so also does it provide a basis for understanding his freedom. In
direct contrast with Spinoza, St. Thomas' doctrine of existing indicates
that a man subsists in having his own act of existing; he *acts* and is not
merely acted upon. God makes him to be; but that means He makes a
man precisely so that *he* can act. Indeed, as we shall have occasion to
see more fully later, if man is one of God's effects, he will be in his own
small way an agent *in his own right*. And in existing, man also inclines
to what is good for him; he necessarily seeks what he understands to be
good for man as an intellectual substance. His will is necessarily determined only by the good in general; it stands freely disposed to choose
any particular thing that he decides is for his good. Being as act, therefore, provides a guide for our understanding of man's being free.

Is a man prevented from being free because he is an *incarnate* intellectual substance and, hence, a very real participant in his world? No. In fact, being a part of his world even serves to *explain* the freedom a man enjoys. For it is precisely because he *is* part of a material, physical world of individual entities that he only finds particular and contingent goods to enjoy, that he has to choose among them, that his freedom is one of choice. Man does share in the physical world around him and he cannot defy the laws of bodies, living things, and the animal kingdom. But he can use those laws for his own purposes. He is not free in the sense that he acts entirely apart from the world of physical laws as a pure intelligence or noumenal self might act. That is not human—and man can only enjoy *human* freedom, just as he can only exercise *human* being. But as a part of nature that exists rationally, he can understand nature, dominate it, and, by using its laws, achieve purposes that he himself sets. In short: a man can act for ends that he himself determines.

Is man free because he is set in opposition to both nature and God? No. For St. Thomas nature is not merely material, physical nature; all nature does not move through fixed means to determined ends in consequence of necessary, intrinsic, material principles. In that order agents *do* only act in accordance with physical laws. Man is not a member of the world of nature in that sense; he does not have a nature as a stone or a tree has a nature. But he does have a nature, he is not a completely undetermined being. He is not God, but a specific kind of finite being. His nature is a *human* nature; his nature enables him to understand, reason, judge freely in practical affairs where his actions are concerned. It is his nature to be free, to take his own counsel, to determine the things he will pursue, the virtues he will develop, the kind of human being he wants to be. He is free *by* nature, not *in spite of* nature. Nor is he free because he is opposed by God, or to God, and threatened by Him. He is a free being because God made him to be, and to be free; indeed, it is by being free in his own human manner, i.e. by free choice, that he most resembles God. He stands over against God only in the very limited sense that he does act freely and is not merely moved to act. He stands on his own feet; indeed, as a free being he is totally responsible for himself and for the kind of human being he will make of himself. To say that he is not free because he cannot act except as a human being really serves to prove St. Thomas' main thesis!

Is man doomed to have no other law than his own? No. He does have other laws besides those of positive human enactment, but they do not threaten his freedom. Man has nothing to fear from law. Law is always at hand to enable him to be more fully man, to be more fully free. In man's case law does not act as the laws of physical natures do, compelling him to act as the stone is compelled to fall. Law is not a set of rules foreign to man's freedom, expressing the good of some other kind of being, a code before which he must slavishly bow; a law is a conclusion about the way man is to exercise his freedom. For St. Thomas laws are so many expressions of what is good for man; and being the laws of a free being, they have to be freely incorporated into his actions. In the final analysis, in the existential moment of prudential judgment and free choice, the individual must make the law for the moment in his own well-considered and morally disciplined practical judgment; and he has to accept the sole responsibility for doing so. It is his closest approach to a creative act, for he makes *the* good for a moment. Either he imitates God's act thereby or he is at fault. In a very real sense, he is alone; nature, virtue and law are there to help him, but he must freely decide what is to be done and what he is to be. As a Christian he has the aid of grace to sustain him, but he must still suffer the loneliness of a repeated act of faith.

Orestes' passionate outcry suggests two questions that we have left to the end. Must man find his way alone? Must he turn from paths he finds in nature leading to God for fear of losing his freedom and destroying his humanity? Our last two chapters will be devoted to answering these questions.

# CHAPTER VII

# MAN'S SOCIAL BEING

In every sphere, physical no less than intellectual and moral, and whether it be a question of flowing water, a traveller on a journey, or a thinker or mystic engaged in the pursuit of truth, there inevitably comes a point in time and place when the necessity presents itself, to mechanical forces, or to our freedom of choice, of deciding once and for all which of two paths is the one to take. The enforced, irrevocable choice at a parting of the ways that will never occur again: which of us has not encountered that dilemma? But how many of us realise that it is precisely the situation in which social man finds himself, *here and now*, in the face of the rising tide of socialisation? . . . As I have also shown, two attitudes are possible in this situation, two forms of "existentialism." We can reject and resist the tide, seeking by every means to slow it down and even to escape individually (at the risk of perishing in stoical isolation) from what looks like a rush to the abyss; or we can yield to it and actively contribute to what we accept as a liberating and life-giving movement.[1]

Jean-Paul Sartre insists that man's freedom demands that he make his way alone. If a person has to live face to face with God, he cannot make himself whatever he wants to be. His freedom is thwarted. But what of his life with other men? Does life in society likewise make it impossible for man to exercise his freedom? Must he become one of the masses, a conformist? If he lives in society, does he always have to play a role, be outer-directed? Sartre is convinced that we have to lose our subjectivity and become objects in the presence of others.

Here we have arrived at the end of this exposition. We have learned that the Other's existence was experienced with evidence in and through the fact of my objectivity. We have seen also that my reaction to my own alienation for the Other was expressed in my grasping the Other as an object. In short, the Other can exist for us in two forms: if I experience him with evidence, I fail to know him; if I know him, if I act upon him, I only reach his being-as-object and his probable existence in the midst of the world. No synthesis of these two forms is possible.[2]

As long as a man is with other men, he is aware of himself as object: he has to be looked at, to be seen by them, to be ashamed in their presence, to be used and manipulated by them. Conversely, they, too, have to lose their subjectivity in becoming objects for him. Together, they must lose their subjectivity, freedom and humanity. There is no authentic experience of a We-subject, i.e. of a self in the presence of other selves wherein each *I* retains its subjectivity in a *We.*

> These few remarks do not claim to exhaust the question of the "We." They aim only at indicating that the experience of the We-subject has no value as a metaphysical revelation; it depends strictly on the various forms of the for-others and is only an empirical enrichment of certain of these forms. It is to this fact evidently that we should attribute the extreme instability of this experience. It comes and disappears, leaving us in the face of others-as-objects or else of a "They" who look at us. It appears as a provisional appeasement which is constituted at the very heart of the conflict, not as a definitive solution of this conflict. We shall hope in vain for a human "we" in which the intersubjective totality would obtain consciousness of itself as a unified subjectivity. Such an ideal could be only a dream produced by a passage to the limit and to the absolute on the basis of fragmentary, strictly psychological experiences. Furthermore this ideal itself implies the recognition of the conflict of transcendences as the original state of being-for-others.[3]

As Garcin cries out in Sartre's play *No Exit:* "Hell is—other people." [4] In this life Garcin, Inez and Estelle had all succumbed to the human temptation of seeking to enjoy the security of things; they had lost their subjectivity in the solidity of objectivity. Now, in hell, they were to experience the consequences: each was condemned to be an object for the other. The reason is a metaphysical one:

> It appears therefore that the experience of the "We" and the "Us" although real, is not of a nature to modify the results of our prior investigations. As for the Us-object, this is directly dependent on the Third—i.e., on my being-for-others—and it is constituted on the foundation of my being-outside-for-others. And as for the We-subject, this is a psychological experience which supposes one way or another that the Other's existence as such has been already revealed to us. It is therefore useless for human-reality to seek to get out of this dilemma: one must either transcend the Other or allow

oneself to be transcended by him. The essence of the relation between consciousnesses is not the *Mitsein:* it is conflict.[5]

Jean-Paul Sartre's defense of human freedom, then, raises the whole question of the viability of social relationships. Can a person retain his subjectivity, his freedom to say *No* and still exist with other free beings? Or
must each one remain an isolated individual so as to be free and human?

Throughout our Western tradition men have asked: Are human freedom and life in society compatible? Thomas Hobbes and Karl Marx represent one effort to provide an answer; John Locke and John Stuart Mill
are typical of those who would offer quite a different solution.

Karl Marx tells us that the isolated individual is nothing but an abstraction; man, on the contrary, is not an abstraction at all but a concrete,
historical reality and, as such, thoroughly social.

> Feuerbach resolves the religious essence into the *human* essence.
> But the human essence is no abstraction inherent in each single in-
> dividual. In its reality it is the ensemble of the social relations.
>
> Feuerbach, who does not enter upon a criticism of this real es-
> sence, is consequently compelled: 1) To abstract from the historical
> process and to fix the religious sentiment (*Gemüt*) as something by
> itself, and to presuppose an abstract—*isolated*—human individual.
> 2) The human essence, therefore, can with him be comprehended
> only as "genus," as an internal, dumb generality which merely
> *naturally* unites the many individuals.[6]

He is an ensemble of social relations and economic processes; he is not
an isolated thing, but a product of historical developments. In a clear
statement notable for its use of a favorite nineteenth-century machine-
image, Friedrich Engels describes man in this way:

> . . . history is made in such a way that the final result always arises
> from conflicts between many individual wills, of which each in turn
> has been made what it is by a host of particular conditions of life.
> Thus there are innumerable intersecting forces, an infinite series
> of parallelograms of forces which give rise to one resultant—the
> historical event. This may again itself be viewed as the product of a
> power which works as a whole *unconsciously* and without volition.
> For what each individual wills is obstructed by everyone else, and
> what emerges is something that no one willed. Thus history has
> proceeded hitherto in the manner of a natural process and is essen-
> tially subject to the same laws of motion. But from the fact that the
> wills of individuals—each of whom desires what he is impelled to
> by his physical constitution and external, in the last resort economic,

circumstances (either his own personal circumstances or those of society in general)—do not attain what they want, but are merged into an aggregate mean, a common resultant, it must not be concluded that they are equal to zero.[7]

Individual men are the results of the particular stage of historical development in which they live. Man is a product of history; whatever freedom he may accidentally appear to enjoy as an individual is determined by political and, ultimately, economic realities.

Men make their history themselves, only they do so in a given environment, which conditions it, and on the basis of actual relations already existing, among which the economic relations, however much they may be influenced by the other, the political and ideological relations, are still ultimately the decisive ones, forming the keynote which runs through them and alone leads to understanding.

Men make their history themselves, but not as yet with a collective will according to a collective plan, or even in a definite, delimited given society. Their aspirations clash, and for that very reason all such societies are governed by *necessity*, the complement and form of appearance of which is *accident*. The necessity which here asserts itself athwart all accident is again ultimately economic necessity. That is where the so-called great men come in for treatment. That such and such a man and precisely that man arises at a particular time in a particular century is, of course, pure chance. But cut him out and there will be a demand for a substitute, and this substitute will be found, good or bad, but in the long run he will be found.[8]

As the individual is an instance of historic process, so, too, is human liberty but an appearance of economic necessity. Both the individual and his freedom are swallowed up in social process.

The general conclusion at which I arrived and which, once reached, continued to serve as the leading thread in my studies may be briefly summed up as follows. In the social production which men carry on they enter into definite relations that are indispensable and independent of their will; these relations of production correspond to a definite stage of development of their material powers of production.[9]

The individual's fate is not nearly so completely sealed by Thomas Hobbes' conception of man in society. Taking reason and nature as his guides, he discovers that every individual is endowed with a natural right to use his powers as he himself wills to do, to do whatever reason tells him he must do to preserve his life against every other man who is similarly endowed.

> The right of nature, which writers commonly call *jus naturale*, is the liberty each man hath to use his own powers, as he will himself, for the preservation of his own nature; that is to say, of his own life; and consequently of doing anything, which in his own judgment and reason, he shall conceive to be the aptest means thereunto. By *liberty*, is understood, according to the proper signification of the word, the absence of external impediments: which impediments, may oft take away part of a man's power to do what he would; but cannot hinder him from using the power left him, according as his judgment and reason shall dictate to him.[10]

Man is naturally free, but such a condition of freedom inevitably gives rise to a condition of war of everyone against everyone.

> Hereby it is manifest that during the time men live without a common power to keep them all in awe, they are in that condition which is called war; and such a war as is of every man against every man. . . . Whatsoever therefore is consequent to a time of war, where every man is enemy to every man; the same is consequent to the time, wherein men live without other security than what their own strength and their own invention shall furnish them withal. In such condition there is no place for industry, because the fruit thereof is uncertain: and consequently no culture of the earth; no navigation nor use of the commodities that may be imported by sea; no commodious building; no instruments of moving and removing, such things as require much force; no knowledge of the face of the earth; no account of time; no arts; no letters; no society.[11]

Such a condition is intolerable, so men enter into society. They agree "to confer all their power and strength upon one man, or upon one assembly of men, that may reduce all their wills, by plurality of voices, unto one will."[12] More than mere general consent is thereby achieved; there is, rather, a real unity of many in the one person of the sovereign. The multitude of isolated individuals becomes a commonwealth; the *Leviathan* or mortal god capable of guaranteeing our peace and defense comes into being. Moreover, as a result of the contract the sovereign embodies all the power needed to carry out his side of the bargain, i.e. to protect all who enter into the covenant. Civil society in the person of the sovereign has all the power needed, by awe and terror, to coerce the wills of individual subjects to the common benefit. The sovereign alone has the right to determine what is good for the individual; the subject retains only the right to defend his own body (a right that he cannot transfer) and the liberty to do things not actually proscribed by the sovereign's civil laws. For liberty or freedom, according to Hobbes, is the same as an absence of opposition; there is a compatibility, not a contradiction, between necessity and liberty.

> Liberty and necessity are consistent: as in the water, that hath not only *liberty*, but a *necessity* of descending by the channel; so likewise in the actions which men voluntarily do: which, because they proceed from their will, proceed from *liberty*; and yet, because every act of man's will, and every desire, and inclination proceedeth from some cause, and that from another cause, in a continual chain, whose first link is in the hand of God the first of all causes, proceed from *necessity*. So that to him that could see the connection of those causes, the necessity of all men's voluntary actions, would appear manifest. And therefore God, that seeth and disposeth all things, seeth also that the liberty of man in doing what he will, is accompanied with the necessity of doing that which God wills, and no more nor less.[13]

As subjects of the commonwealth men retain the liberty to do whatever is not impeded by civil law.

> In relation to these bonds only (i.e. of civil laws) it is, that I am to speak now of the *liberty of subjects*. For seeing there is no commonwealth in the world wherein there be rules enough set down, for the regulating of all the actions and words of men; as being a thing impossible: it followeth necessarily that in all kinds of actions by the laws pretermitted, men have the liberty of doing what their own reasons shall suggest, for the most profitable to themselves. . . . The liberty of the subject lieth therefore only in those things which in regulating their actions, the sovereign hath pretermitted: such as is the liberty to buy, and sell, and otherwise contract with one another; to choose their own abode, their own diet, their own trade of life, and institute their children as they themselves think fit; and the like.[14]

In short: by entering civil society, an individual's liberty is very severely circumscribed in the interest of peace and security.

Locke and Mill, on the other hand, are far more concerned with *preserving* the individual's liberty and defending its survival within society. Locke tells us that all men are *naturally* free and equal, and that an individual's natural liberty consists in his being free to dispose of his person and possessions, free to live according to reason. He is not free to destroy himself or any creature in his possession except where some nobler purpose dictates.

> To understand political power aright, and derive it from its original, we must consider what state all men are naturally in, and that state is one of perfect freedom to order their actions and dispose of their possessions and persons as they think fit, within the bounds of the law of nature, without asking leave, or depending upon the will of any other man.
>
> A state also of equality, wherein all the power and jurisdiction is reciprocal, no one having more than another, there being nothing more evident than that creatures of the same species and rank, promiscuously born to all the advantages of nature, and the use of the same faculties, should also be equal one amongst another without subordination or subjection, unless the Lord and Master of them all should by any manifest declaration of His will set one above another, and confer on him by an evident and clear appointment an undoubted right to dominion and sovereignty.[15]

However, even though each man is *naturally* free, the fact is that the *enjoyment* of his rights is uncertain and constantly exposed to invasion by other men; a right conferred by nature is one thing, exercising it is quite another. To remedy this condition a man is willing to agree with other similarly free men to join in society for the mutual preservation of life, liberty and estate.

> Man being, as has been said, by nature all free and equal, and independent, no one can be put out of this estate, and subjected to the political power of another, without his own consent, which is done by agreeing with other men to join and unite into a community for their comfortable, safe and peaceable living one amongst another, in a secure enjoyment of their properties, and a greater security against any that are not of it. This any number of men may do, because it injures not the freedom of the rest; they are left as they were in the liberty of the state of nature. When any number of men have so consented to make one community or government, they are thereby presently incorporated, and make one body politic, wherein the majority have a right to act and conclude the rest.[16]

In so doing, a person enters into a contract whereby he *wholly* surrenders his right to punish those who transgress the law of nature, and *partially* relinquishes his right to determine what is needed for his own preservation. In return he gains a settled and established law and judgment by impartial magistrates. The consequence is that liberty and the free use of property are assured because the exercise of legislative power, fully placed within the hands of rulers, is very severely circumscribed so as to guarantee respect for liberty and property.

> These are the bounds which the trust that is put in them by the society, and the law of God and Nature, have set to the legislative power of every commonwealth, in all forms of government.
> First, they are to govern by promulgated laws, not to be varied in particular cases, but to have one rule for rich and poor, for the favorite at court and the countryman at plough.
> Secondly, these laws also ought to be designed for no other end ultimately but the good of the people.
> Thirdly, they must not raise taxes on the property of the people without the consent of the people, given by themselves or their deputies. . . .
> Fourthly, the legislative neither must nor can transfer the power of making laws to anybody else, or place it anywhere but where the people have.[17]

Society, then, is intended to make it possible for free men to exercise their natural rights to life, liberty and estate.

John Stuart Mill was keenly aware that, important though these *principles* are in theory, in *practice* they are not enough. Let us grant that government must be benevolent in the way Locke describes it. How can we be sure that legislative power actually will be exercised in the best interest of the people? Mill notes that there are many ways in which a society may try to guarantee that such powers will be properly wielded: by gaining specific recognition for various immunities or political liberties, by establishing constitutional checks on legislative and executive authority, by assuring that magistrates will be sensitive to the people's pleasure. But even when these protective devices have been put into effect, even when we can speak of "self-government" and "the power of the people over themselves," popular government in practice reveals hitherto unsuspected dangers. The greatest of these, in Mill's eyes, is the tyranny of the majority, the tyranny of imposing prevailing public views on individuals.

> Like other tyrannies, the tyranny of the majority was at first, and is still vulgarly, held in dread chiefly as operating through the acts of the public authorities. But reflecting persons perceived that when society is itself the tyrant—society collectively over the separate individuals who compose it—its means of tyrannizing are not restricted

to the acts which it may do by the hands of its political function-
aries. . . . Protection, therefore, against the tyranny of the magis-
trate is not enough: there needs protection also against the tyranny
of the prevailing opinion and feeling; against the tendency of society to impose, by other means than civil penalties, its own ideas
and practices as rules of conduct on those who dissent from them;
to fetter the development, and, if possible, prevent the formation,
of any individuality not in harmony with its ways, and compels all
characters to fashion themselves upon the model of its own.[18]

To the question: How can we adjust the individual's liberty to social control?, his answer is that we must be guided by a single principle:

The object of this essay is to assert one very simple principle, as
entitled to govern absolutely the dealings of society with the individual in the way of compulsion and control, whether the means
used be physical force in the form of legal penalties, or the moral
coercion of public opinion. That principle is, that the sole end for
which mankind are warranted, individually or collectively, in inter-
fering with the liberty of action of any of their number, is self-protection. That the only purpose for which power can be rightfully
exercised over any member of a civilized community, against his
will, is to prevent harm to others. His own good, either physical or
moral, is not a sufficient warrant. . . . The only part of the conduct
of anyone, for which he is amenable to society, is that which concerns others. In the part which merely concerns himself, his independence is, of right, absolute. Over himself, over his own body
and mind, the individual is sovereign.[19]

Spelling that principle out in more concrete and practical detail, Mill
designates various areas of human liberty that have become very familiar
to us in our own lives and discussions: liberty of *consciousness*—including
liberty of conscience, thought, feeling and opinion—; liberty of *taste
and pursuit*—the freedom to pursue our lives as we see fit and of doing
what we like so long as no harm to others results—; liberty of *association*
—the freedom to unite with other men so long as no other is injured.

No society in which these liberties are not, on the whole respected,
is free, whatever may be its form of government; and none is completely free in which they do not exist absolute and unqualified.
The only freedom which deserves the name, is that of pursuing our
own good in our own way, so long as we do not attempt to deprive
others of theirs, or impede their efforts to obtain it. Each is the
proper guardian of his own health, whether bodily, or mental and

spiritual. Mankind are greater gainers by suffering each other to live as seems good to themselves, than by compelling each to live as seems good to the rest.[20]

In short: individual liberty is protected within society by cultivating individuality.

Now where does St. Thomas stand on these great questions of liberty and social life? We have seen in Chapter VI that his doctrine of being has provided a basis for understanding man's freedom as a freedom of choice. But what does he have to say of man's life with other men in society? Above all, do his views on man's social being find inspiration in his general approach to being as act?

We have already uncovered a clue to the answer in the same Chapter VI wherein we compared St. Thomas' conception of man with Sartre's. In discussing *Man's Being Free*, we saw that for Sartre man is a consciousness-self. Basically, he is the Cartesian man, an intelligence, interpreted as consciousness and freedom. And that is why "Hell is . . . other people." As a consciousness each man has to look upon other men in the same way; to *him* they are objects, and to *them* he is an object. In a society composed of Sartrean men, each person has to be aware of himself as an object to be used by others; he has to forfeit his subjectivity in the society of others. Thus, for example, in experiences of friendship or generosity as Sartre interprets them one is never aware of being a subject in the presence of another subject, of another being concerned for one's own self. One is not given a gift or shown a favor for oneself. A person is, rather, alienated in friendship; he is aware that someone else is using him for *their* purpose. So, too, a gift is never given because of what one is, but instead, for the advantage it gives someone else. If I accept a gift, I am in someone's debt; in Sartre's view he now has a hold on me.[21] And behind these attitudes rests the conviction that the reality we experience is our consciousness—the awareness of a subject-object relationship. So society at all levels—personal acquaintance, love, family-life, social contacts—involves a loss of identity and a loss of liberty. And the reasons are ontological.

With St. Thomas it is quite different. As we have seen, for him man is neither a Cartesian intelligence nor a Sartrean consciousness; he is an intellectual substance informing a physical, organic body, an incarnate intelligence. The *being* proper to man is the being of a unique kind of intelligence, one that can only *be* an intelligence through his body and senses. He has to *become* an intelligence in act by reasoning, and he has to reason precisely because his understanding is intrinsically bound up with and dependent on his senses. We have seen, too, that man, like any other finite being, naturally tends to anything that will perfect him in being, to anything good for him. But he does so intelligently and rationally, i.e. by freely choosing the means to his good. A man is not only capable of knowing but of loving as well. Now in knowing other things and other human beings speculatively, they *do* become objects for us; knowing is concerned with the being things have for the intellect, i.e. their truth. But we can also be interested in things for the being they have as they exist *in themselves;* we can reach out to possess *the being they have* as beings, i.e. their goodness. We can desire and love them when we foresee an identity between their being and ours.

> The true and the good must therefore add to the concept of being, a relationship of that which perfects. But in any being there are two aspects to be considered, the formal character of its species and the act of being by which it subsists in that species. And so a being can be perfective in two ways. (1) It can be so just according to its specific character. In this way the intellect is perfected by a being, for it perceives the formal character of the being. But the being is still not in it according to its natural existence. It is this mode of perfecting which the true adds to being. For the true is in the mind, as the Philosopher says; and every being is called true inasmuch as it is conformed or conformable to intellect. For this reason all who correctly define *true* put intellect in its definition. (2) A being is perfective of another not only according to its specific character but also according to the existence which it has in reality. In this fashion the good is perfective; for the good is in things, as the Philosopher says. Inasmuch as one being by reason of its act of existing is such as to perfect and complete another, it stands to that other as end.[22]

When a person loves a thing, then, he is concerned with *its* being. Now the reason for that concern may either be that he finds the other thing's being good *for him,* or that he is intent upon insuring the *other's* being.

Thus, in desiring anything, even another human being, we may experience it insofar as it is good *for us;* if so, that person is loved with a love of concupiscence. But, according to St. Thomas, beyond this there is also the love of friendship. It is a love that is not directed towards another as good for us; rather, the other is looked upon as *another self* and is loved for *his* good.

> As to the appetitive power, the object loved is said to be in the lover, inasmuch as it is in his affections, by a kind of complacency: causing him either to take pleasure in it, or in its good, when present; or, in the absence of the object loved, by his longing, to tend towards

it with the love of concupiscence, or towards the good that he wills to the beloved, with the love of friendship: . . . On the other hand, the lover is in the beloved, by the love of concupiscence and by the love of friendship, but not in the same way. For the love of concupiscence is not satisfied with any external or superficial possession or enjoyment of the beloved; but seeks to possess the beloved perfectly, by penetrating into his heart, as it were. Whereas, in the love of friendship, the lover is in the beloved, inasmuch as he reckons what is good or evil to his friend, as being so to himself; and his friend's will as his own, so that it seems as though he felt the good or suffered the evil in the person of his friend. Hence it is proper *to friends to desire the same things, and to grieve and rejoice at the same*, as the Philosopher says (*Ethic.* ix and *Rhet.* ii.). Consequently in so far as he reckons what affects his friend as affecting himself, the lover seems to be in the beloved, as though he were become one with him.[23]

In friendship, then, a person seeks the other's good; attaining *his* good is good for us! The other's good becomes our good. And in generosity the claims of justice, suggested by the indebtedness of one object before another, is transcended. In giving a gift or performing an act of generosity, or in receiving a gift or being favored by a generous act, one is not indebted to another or involved in justice—a person is not confronted with giving another what is due to him. Justice *is* recognized inasmuch as the other person is seen to be an *equal*—but equally a *self* as well! A friend's enjoyment of the good that is offered to him—an enjoyment possible only to another self—determines the act. So for St. Thomas, man can grow in knowledge, friendship and generosity; indeed, to be fully an intelligence he has to grow in these and in all the other virtues. Now it is precisely at this point, at a point determined by his incomplete human *being,* that society enters the human situation.

In his work entitled *On Kingship,* St. Thomas sets forth various reasons why men enter social groups, and all of them stem from demands of human nature. It should be noted at once that St. Thomas' appeal to nature is fundamentally different from John Locke's examination of a state of nature. The former refers to the requirements of a being, man, if it is to complete itself; the latter concerns a historical condition in which man finds himself before he enters society.

'Tis often asked as a mighty objection, Where are, or ever were there, any men in such a state of nature? To which it may suffice as an answer at present: That since all princes and rulers of independent government all through the world are in a state of nature, 'tis plain the world never was, nor ever will be, without numbers of men in that state. I have named all governors of independent communities, whether they are or are not in league with others. For 'tis not every compact that puts an end to the state of nature between men, but only this one of agreeing together mutually to enter into one community, and make one body politic; other promises and compacts men may make one with another, and yet still be in the state of nature. The promises and bargains for truck etc. between the two men in Soldania, in or between a Swiss and an Indian, in the woods of America, are binding to them, though they are perfectly in a state of nature in reference to one another.[24]

For St. Thomas the requirements of nature remain whether man is in society or not—indeed, they remain whether he is in a state of grace or not. Thus, in discussing the human condition in a state of innocence, St. Thomas repeatedly returns to the many things his nature demands; indeed, he finds it quite proper that men should have led a social life even in a state of innocence.

But a man is the master of a free subject by directing him either towards his proper welfare, or to the common good. Such a mastership would have existed in the state of innocence between man and man, for two reasons. First, because man is naturally a social being, and so in the state of innocence he would have led a social life. Now a social life cannot exist among a number of people unless under the guidance of one to look after the common good; for many, as such, seek many things, whereas one attends only to the one. Hence the Philosopher says, in the beginning of the *Politics,* that wherever many things are directed to one, we shall always find one at the head directing. Secondly, if one man surpassed another in knowledge and justice, this would not have been fitting unless these gifts conduced to the benefit of others.[25]

By what demands of human being is St. Thomas convinced that man is by *nature* a *social* being?

In one argument he examines the kind of knowledge man has as distinct from the other animals, and he concludes that the way man knows points to his being a social animal. Some animals, St. Thomas points out, have an instinctive knowledge of things useful or harmful to them—as the sheep knows by instinct that the wolf is his enemy. Other animals have a kind of instinctive knowledge of medicine, for they know various herbs that are of medicinal value to them. Man, on the other hand, has by natural endowment only a general knowledge of things necessary for his life. As an intellectual substance, he knows the principles that are most universal and common, for example, "The good is to be done." Such principles express a kind of instinctive knowledge. However, he is not simply an intelligence and is not intended to live by such purely intellectual principles. To live as an intellectual substance informing a body, he has to make the universal good precise and particular by reasoning and sensing.

> Being gifted with reason he has to use it to pass from such universal principles to the knowledge of what in particular concerns his well-being.[26]

Now according to St. Thomas one man alone cannot do that all by himself and by his own individual reason alone. To discover the precise, individual things that are good for him, he has to share and communicate his discoveries with other men.

> It is therefore necessary for man to live in a multitude so that each one may assist his fellows, and different men may be occupied in seeking, by their reason, to make different discoveries—one, for example, in medicine, one in this and another in that.[27]

The full thrust of St. Thomas' argument may be felt by pausing for a moment and trying to isolate the knowledge we as individuals have of what is good for us. Compare it with the knowledge we have gained for ourselves without benefit of associating with others. The latter is very scant, indeed. The fact, then, that man is the kind of intelligent being that has to arrive at knowledge gradually is proof to St. Thomas that he is naturally intended to join with other men to share his discoveries. The very character of human reason is itself proof that man is a social being *by nature*—not, indeed, that society is ready-made for him "by nature." Society is, rather, made by *his* natural talents to satisfy his needs; it is artificial in the sense that man makes it as a work of art. But in making it he uses natural endowments to fill needs nature has left him.

St. Thomas follows Aristotle in developing a further proof, also based on man's rational nature. It is a proof that rests on the human capacity for communicating by words, and it concludes that the social condition is natural to man, not a state of war of man against man as Hobbes concluded.[28] As propounded by St. Thomas the argument unfolds in this way. Only men have the power of speaking, whereby they are able to communicate their knowledge to others. Other animals, it is true, have a capacity for communicating by sound, but according to St. Thomas they only express their passions, and that in a general way only (as a dog displays anger by barking). Men, on the other hand, communicate their thoughts and judgments about what is true and useful, just and good, and that requires an ability beyond the powers of the other animals. Such judgments need the power to grasp the universal and to judge the suitability of a means for an end. Moreover, he points out, even the character of the sound used in the two types of communication is different. Animal sounds are natural and instinctive; human words are works of art and require agreement among the many men who use them so that they will stand for and convey the thought that is intended.[29] A whole multitude of men must *agree* that the articulated sound "man" will be accepted as a means of communicating what they mean by man —and the way each group generalizes the meaning of man will differ. The very character of words—products of reason fashioned to communicate knowledge gained by reason and experience—is once again proof that man's rational nature is social. And immediately after using this argument from Aristotle's *Politics,* St. Thomas adds:

> Solomon had this in mind when he said (*Ecclesiastes* iv, 9): it is better for two to live together than solitary, for they gain by mutual companionship.[30]

Could we have a clearer example of the Christian theologian's method of seeking understanding through philosophy than this juxtaposing of Aristotle and Solomon?

St. Thomas uses the same method in a third argument. He is convinced that man is an *incarnate* intelligence: surely his body will share in the proof that he is by nature social. Avicenna provides such an argument and St. Thomas takes it over.

> Man's actions possess certain properties which proceed from his soul and are not found in other animals. The first of these is that man's being in which he is created, could not last if he did not live in society. Man is not like other animals, each of which is self-sufficient for living with what it has by its nature. One man, on the contrary, if he were alone and left to rely on nothing but what he has by nature, would soon die, or at least his life would be miserable and certainly worse than it was meant to be. This is because of the nobility of man's nature and the ignobility of the nature of other beings. . . . It is necessary for man to add certain things to what nature gives him; for raw food, not treated by art, is unbecoming to him: he would not be able to live well with it. Likewise does he have to treat certain materials and make them into garments, while other animals have their covering by nature. First of all, then, man needs the art of agriculture, and, in the second place, many other

arts. Now one man would be unable to acquire all these necessities of life, if he were alone. . . . He can do so, however, in society where one bakes the other's bread and the latter in turn weaves the former's clothes, and one man imports wares from far-away lands for which he receives remuneration from the produce of another man's country. These are the most evident among many other reasons why it is necessary for man to possess the natural ability to express to his fellowmen what is in his mind.[31]

Animals other than man, then, have their food provided by nature, they have a natural coat of fur, teeth, horns or claws for defence—or at least speed of flight! Man is not so provided. Instead he has the power of reason to grow his own food and prepare it, and to fashion weapons for defence, and to erect buildings to protect him from the weather. One man alone can provide enough of these things so that he can survive, but not sufficient to provide for a good human life. To have the things man needs to live a *human* life (i.e. to live *well* as a human being and not merely to have the physical necessities he requires; to have the emotional, educational, moral, artistic, and religious assistance he needs as well), he has to live in the society of a multitude of other men. On this account St. Thomas once more concludes that man is by nature a social being. He is not by nature an individual, isolated in his liberty from other men as he is for John Locke (society being a convention and a convenience), nor is he a product of social process as he is for Karl Marx. He is, rather, by nature a social being capable of fashioning society to his own needs and purposes.

St. Thomas is convinced, then, that man needs society to help him to be more fully man, i.e. to gain the knowledge and virtue that will make him actually *be* the mature intellectual and moral being he was born to be. Society is not intended to protect his property but to help him attain fulness and happiness; society is a means to man's happiness, a means he has to make himself. Now as we have seen earlier in Chapter VI, men have to take counsel and freely choose the means that will best bring them to the end they set for themselves. Perhaps the nature of that end will differ in definition as men see themselves naturally constituted in different ways, but even granting that there is some agreement about the *end* men are trying to gain—the happiness they want to enjoy by living together—there may still be disagreement about the *means* to that end. This aspect of the human condition suggests to St. Thomas that the very constitution of man's nature as a rational, free, social being demands that there be some ruling principle in society if the end is to be reached most expeditiously.

If then, it is natural for man to live in the society of many, it is necessary that there exist among men some means by which the group
may be governed. For where there are many men together and each
one is looking after his own interest, the multitude would be broken
up and scattered unless there were also an agency to take care of
what appertains to the common weal. In like manner, the body of
a man or any other animal would disintegrate unless there were a
general ruling force within the body which watches over the common good of all members. With this in mind, Solomon says: "Where
there is no governor, the people shall fall (*Proverbs* xi, 14)." [32]

He gives an example to illustrate just what he has in mind. A ship might
be blown in different directions by the various winds it encounters and
would not reach its destination if it were not for the skill of the helms-
man steering it to port. Now man is an agent who acts through intelligence, and it is proper to such an agent to act for an end. So man's
whole life and his every human action are directed to some end. The
diversity of human interests and pursuits, however, makes it quite clear
that many courses are open to men seeking the end they desire. Each
could reason out for himself the best way for him to gain happiness and
if it befitted men to live solitary lives, he would require no one to direct
him. His reason would suffice and, St. Thomas says very significantly, each
would be a king under God, the king of kings. However, man is not a
solitary but a social being, and every group requires some unifying direction to gain its ends effectively.

It is fascinating and instructive to compare St. Thomas and John Locke
on this fundamental point. St. Thomas says:

To be sure, the light of reason is placed by nature in every man, to
guide him in his acts towards his end. Wherefore, if man were intended to live alone, as many animals do, he would require no other
guide to his end. Each man would be a king unto himself, under
God, the highest King, inasmuch as he would direct himself in his
acts by the light of reason given him from on high. Yet it is natural
for man, more than for any other animal, to be a social and political
animal, to live in a group.[33]

Contrast this with John Locke's statement:

If man in the state of nature be so free, as has been said, if he be
absolute lord of his own person and possessions, equal to the greatest, and subject to nobody, why will he part with his freedom, this
empire, and subject himself to the dominion and control of any other
person? To which, it is obvious to answer, that though in the state

of nature he hath such a right, yet the enjoyment of it is very uncertain, and constantly exposed to the invasion of others. For *all being kings* as much as he, every man his equal, and the greater part no strict observer of equity and justice, the enjoyment of the property he has in this state is very unsafe, very unsecure.[34]

For Locke each man is a king because he is free and equal to the next; for St. Thomas he would be a king if he were not social by nature. But for him the solitary life is *not* natural to men. The hermit or criminal may shun society because the one lives with God and the other is unfit for the company of men. But by nature and normally, apart from extraordinary acquired virtue or vice, man does live in society with other men and construct civil communities. And just as it is natural for him to live with others, so is it natural that some principle rule the multitude he forms so that as a social being he may gain his happiness in a way befitting a social being, i.e. while other men do the very same thing. It is *natural*, then, for men to be governed in society, but, as we shall see in a moment, government is not supreme and capable of determining what is good for the individual, as it is for Hobbes.

Fourthly, because every subject is by this institution author of all the actions and judgments of the sovereign instituted, it follows that whatsoever he doth, it can be no injury to any one of his subjects, nor ought he to be by any of them accused of injustice. For he that doth anything by authority from another, doth therein no injury to him by whose authority he acteth: but by this institution of a commonwealth, every particular man is author of all the sovereign doth: and consequently he that complaineth of injury from his sovereign, complaineth of that whereof he himself is author; and therefore ought not to accuse any man but himself; no nor himself of injury, because to do injury to one's self is impossible. It is true that they that have sovereign power may commit iniquity, but not injustice or injury in the proper signification.[35]

Government must act to gain the citizen's good; government is required by nature, even though it *is* artificial to the extent that men have to construct the precise instruments by which they are to be governed. But government is thoroughly artificial for Locke. Solitary men enter into society through an agreement or contract; so, too, any ruling power exercised over such men must be artificial. It would be better for men if it were possible for them to persist in their individual, free and equal status. But it is not possible, and life in society is the next best thing. For St. Thomas, on the other hand, society is natural to man and so, too, is the power to rule; it is not artificial or conventional. Actually, inasmuch as St. Thomas and John Locke are not operating on the same level, they would undoubtedly agree that at the *historical* level society is artificial; they would disagree at the metaphysical level because in St. Thomas' eyes society and government derive from principles in man's nature rather than from historical or factual circumstances. As we have already seen, St. Thomas once pointed out that even in the state of innocence without original sin, there would be a disparity among men inasmuch as some would be more wise and righteous than others.[36] It would be unseemly, he concludes, if those who had such gifts did not exercise them for the benefit of others and lead them to the happiness they all seek.

Does this mean that men are *not* naturally equal in St. Thomas' eyes? Yes. He discusses disparities among men in a context wherein it is impossible to attribute inequalities to sinfulness; they are natural.[37] In the state of innocence men would differ at least in these ways: *sex* (for otherwise there would be no procreation), *age* (for procreation begets children who must differ in age from their parents), *physical powers* (food, climate, the stars would influence people differently in virtue of dissimilar physical constitutions), and *spiritual capacities* (as free agents men would cultivate knowledge, justice and the other virtues in varying degrees because they would not apply their intellects and wills in the same way). They would be free, then, but unequal—yet not free with the full-blown autonomy Locke seems to feel men possess. Their freedom would be an embryonic freedom of choice that they would have to learn to exercise by cultivating the moral virtues. And, unlike man's social condition in Hobbes' *Leviathan*, human freedom would not be diminished, in St. Thomas' thought, when men live socially. When they live in society, men are existing in a natural way, and that not only means existing freely, but growing and maturing in freedom.

Now inasmuch as the disparities that St. Thomas recognizes *do* exist among men, then living together in society requires that such inequalities be rectified. And that is the work of justice. There is a sense in which every person who cultivates the sciences and moral virtues so as to be a mature human being is said to be just, for his life is rectified by moral law and properly ordered to the common good.

A thing is said to be *general* in two ways. First, by *predication*: thus *animal* is general in relation to man and horse and the like: and in this sense that which is general must needs be essentially the same as the things in relation to which it is general, for the reason that the genus belongs to the essence of the species, and forms part of its definition. Secondly a thing is said to be general *virtually*; thus a universal cause is general in relation to all its effects, the sun, for instance, in relation to all bodies that are illumined or transmuted by its power; and in this sense there is no need for that which is *general* to be essentially the same as those things in relation to which it is general, since cause and effect are not essentially the same. Now it is in this latter sense that, according to what has been said, legal justice is said to be a general virtue inasmuch, to wit, as it directs the acts of the other virtues to its own end, and this is to move all the other virtues by its command; for just as charity may be called a general virtue insofar as it directs the acts of all the virtues to the Divine good, so too is legal justice, insofar as it directs the acts of all the virtues to the common good. . . . However the name legal justice can be given to every virtue insofar as every virtue is directed to the common good by the aforesaid justice, which though special is nevertheless virtually general. Speaking in this way, legal justice is essentially the same as all virtues, but differs therefrom logically.[38]

Justice may, then, be equated with the whole moral life as such. However as regards the precise inequalities existing among men in society, justice has a more specific task to accomplish. For one thing, it must see to it that inequality is not perpetuated within society in, for example, unfair dealings in trade, barter and exchange, usurious lending of money, exorbitant prices etc. St. Thomas calls that special kind of justice *commutative* justice.

There are two kinds of justice. The one consists in mutual giving and receiving, as in buying and selling, and other kinds of communication and exchange. This justice the Philosopher calls *commutative justice*, which directs exchange and the communication of business.[39]

It is a virtue concerned with ensuring that things passing between men in their daily business dealings maintain a fair balance. It aims at guaranteeing that each person will get his due in the sense that a balance is struck between the things exchanged, whether a balance of article with money or of article with article. As Aristotle says, commutative justice is concerned with things and not with the men involved in a transaction.

But the justice in transactions between man and man is a sort of equality indeed, and the injustice a sort of inequality; not according to that kind of proportion, however, but according to arithmetical proportion. For it makes no difference whether a good man has defrauded a bad man or a bad one a good one, nor whether it is a good or a bad man that has committed adultery; the law looks only to the distinctive character of the injury, and treats the parties as equal, if

one is in the wrong and the other is being wronged and if one in-
flicted injury and the other has received it.[40]

In quite a different way inequalities among citizens precisely as persons and human beings is the target of a more important kind of justice,
*distributive justice.*

As stated above, in distributive justice something is given to a private
individual insofar as what belongs to the whole is due to the part,
and in a quantity that is proportionate to the importance of the position of that part in respect of the whole. Consequently in distributive justice a person receives all the more of the common goods according as he holds a more prominent position in the community.
This prominence in an aristocratic community is gauged according
to virtue, in an oligarchy according to wealth, in a democracy according to liberty, and in various ways according to various forms of
community. Hence in distributive justice the mean is observed, not
according to equality between thing and thing, but according to proportion between things and persons; so that which is given to one
person surpasses that which is allotted to another. Hence the Philosopher says ( *Ethic.* v, 3, 4) that the mean in the latter case follows geometrical proportion, wherein equality depends not on quantity but on proportion.[41]

It is a justice that aims at establishing an equality among persons; it is
not concerned with the things that are exchanged, but with persons living
together and sharing in the common good of society. Distributive justice
tries to ensure an equitable distribution of honors and burdens, duties
and responsibilities, in the common life. Distributive justice looks to
inequalities among persons as such and tries to guarantee that each person will share in society's goods and responsibilities in proportion to his
or her contribution to the common good of the whole. In maintaining a
balance or restoring one it does not try to have everyone share alike in
an arithmetic sense; it recognizes, rather, that one person does not have
the same natural and acquired endowments as his neighbor and cannot
make a similar contribution to the common life. But by the same token
it recognizes that each person has a right to a proportionate share in the
goods of the common life. Distributive justice takes the geometric mean
as its model. Aristotle explains that mean in this way:

The just, then, is a species of the proportionate ( proportion being
not a property only of the kind of numbers which consists of abstract
units, but of number in general). For proportion is equality of ratios,

and involves four terms at least (that discrete proportion involves four terms is plain, but so does continuous proportion, for it uses one term as two and mentions it twice, e.g. "as the line A is to the line B, so is the line B to the line C;" the line B, then, has been mentioned twice, so that if the line B be assumed twice, the proportional terms will be four); and the just, too, involves at least four terms, and the ratio between one pair is the same as that between the other pair; for there is a similar distinction between the persons and between the things. As the term A, then, is to B, so will C be to D, and therefore, *alternando*, as A is to C, B will be to D. Therefore also the whole is in the same ratio to the whole; and this coupling the distribution effects, and, if the terms are so combined, effects justly. The conjunction, then, of the term A with C and of B with D is what is just in distribution.[42]

Both Aristotle and St. Thomas would expect that this threefold work of justice—conformity with the laws of morality, equity in the exchange of things, proportional equality among persons—would result in a mutual good-will among the members of society. Justice prepares the ground for mutual trust and benevolence by reducing the inequalities among men as far as possible; it clears the way for the real bond that holds men together in society, *friendship*. A friend is another self, and this at once suggests that friendship can only exist between equals; men are friends, a man is not his dog's friend.

Friendship cannot exist except towards rational creatures, who are capable of returning love and of communicating with one another in the various works of life, and who may fare well or ill, according to the changes of fortune and happiness; even as towards them is benevolence, properly speaking, exercised. But irrational creatures cannot attain to loving God, nor to any share in the intellectual and beatific life that He lives. Strictly speaking, therefore, God does not love irrational creatures with the love of friendship.[43]

In friendship a person desires his friend's good, not his own. In other words, a friend wishes that another person have his proper share of the good of the particular society within which the friends exist, be it a familial society or a political society.

According to the Philosopher (*Ethic.* viii, 2, 3) not every love has the character of friendship, but that love which is together with benevolence, when, to wit, we love someone so as to wish good to him. If, however, we do not wish good to what we love, but wish its good for ourselves (thus we are said to love wine, or a horse, or the like), it is love not of friendship, but of a kind of concupiscence. For it would be absurd to speak of having friendship for wine or for a horse.

Yet neither does well-wishing suffice for friendship, for a certain mutual love is requisite, since friendship is between friend and friend: and this well-wishing is founded on some kind of communication.[44]

Friendship, then, implies a communicating or sharing in some good. It is, indeed, almost synonymous with society. So as a result of justice and friendship, there is a structural order in society.

For St. Thomas society is an *order;* its unity is brought about by the order that relates the members of a society or the citizens of a civic community to the common good; the sovereign does not constitute society's unity, as it does for Hobbes. At best the sovereign is the symbol of a unity that exists for quite different reasons and rests on very different grounds. It is interesting to follow St. Thomas as he examines the unity of society and the body politic; he finds that the unity of society is a *unity of order* or structure. The domestic family and civic community have a peculiar unity: they are multitudes with a unity of order only. Other totalities or wholes do not have that kind of unity; they are one by composition, collection or continuity. For example, a house is made of parts conjoined by contact; the components of a chemical compound are mixed together, interact and form *one* mixture. In these cases the parts have no operation that is not the operation of the whole. In continuous things like pencils, the motion of the whole and part are identical; in composites or collectives the operation is principally that of the whole; this is not true of a whole that is one by order *only.* Each part of a multitude or social group is a *person* and as such can have an operation that is not the operation of the whole. The individual is not swallowed up in the social process, as he is for Karl Marx, but has, retains and develops his *own* personality. Nor is that personality the necessary result of economic development; it comes into being, rather, through the activity of an intelligent and free being, a *person.* A family or an army is just such a multitude, and each member of the family or each soldier can have an operation that is not that of the whole family or army—indeed, the members of a family (and especially the father and mother) must exercise different operations and perform acts different from those of the family as a whole; and if each soldier does not have a distinct function (communication, supply, medical, infantry) the army as a whole *cannot* have an operation. But considered as a family or an army, they have an operation that does not belong to any of the parts but to the whole multitude *only;* the whole family combines as a unit to educate and develop the personalities of each of the members, and the operations of waging war and gaining victory are works of the whole army.[45]

Now in an earlier examination of the being of an agent in Chapter VI, we have seen that a thing becomes an agent in virtue of some end, and that ends are arranged in an order of dependence one upon the other to the extent that gaining one hinges on attaining others. In this way each person becomes a locus upon whom many societies focus because each society is organized to gain some specific good and contribute something to each person's overall perfection. Thus, for instance, a person finds that he needs recreation, help in caring for his health, assistance in teaching and learning, so he becomes a member of several societies dedicated to those purposes: bridge club, health program, school. To mature physically, emotionally, morally and intellectually he finds the need of a wife and children, so he founds his own personal society, his family. And when he discovers that all by himself he cannot feed the members of his family adequately, clothe them properly or educate them in satisfactory fashion, he finds that he has to have the help of the many groups provided by a local community. Ultimately, his desire to protect their health, to have them learn through study in schools, to support and educate his family is found to depend on a more or less self-sufficient community, the total civil community or body politic. In this way each person becomes a center of many activities, each one inspired by a distinct goal or end, each satisfied through a social group; and the capacity of each group to help him rests on the prosperous functioning of another group. St. Thomas expresses this fact in technical language by saying that there is a subalternation of ends and that the body politic is a final cause making the attainment of other final causes possible.

Moreover, in every ordered series of ends the ultimate end must be the end of all preceding ends. For instance, if a potion is mixed to be given to a sick man, and it is given in order to purge him, and he is purged in order to make him thinner, and he is thinned down so that he may become healthy—then health must be the end of the thinning process, and of the purging, and of the other actions which precede it. But all things are found, in their various degrees of goodness, to be subordinated to one highest good which is the cause of all goodness. Consequently, since the good has the essential character of an end, all things are subordinated to God, as preceding ends under an ultimate end. Therefore, God must be the end of all things.

Furthermore, a particular good is ordered to the common good as to an end; indeed, the being of a part depends on the being of the whole. So, also, the good of a nation is more godlike than the good of one man. Now, the highest good which is God is the common good, since the good of all things taken together depends on Him; and the good whereby each thing is good is its own particular good, and also is the good of the other things that depend on this thing. Therefore, all things are ordered to one good as their end, and that is God.[46]

The good of the civil community, a good in which all citizens are to share commonly, becomes a common goal or good. As the members of a family or army share in the common good of society, so, too, does each citizen share in the common good of the body politic. The common good is primary and most universal for each self-sufficient civil community; it is *not* the sum-total of all the particular goods sought by individuals. The common good is, rather, a *distinct* good for the attainment of which the whole society must strive and by the enjoyment of which each member of the group is aided in gaining his own particular good. Peace, justice, the protection of law and courts, a high level of public morality, respect for human rights and personal dignity, an adequate standard of living make it possible for health programs, schools, churches and families to make their proper contribution to the individual person's happiness.

This is the aspect of social life with which Mill is concerned in the texts we have quoted; but in his preoccupation with individual liberty, as he conceives it, and with self-protection, the individual as sovereign agent obliterates the common good of society as a whole and the principle of subalternating ends is lost. For St. Thomas, on the other hand, each member of a society is a *person;* he is a subsistent, rational, free agent with duties and rights of his own. The society or political community cannot violate those prerogatives. But as a person he is also social and dependent upon others if he is to gain his own good; unless the whole social unit gains a common good and shares in it, there will be no society—and the possibility of each person gaining his own personal good will become well-nigh impossible. The common good, then, assumes a priority over the personal good of each member of the family or of each citizen in the body politic. As St. Thomas says in one place:

> Each part naturally loves the common good more than his own particular good. And this is clear from his actions, for every part has its principal inclination to an action common to the usefulness of the whole. It is clear, too, in political virtues according to which citizens

suffer the loss of their own goods and even of their persons at times in virtue of the common good.[47]

As the most universal good of a multitude, the common good makes all particular goods to be good; it is, then, according to Aristotle, more *divine* than all human goods. St. Thomas explains the adjective "divine" in a way that completely transforms everything he has borrowed from Aristotle. He says:

The common good is said to be more divine inasmuch as it pertains most to the likeness of God who is the ultimate cause of all goods.[48]

All human societies—families, social groups, local communities, bodies politic—are unified in their own order by a common good that is supreme in that order. But all societies share in one common end, the end of serving man in some way or other. Serving man, whether in a subalternated or primary society, unifies the whole order of human social striving. In this way the common good best exemplifies the way in which God unifies all things as their end; the common good is godlike in each order. But there is more to the godlike character of the common good than that. For St. Thomas all men are struggling socially for a good common to all and beyond the common good of any human society, namely, God. He is, in truth, their one common good and the final end that makes all final ends to be final ends. In short: gaining each lesser common good, the goal of a subalternated society, brings each person a step closer to God. Seeking God, then, does not alienate man or human society from their proper happiness; seeking God as a final end demands that one seek to accomplish the ends of various human societies. But the seeking must be an *ordered* seeking.

Furthermore, a particular good is ordered to the common good as to an end; indeed, the being of a part depends on the being of the whole. So, too, the good of a nation is more godlike than the good of one man. Now, the highest good which is God is the common good, since the good of all things taken together depends on Him; and the good whereby each thing is good is its own particular good, and also is the good of the other things that depend on this thing. Therefore, all things are ordered to one good as their end, and that is God.[49]

God, then, becomes a being of real social concern. In the final analysis each social group assumes its ordered significance from the contribution it makes to each man's approach to God. But each society has to gain its own *specific* goal if it is to make its proper contribution to the whole; each common good retains its integrity and motivates in its own way. Thus, at the level of the body politic—whether, in contemporary language, it be a national state or the international community—making it possible for *all* men to enjoy God is a condition for each individual person enjoying Him. For a Christian, commitment to man's good in *human* society becomes a prerequisite for his own personal happiness. It is not enough for him to say that, as a Christian, he is "trying to live with God;" he has to respect the subalternation of ends and admit in his actions that the ends of human society, man's natural perfection or human betterment, must be realized if he is to be happy as a Christian. God becomes a concern for man living in society; society becomes a concern for man living with God.

That is a step Aristotle could not take. For Aristotle justice establishes an equality only among *men;* and friendship, too, is possible only among men.

> But equality does not seem to take the same form in acts of justice and in friendship; for in acts of justice what is equal in the primary sense is that which is in proportion to merit, while quantitative equality is secondary, but in friendship quantitative equality is primary and proportion to merit secondary. This becomes clear if there is a great interval in respect of virtue or vice or wealth or anything else between the parties; for then they are no longer friends, and do not even expect to be so. And this is most manifest in the case of the gods; for they surpass us most decisively in all good things. But it is clear also in the case of kings; for with them, too, men who are much their inferiors do not expect to be friends; nor do men of no account expect to be friends with the best or wisest men. In such cases it is not possible to define exactly up to what point friends can remain friends; for much can be taken away and friendship remain, but when one party is removed to a great distance, as God is, the possibility of friendship ceases. That is in fact the origin of the question whether friends really wish for their friends the greatest good, e.g. that of being gods; since in that case their friends will no longer be friends to them.[50]

Human society, therefore, has to be limited to the order of human and purely natural goods; the common good of the body politic or city must be those natural conditions of peace and prosperity that make it possible for a man to enjoy his highest natural activity, contemplation.

This is indicated, too, by the fact that the other animals have no
share in happiness, being completely deprived of such activity. For
while the whole life of the gods is blessed, and that of men too in
so far as some likeness of such activity belongs to them, none of the
other animals is happy, since they in no way share in contemplation.
Happiness extends, then, just so far as contemplation does, and those
to whom contemplation more fully belongs are more truly happy, not
as a mere concomitant but in virtue of the contemplation; for this is
in itself precious. Happiness, therefore, must be some form of contemplation. But, being a man, one will also need external prosperity;
for our nature is not self-sufficient for the purpose of contemplation,
but our body also must be healthy and must have food and other
attention.[51]

St. Thomas could take the step he did because he was a Christian
philosopher; as a man of faith he could answer Aristotle's question (to
wit, do friends really wish the greatest good for their friends?). Yes. We
do want our friends to enjoy the greatest of goods; we do want them
to share in the life of God. Human society is ultimately intended to
produce saints. He knew from his Christian faith that God had, indeed,
entered into fellowship with man in the Incarnation, that divine grace
effected a kind of equality between men and God, that men can be
friends of God in charity, that man's life on earth is subalternated or
further directed to life with God. These things he knew from faith, not
philosophy. But in virtue of his conviction that nature remains integral
under the influence of grace, that nature is made more perfect (precisely as nature) by divine grace and is not destroyed or replaced by it,
St. Thomas could go ahead and see the nature of society and the body
politic much as Aristotle did. Society is a result of man's social being;
justice reduces natural and artificial inequalities; friendship binds equal
citizens together; and society has a finality of its own. Only its *status*
was changed in the Christian dispensation; its *nature* remains whole
and entire. In a very true sense Aristotle's view of the *polis,* including
as it did worship of the gods and moral life, becomes universal because
it is subalternated to a further common good, God, which *all* can enjoy.
Man's nature remains open to grace and life with God, not closed to
life in this world with other men alone; society, too, while remaining
integrally *society* is left open in its existence to divine intervention. Thus
the Christian, while working in the daily temporal order of factory,
office or school, can be on the watch for God's intervention in the affairs of men, he can proclaim what he believes to be God's hand at
work, and he can work for human betterment in that area, the while

convinced *in faith* that he is doing God's work in the world. But that
assurance is a reward of faith: faith in God and trust in man.

   In according or recognizing an integrity and finality proper to temporal society, St. Thomas gave it a dignity it had lacked in previous
Christian thought. Society was no longer St. Augustine's earthly city
founded in pride and concerned with love of worldly things; it was
founded by God in man's nature and concerned with the *use* of worldly
things.

> There was indeed on earth, so long as it was needed, a symbol and
> foreshadowing image of this city, which served the purpose of re-
> minding men that such a city was to be, rather than of making it
> present; and this image was itself called the holy city, as a symbol
> of the future city, though not itself the reality. Of this city which
> served as an image, and of that free city it typified, Paul writes to
> the Galatians in these terms: "Tell me, ye that desire to be under
> the law, do ye not hear the law? For it is written that Abraham had
> two sons, the one by a bond maid, the other by a free woman. But
> he who was of the bond woman was born after the flesh, but he of
> the free woman was by promise. Which things are an allegory: for
> these are the two covenants; the one from the mount Sinai, which
> gendereth to bondage, which is Agar. . . ." In the earthly city, then,
> we find two things—its own obvious presence, and its symbolic pres-
> entation of the heavenly city. Now citizens are begotten to the
> earthly city by nature vitiated by sin, but to the heavenly city by
> grace freeing nature from sin; whence the former are called "vessels
> of wrath," the latter "vessels of mercy." And this was typified in the
> two sons of Abraham—Ishmael, the son of Agar the handmaid, be-
> ing born according to the flesh, while Isaac was born of the free
> woman Sarah, according to the promise. Both, indeed, were of Abra-
> ham's seed; but the one was begotten by natural law, the other was
> given by gracious promise. In the one birth, human action is re-
> vealed; in the other, a divine kindness comes to light.[52]

It was a daring thing for St. Thomas to do—to espouse Aristotle's
view that man naturally *needed* earthly society, that the common good
of the body politic has a worth of its own that men have to respect and
for which they *must* strive, that the civil community has its own rights.
In contemporary terms we would have to say that sociology has its own
end; politics and economics have their proper purposes. And just as
the Christian philosopher has to respect the finality of philosophic reason not only as a philosopher but as a Christian, so, too, must we respect
the finalities of sociology, politics and economics. As St. Thomas had
recognized that man has a being of his own, a capacity to know by

himself, a freedom to choose as he sees fit, so, too, did he accord society and the political community a being of their own. But as human being, although independent, is integral with being Christian, so, too, does temporal society find its place within a unifying Christianity—not a unified political *Christendom*, but a unifying Christian life capable of expressing itself in many diverse political forms.

The finality of society and the body politic is, then, caused by God as ultimate cause of all final causes. So once again man is brought face to face with God; this time society is the path. Once more Sartre's challenge confronts us: can man remain human and follow the path of a society that leads him to God? If he is not alone in this world, is it only because he is condemned socially to be alienated before God? In apparently salvaging man as a social being, we would appear to have succeeded only in preparing him for an ultimate alienation before God. Must he not forsake society, therefore, make his own solitary way, remain human rather than come face to face with God in the company of others? Man before God will be the theme of the last chapter.

# CHAPTER VIII

# PHILOSOPHIC KNOWLEDGE OF GOD

Only from the truth of being can the essence of the holy be thought. Only from the essence of the holy is the essence of deity to be thought. Only in the light of the essence of deity can that be thought and said which the word "God" should name. Do we not have to be able first to understand and hear carefully all these words, if we as men, i.e. as ek-sistent beings, are to experience a relation of God to man? For how could man in contemporary world history ever ask seriously and rigorously whether God is drawing near or withdrawing himself, if man neglects first of all to think his way into the only dimension in which such a question can be asked? But that is the dimension of the holy, which even as a dimension remains closed if the openness of being does not become clear and in its clearing is not near to man. Perhaps the outstanding characteristic of this age consists in the closedness of the dimension of the whole.[1]

St. Thomas' Christian philosophy provokes a great many fears in modern minds when it undertakes to approach God. Inasmuch as philosophy is logical, reasoned knowledge, it arouses the fear among some Christians that it will destroy divine transcendence, make the Christian God into a rational Absolute and, thereby, undermine Christian belief. On the other hand, to many non-Christians it stirs up the spectre of a God who will threaten man's true humanity and demolish his freedom by creating human nature and imposing on man a law by which he must live, a law not of man's own making.

Søren Kierkegaard is one of the sources and earliest modern spokesmen of the first fear. He says:

. . . one can certainly cast the horoscope of any generation with regard to their ethics and religion by discerning what they think about "science" in the religious sphere. "Minerva's owl only flies when it gets dark" and science always follows after. What Johannes Climacus says is perfectly true: to transform Christianity into a science is the greatest of all errors and when it is completely achieved (how everyone will rejoice) Christianity will have been completely abolished.[2]

Friedrich Nietzsche expresses the second fear in that famous passage from his work *The Joyful Science* that runs as follows:

> Have you not heard of that madman who lit a lantern in the bright morning hours, ran to the market place, and cried incessantly, "I seek God! I seek God!" As many of those who do not believe in God were standing around just then, he provoked much laughter. Why, did he get lost? said one. Did he lose his way like a child? said another. Or is he hiding? Is he afraid of us? Has he gone on a voyage? or emigrated? Thus they yelled and laughed. The madman jumped into their midst and pierced them with his glances. "Whither is God," he cried. "I shall tell you. We have killed him—you and I. All of us are his murderers. But how have we done this? How are we able to drink up the sea? Who gave us the sponge to wipe away the entire horizon? What did we do when we unchained this earth from its sun? Whither is it moving now? Whither are we moving now? Away from all suns. Are we not plunging continually backward, sideward, forward in all directions? Is there any up or down left? Are we not straying as through an infinite nothing? Do we not feel the breath of empty space? Has it not become colder? Is not night and more night coming on all the while? God is dead. God remains dead. And we have killed him." [3]

This was the very same dread Orestes proclaimed in Jean-Paul Sartre's play *The Flies*.[4]

How have we killed God? Philosophically. The Western tradition has gradually robbed God of all reality by making Him a creation of human reason; philosophers have said that God is an *idea*. Thus in the Dialectic of his *Critique of Pure Reason,* Kant examines in turn each of the three kinds of argument for God's existence that he considers to be the traditional theological paths to God. He calls the arguments respectively ontological, cosmological, and physico-theological. According to Kant all three involve at least one major fallacy: principles valid in the order of phenomenal objects are applied to thinking about God, an "object" that cannot possibly fall within sensible experience. We can never come upon God spatio-temporally in any sensible intuition; as a result, we cannot apply to Him principles that can only validly be used when we experience objects in space and time, i.e. as having geometric dimensions of length, breadth and depth, and as enduring through a succession of moments of time. For God is not a sensible object; indeed, He is not properly-speaking an object at all! God is an *idea* generated by pure reason when it tries to achieve "the dimension of the whole," a complete synthesis in its thinking. He is an idea or, better still, an ideal that reason fashions or conceives to inspire it in its attempt to organize human knowledge, i.e. scientific knowledge, into more and more completely unified patterns.

If, in following up this idea of ours, we proceed to hypostatise it, we shall be able to determine the primordial being through the mere concept of the highest reality, as a being that is one, simple, all-sufficient, eternal etc. In short, we shall be able to determine it, in its unconditioned completeness, through all predicaments. The concept of such a being is the concept of *God*, taken in the transcendental sense; and the ideal of pure reason, as above defined, is thus the object of a transcendental *theology*.

In any such use of the transcendental idea we should, however, be overstepping the limits of its purpose and validity. For reason, in employing it as a basis for the complete determination of things, has used it only as the *concept* of all reality, without requiring that all this reality be objectively given and be itself a thing. Such a thing is a mere fiction in which we combine and realise the manifold of our idea in an ideal, as an individual being. But we have no right to do this, nor even to assume the possibility of such an hypothesis. Nor do any of the consequences which flow from such an ideal have any bearing upon the complete determination of things, or exercise in that regard the least influence; and it is solely as aiding in their determination that the idea has been shown to be necessary.[5]

As an ideal God rules our thinking; He does not and, indeed, cannot constitute an object of our *knowledge*. Principles of understanding and intuition *alone* have objective validity, and objective validity is interpreted by Kant as referring to things given in experience, not to things in themselves.[6] Intuition is restricted to sensible intuition and, hence, to things that are spatio-temporal; an intuition of anything intelligible—even the intelligibility of anything sensible!—is explicitly ruled out.[7]

Three points in Kant's position are absolutely fundamental: first, the conviction that the only data available to human, scientific knowledge is sensible in the sense of being atomic, unrelated, spatio-temporal information; second, the view that scientific knowledge is formulated in synthetic a priori propositions; third, the belief that Newtonian physics is the model of all theoretical knowledge. One immediate result is that there is no *science* of theology because God does not satisfy the conditions of a *Newtonian* object—He cannot be experienced sensibly as a space-time object and no objectively valid synthetic a priori proposition can be formulated about Him. However, where reason (in its theoretical usage) finds itself incapable of leading us to God except as an idea, it finds that it *must* posit God's existence as a purely practical postulate. Reason is compelled to grant that God certainly does exist, but it is not forced to do so by theoretical reasons or arguments but, rather, as the ultimate justification of *moral* experience. For morality is only possible if reason conceives of the moral agent as a person acting in a purely intelligible order without any sensible determination; to safeguard morality reason postulates God's existence as the greatest Good in Whom progress towards happiness and virtue may find completeness. Reason, then, lacking insight into the intelligibility of things and discovering that it is restricted to generating *ideas*, finds that it cannot *know* God, i.e. have scientific (in the Newtonian sense) knowledge of Him, but can only *postulate* His existence *practically*.

God, then, is a product of human consciousness; He serves a demand of human experience. And philosophers have gradually come to realize the implications of a God fashioned to serve and satisfy human needs. They have become convinced that, when man really comes to know *him*-self fully, i.e. when he achieves total self-consciousness, he will see that *he* has created God and attributed to Him all that he finds best in human experience. Thus Hegel, for example, considers the god of any religious experience to be a representation of the infinite in the form of some natural force or phenomenon; Christianity has simply pushed the process of representation to its ultimate by taking man as its model. The Incarnation simply presents God as man:

> That Absolute Spirit has taken on the shape of self-consciousness inherently, and therefore also consciously to itself—this appears now as the belief of the world, the belief that spirit exists *in fact* as a definite self-consciousness, i.e. as an actual human being; that spirit is an object for immediate experience; that the believing mind *sees*, *feels*, and *hears* this divinity. Taken thus it is not imagination, not a fancy; it is actual in the believer. Consciousness in that case does not set out from its own inner life, does not start from thought, and in itself combine the thought of God with existence; rather it sets out from immediate present existence, and recognizes God in it.
>
> . . . This Incarnation of the Divine Being, its having essentially and directly the shape of self-consciousness, is the simple content of Absolute Religion. Here the Divine Being is known as Spirit; this religion is the Divine Being's consciousness concerning itself that it is Spirit. For spirit is knowledge of self in a state of alienation of self: spirit is the Being which is the process of retaining identity with itself in its otherness. This, however, is substance, so far as in its

accidents substance at the same time is turned back into itself; and is so, not as being indifferent towards something unessential and, consequently, as finding itself in some alien element, but as being there within itself, i.e. so far as it is subject or self.

In this form of religion the Divine Being is, on that account *revealed*. Its being revealed obviously consists in this, that what it is, is known. It is, however, known just in its being known as spirit, as a Being which is essentially self-consciousness.[8]

With the discovery that God is really made in the image of man, as Ludwig Feuerbach has expressed it, will come the full realization that God is, indeed, dead.

Man, as an emotional and sensuous being, is governed and made happy only by images, by sensible representations. Mind presenting itself as at once type-creating, emotional and sensuous, is the imagination. The second Person in God, who is in truth the first person in religion, is the nature of the imagination made objective. The definitions of the second Person are principally images or symbols; and these images do not proceed from man's incapability of conceiving the object otherwise than symbolically,—which is an altogether false interpretation,—but the thing cannot be conceived otherwise than symbolically because the thing itself is a symbol or image. The Son is, therefore, expressly called the Image of God; his essence is that he is an image—the representation of God, the visible glory of the invisible God. The Son is the satisfaction of the need for mental images, the nature of the imaginative activity in man made objective as an absolute, divine activity. Man makes to himself an image of God, i.e. he converts the abstract being of the reason, the being of the thinking power, into an object of sense or imagination. But he places this image in God himself, because his want would not be satisfied if he did not regard this image as an objective reality, if it were nothing more for him than a subjective image, separate from God, —a mere figment devised by man. And it is in fact no devised, no arbitrary image; for it expresses the necessity of the imagination, the necessity of affirming the imagination as a divine power. The Son is the reflected splendour of the imagination, the image nearest to the heart; but for the very reason that he is only an object of the imagination, he is only the nature of the imagination made objective.[9]

Therefore, the path leading to the death of God is not a path traced out in nature; it is a path that man has made for himself. The moment philosophers began to look upon nature as merely a totality of sensible phenomena, as Kant did, and to interpret the laws of nature as so many impositions of human reasoning, nature ceased to reveal paths leading to God as a being, rather than as an idea. If men cannot know things as beings, they will never know that the cause of things is a being; if nature is a product of human reasoning, so, too, will be the paths leading to God—so, too, will be the God found at the end of those paths. Kant's charge of fallacy in the theoretical proofs of God's existence and his restricting certitude about His existence to moral conviction and practical necessity do not touch St. Thomas' position at all—the ultimate reason being that Kant is concerned with the *idea* of God, whereas St. Thomas is trying to understand His *being!* For St. Thomas, philosophy and experimental science consider quite distinct objects; philosophy must and, indeed, does examine things that fall under the senses, but it is not confined to doing that alone at the expense of losing its objective validity. Indeed, Kantian objective validity is meaningless within St. Thomas' approach to being.

For St. Thomas reality is *being, not* objective validity! Philosophy is always interested in the being of *things*—and not always or exclusively *sensible* things—rather than with *phenomena.* Human understanding, as St. Thomas sees it, *can* grasp what is intelligible about things, including *sensible* things; understanding is *not* responsible for organizing the purely spatio-temporal data provided in sensation (interpreted mechanistically as being merely the physical action of body on body) by *a priori* principles supposedly proper to understanding. Sensation remains *human* and involves the presence of the *whole* sensing being to the thing sensed, including the intellect's contact with the thing's being; and intellect derives its principles and concepts *from* what is sensed instead of imposing them as forms *totally* derived from the understanding. And reason stands in quite a different relation to understanding, according to St. Thomas, than it does in Kant's critical view of knowledge. As we have seen, reason and understanding are *not* distinct faculties; they are one faculty distinct only as rest and motion are distinct. Reason does not generate *ideas*—indeed, except in practical knowledge (practical in St. Thomas' sense, not Kant's!), wherein the human intellect is intent on producing an artistic product, ideas play no role in the work of the human intellect. Man's intellect produces *concepts* and, through them, judgments and demonstrations, but only with a view to coming to rest in the understanding of a conclusion. Indeed, concept, proposition and demonstration are ultimately but the *means* used by the human intellect to effect an intentional identification with things. Thus, when a man's reason tries to understand the truth of the proposition "God exists," it is not in search of systematic completeness or synthetic totality; it is, rather, in search of the ultimate evidence of being. When, after reason has performed its task of constructing a demonstration, the intellect gives its assent, it is not to an *idea* or an *ideal,* but to a *Being.* On the other hand, practical reason cannot produce a knowledge or certitude about God's existence for the very reason that it is not concerned with existence or being and does not yield an evidence to which assent has to be given; the practical intellect is interested in an existence that is *to be.* It deals with acting and making. In short: Kant's presentation and criticism of the cosmological and physico-theological arguments do not come to grips with St. Thomas' proofs.

Their respective criticisms of the so-called ontological argument are sufficient to mark off the different ways in which the two men philosophize. For Kant, existence is a category of understanding and to say that anything exists adds nothing to the understanding of the thing:

> If, now, we take the subject (God) with all its predicates (among which is omnipotence) and say "God is" or "There is a God," we attach no new predicate to the concept of God, but only posit the subject in itself with all its predicates, and indeed posit it as being an *object* that stands in relation to my *concept.* The content of both must be one and the same; nothing can have been added to the concept, which expresses merely what is possible, by thinking its object (through the expression "it is") as given absolutely. Otherwise stated, the real contains no more than the merely possible. A hundred real thalers do not contain the least coin more than a hundred possible thalers.[10]

For St. Thomas, existence is the first act of being and it makes all the difference in the world; without the act of existing there is no being and no essence. One cannot, then, argue from essence *to* existence.

> . . . granted that everyone understands that by this name *God* is signified something than which nothing greater can be thought, nevertheless, it does not therefore follow that he understands that what the name signifies exists actually, but only that it exists mentally. Nor can it be argued that it actually exists unless it be admitted that there actually exists something than which nothing greater can be thought; and this precisely is not admitted by those who hold that God does not exist.[11]

In short: if a person is going to attempt a demonstration of God's existence, he must begin with the act of existing of something that exists. Kant and St. Thomas, then, represent two approaches to God through quite distinct philosophies. For Kant, scientific or theoretical knowledge

of God's existence is impossible because science is knowledge of phenomena and philosophy is critique; for St. Thomas, scientific or speculative knowledge of God's existence is possible because all scientific
knowledge is knowledge of being in some way or other, and *some*
knowledge of being—metaphysical knowledge—leads the human intellect to God.

However, this question at once arises: *can* we follow the path of
being, a path traced out in nature as it *is* rather than as we *think* it?
Is not the path of being blocked the moment we try to follow it *rationally*, as St. Thomas does? Is not Kierkegaard's fear a very real one,
the fear that reason must always treat being as an abstraction and,
consequently, that God's existence can never emerge from reason's effort to prove it? For Kierkegaard was as suspicious of the theoretical
approach to God as Kant was and he was, moreover, convinced that the
path to God by way of being was blocked precisely by *being* itself. Science, in Kierkegaard's eyes, has done irreparable harm to Christianity; and
existence necessarily escapes understanding because it becomes a *concept*
the very moment it is known.

> No, the thing is that when "science" is undoubtedly the highest,
> then religion has as good as completely disappeared. Those are the
> two poles and one can certainly cast the horoscope of any generation
> with regard to their ethics and religion by discerning what they think
> about "science" in the religious sphere. "Minerva's owl only flies
> when it gets dark" and science always follows after. What Johannes
> Climacus says is perfectly true: to transform Christianity into a sci-
> ence is the greatest of all errors and when it is completely achieved
> (how everyone will rejoice) Christianity will have been completely
> abolished.[12]

Kierkegaard's fear that science is ultimately destructive of Christianity is
a result of his complete disillusionment with Hegel. He was above all
afraid of the fate Christianity suffers when it is sublimated by philosophy.
Hegel, in Kierkegaard's eyes, robbed Christianity of all uniqueness and
vitality by making it—indeed, *all* religion—a moment of self-realization
or self-consciousness inferior to the self-awareness that is philosophy.
Thus, Hegel says of religion:

> Religion brings God close to a people's mind in mythical represen-
> tations, involving feelings and thoughts. In worship the religious
> mind forgets itself and also forgets the mediating means of its ele-
> vation; it is unaware of the particular imagery which is necessarily
> connected with cultic actions honoring the absolute relation of man

to God. *God is the absolute spirit:* in its non-mythical truth, it is the
pure dialectical essence of all Being which objectifies itself in its own
otherness, by means of which it returns eternally to itself; it maintains its identity in and through its non-absolute and finite self-
manifestations. *God is holy* is that absolute whole which has nothing alien outside of itself: which has no "temptation." He is absolute
*power* insofar as he actualizes its concrete wholeness in all indi-
viduations: In mythical language He is "creator" of his "creation."
The Absolute is *wisdom* as its power is one with its holiness. The
Absolute is *good* as it bestows freedom to the individual; and *just*
as it eternally reunites all individuals in its eternal life.[13]

Philosophy takes us beyond religion and its mythical representations
and thereby effects the final liberation of spirit.

Philosophy thus understands religion as one of its own presuppositions and as a particular articulation of the absolute totality. It sees
through the form of mythical representations by virtue of which the
life of the Absolute is pictured in seemingly discreet stories, quasi-
temporal myths, and cultic symbols. Philosophy uses such language
without being taken captive by it. The revelation of the Absolute is
not confined to religion, but can and must also be thought in the
logical form of truth. This comprehensive truth corresponds to the
comprehensiveness and eternal actuality of the Absolute in *all* its
opposite manifestations. In philosophy thought becomes absolutely
free in and for itself.[14]

It is just this subordination of Christianity to philosophy, this loss of
transcendence involved in the logical rendition of Christian thought,
that warns Kierkegaard against following the path of reason and science
to God.

And now what about Christianity, how has it been dealt with? I
entirely agree with your disapproval of the way in which every
Christian concept has been so sublimated, so completely volatilised
into a sea of fog that it is impossible to recognize it again. To such
concepts as faith, incarnation, tradition, inspiration, which in Christianity must be referred to a particular historical fact, it has seemed
good to philosophers to give an entirely different general meaning
whereby faith becomes immediate certainty, which at bottom is
neither more nor less than the vital fluid of the life of the mind, its
atmosphere; tradition has become the summary of a certain world
experience; whilst inspiration has become nothing but the result of
God having breathed the spirit of life into man, and incarnation

nothing else than the existence of one or other ideas in one or more individuals—and still I have not mentioned the idea which has not only been reduced to nothing but even profaned, the idea of salvation, an idea which journalism in particular has taken up with a certain prejudice in its favor, and applies to everyone, utterly regardless whether the man is the greatest hero of liberty or a baker or butcher who save their district by selling their wares a shilling cheaper than the others.[15]

Science, then, does not chart a course to God; and the path of being is no better. Indeed, the way philosophers treat of being actually constitutes a *barrier* on the path to God. And the reason is quite simple: philosophers always handle being through the *concept* of existence and existence can never be properly conceptualized. A concept rests on *similarities* in the objects that are conceptualized, whereas it is the function of existence to *separate* one thing off from another; a concept presents the mind with a *possibility*, whereas existence gives the *actual*.

What confuses the whole doctrine about "being" in logic is that people do not notice that they are always operating with the "concept" existence. But the *concept* existence is an ideality and the difficulty is, of course, whether existence can be reduced to a concept. . . . existence corresponds to the individual thing, the individual, which even Aristotle teaches lies outside, or at least cannot be reduced to a concept. For an individual animal, plant, or man, existence (to be —or not to be) is of quite decisive importance; an individual man has not after all a conceptual existence.[16]

The immediate consequence of this, as far as the present discussion is concerned, is that we cannot prove that God exists by analysing being. Let us once more hear Søren Kierkegaard:

And how does God's existence emerge from the proof? Does it follow straightway, without any breach of continuity? Or have we not here an analogy to the behavior of those toys, the little Cartesian dolls? As soon as I let go of the doll it stands on its head. As soon as I let go—I must therefore let it go. So also with the proof of God's existence. As long as I keep my hold on the proof, i.e. continue to demonstrate, the existence does not come out, if for no other reason than that I am engaged in proving it; but when I let the proof go, the existence is there. But this act of letting go is surely also something; it is, indeed, a contribution of mine. Must not this also be taken into account, this little moment, brief as it may be—it need not be long for it is a *leap*.[17]

If we are going to prove anything about God, whether it be His existence or some attribute, we first have to discover some point of likeness from which to argue. God, however, is precisely the Unknown, the Unlike. To be convinced of His existence, then, we must approach Him through *unlikeness*, rather than through likeness; the approach cannot be through *being*, it has to be through *sin*. For it is by sin that man is totally *unlike* God! In his *Philosophical Fragments* Kierkegaard presents this case as follows:

> Reason, in attempting to determine the Unknown as the unlike, at last goes astray, and confounds the unlike with the like. From this there would seem to follow the further consequence, that if man is to receive any true knowledge about the Unknown (God) he must be made to know that it is unlike him, absolutely unlike him. This knowledge the Reason cannot possibly obtain of itself; we have already seen that this would be a self-contradiction. It will therefore have to obtain this knowledge from God. But even if it obtains such knowledge it cannot understand it, and thus is quite unable to possess such knowledge. For how should the Reason be able to understand what is absolutely different from itself? If this is not immediately evident, it will become clearer in the light of the consequences; for if God is absolutely unlike man, then man is absolutely unlike God; but how could the Reason be expected to understand this? Here we seem to be confronted with a paradox. Merely to obtain the knowledge that God is unlike him, man needs the help of God, and now he learns that God is absolutely different from himself. But if God and man are absolutely different, this cannot be accounted for on the basis of what man derives from God, for insofar they are akin. Their unlikeness must therefore be explained by what man derives from himself, or by what he has brought upon his own head—it is Error or Sin.[18]

Here at last in sin the Christian is certain that God is outside concept, likeness and being. In the medium of abstraction, God does not exist; God only exists for an existing man. And a man only truly exists when he stands outside God, sure of his otherness, but confronting God and persisting in his otherness through faith in God. Faith holds the cleavage of existence together. When an existing individual does not have faith, God *is* not nor does He *exist*—although from the eternal point of view God *is* eternally.

The roots of Kierkegaard's objections to rational proofs for God's existence are to be found in philosophical ideas quite alien to the concepts St. Thomas used to approach God. For Kierkegaard speculates in his own way within the general framework already established by Kant.

According to Aquinas, on the contrary, a concept is not a totality but, rather, a distinct and limited way of being—as known. And being is not a total concept implying, at one extreme, nothing, and at the other, the All; indeed, being is not fundamentally a concept at all—although the philosopher does *try* to fashion a concept of being. Being is any existent; above all it is the act of being that makes an existent to be. Being does not signify the possible; it points to the act of existing, and that is most actual in anything. And, as we shall see in a moment, when St. Thomas explores the path of being as an approach to God, he does not follow the way of univocal likeness—as though by tracing the likenesses of things one suddenly came upon the *Same* that explained all similarity. St. Thomas looks to *unlikeness*—not the unlikeness of sin but, rather, of existing! St. Thomas was as convinced as Kierkegaard was that no human concept, no characteristic of man, could ever adequately represent God. The path of being explored by St. Thomas is the way of analogical or proportionate likeness. And at the end of the path he does not discover an ultimate likeness or the Like; he comes upon the *existence* of the Unlike—not by faith (although most men *do* have to find God in that way), not by a leap or sin (although many men actually *do* come to God by experiencing their own guilt) but, rather, by reason. Not that it is the only way, but it is the approach taken by the metaphysician.

In his own day St. Thomas was surrounded by thinkers who tried to prove God's existence in one way or another—some of his contemporaries, indeed, argued that one *cannot* or *need not* demonstrate that God exists. For, as one argument would have it, anything naturally present to us is self-evident and does not require demonstration. Now according to St. John Damascene knowledge of God is implanted in man by nature. His existence, then, is self-evident. Another argument contended that anything is self-evident when, as soon as the meaning of the terms expressing it become clear, it becomes known. Thus, as soon as the meaning of "whole" and "part" are known, it is at once clear that the whole is greater than the part. Now everyone knows what the term "God" means; God's existence is clearly known, then, because His existence is implied in the very term "God."

Other contemporaries of St. Thomas gave a variety of reasons in defense of their position that God's existence *cannot* be demonstrated. First, God's existence is an article of faith and, inasmuch as faith is precisely an acceptance of things not seen, it is quite impossible to prove or demonstrate anything accepted by faith. Second, according to an argument that seems to be a harbinger of Kierkegaard's reasoning, a person demonstrates when he constructs a syllogism or series of syllogisms in which the middle term is a definition or essence. But we cannot grasp God's essence, and it is impossible to define Him. Consequently, there can be no middle term and, hence, no demonstration. Third, if we could prove that God exists, it would have to be through His effects. But no effect produced by God is proportioned to Him. No effect can, therefore, lead us to grant His existence.

Still others produced arguments that have a remarkably modern ring about them to prove that one can demonstrate that God does *not* exist. The first argument bears on the problem of evil and runs as follows: if one of two contraries be infinite, the other would be altogether destroyed. Now the name "God" signifies absolute goodness; its opposite would be evil. If God existed, then absolute goodness would exist, and one should not be able to find the slightest trace of evil. But evil *does* exist in the world; its infinite contrary, then, absolute goodness or God, does *not* exist.

A second argument centers on the desirability of simplicity in explaining things. It is superfluous, the argument contends, to suppose that anything for which a few principles can account has been produced by many principles. Now it appears that everything we behold in the world around us can be accounted for by a few other principles without supposing that God exists. For all natural things can be reduced to a single principle, nature; all voluntary things can be explained by one principle, too, human reason or will. Consequently, nature or matter and reason would seem to account for everything sufficiently well. In the interest of simplicity, then, we should say that God's existence is superfluous.

Of these three alternatives—the existence of God is self-evident and *needs* no demonstration, His existence *cannot* be demonstrated, it can be shown that God does *not* exist—the first would seem most tempting to a Christian theologian. St. Thomas, however, rejected all three and vigorously defended a fourth possibility: God's existence *can* and, indeed, *must* be demonstrated. The argument from self-evidence drew a quick rebuttal from St. Thomas. No one can mentally admit the opposite of anything self-evident, but men actually *do* deny that God exists. How, then, can a person claim that it is self-evident? Moreover, arguing that the whole is greater than the part presupposes that one knows what the subject, i.e. *whole*, is. But that is the very thing that eludes our grasp in the proposition *God exists;* we do *not* know what God is.

In part, the above opinion arises from the custom by which from their earliest days people are brought up to hear and to call upon the name of God. Custom, and especially custom in a child, comes to have the force of nature. As a result, what the mind is steeped in from childhood it clings to very firmly, as something known naturally and self-evidently.

In part, however, the above opinion comes about because of a failure to distinguish between that which is self-evident in an absolute sense and that which is self-evident in relation to us, for assuredly that God exists is, absolutely speaking, self-evident, since what God is is His own being. Yet, because we are not able to conceive in our minds that which God is, that God exists remains unknown in relation to us. So, too, that every whole is greater than its part is, absolutely speaking, self-evident; but it would perforce be unknown to one who could not conceive the nature of a whole. Hence it comes about, as it is said in *Metaphysics* II, that "our intellect is related to the most knowable thing in reality as the eye of an owl is related to the sun.[19]

We can only naturally know God's effects. So why not start with His effects as they are found in sensible things and proceed to God by demonstration—not using His essence or definition as middle term but, rather, the effects of His activity? For even though those effects are not proportionate to God or adequate to the task of giving us knowledge of God's nature, they are enough to give *some* knowledge of their cause, i.e. *that* their cause *exists*.

From effects not proportioned to the cause no perfect knowledge of that cause can be obtained. Yet from every effect the *existence* of the cause can be clearly demonstrated, and so we can demonstrate the existence of God from His effects; though from them we cannot know God perfectly as He is in His essence.[20]

A variety of factors impelled St. Thomas to make this effort. As a *Christian* and a *man of faith* he knew that he, along with all other men, was destined for saintliness; he knew that his happiness and highest perfection would come in seeing God, that his freedom would find its readiest exercise in loving God, that all the artistic effort expended on fashioning human societies and complex civil communities was ultimately intended to develop man's natural capacities to share in the divine being. What more natural question, for a man convinced of the integrity of human nature and reason even in the presence of sin, than this one: What can reason tell me of the God I am seeking? He was encouraged to find an answer by St. Paul's words to the Romans:

For the invisible things of him, from the creation of the world, are clearly seen, being understood by the things that are made. . . .[21]

As a *theologian* making use of Aristotle's logic, St. Thomas was aware that any scientist has to be sure of the *existence* of his subject before he undertakes to understand it. Thus the natural philosopher supposes there is motion and nature; since these are the subjects he studies and the sources of the principles he uses, he cannot demonstrate that motion and nature exist. The theologian finds himself in a similar situation when he confronts God. As a *scientist* St. Thomas knew, both from the art of demonstration and the order of the sciences, that a demonstration was possible and desirable; the art of demonstration told him that one could arrive at conclusions about causes from their effects, and the order of the sciences assured him that there would be no science above natural science unless there were some knowable substance above sensible substances. As a *historian* he knew that in the past philosophers *had* tried to demonstrate God's existing. And finally, as a *philosopher* he knew that it was his responsibility to plumb being to its depths so as to answer the question: Why is there something rather than nothing? Thus challenged and encouraged, he set forth.

If we review the analysis of being we have made under St. Thomas' direction, we shall see that God is present at every step of the way. Finite things are beings because they have an act of their own, their act of existing. And precisely because they are finite and exist in this or that way, they have to *receive* their act of existing. All finite things are caused in their very being by a primary cause of being; God is ever-present to them as their *efficient* cause. And inasmuch as they continue to exist, God always *remains* there as the cause of their being. In a startling phrase St. Thomas says that God continues to be present to things by His very substance.

> God is said to be in all things by essence, not indeed by the essence of things themselves, as if He were of their essence, but by His own essence, because His substance is present in all things as the cause of their being.[22]

He does not mean that things as beings are parts of God nor that He is a part of things. It means, rather, that He is present to them substantially as their cause, while still not constituting a part of them. The proper way to designate God's being, according to St. Thomas, is to say that He is a subsistent act of being. Consequently, when God is present to things as *beings*, it is as the cause of the existing that makes them beings. His very being causes things to be; His being is not finite and created, whereas the being of things *is* finite and created. So while their being is not His being, He is substantially present to them as the being that causes their being.

Now for God to cause the being of things means, as we have seen, that each being *exists*, subsists by its *own* act, and constitutes a real centre of causality *in its own right;* a being does not exist or produce some effect *merely* in virtue of God's causality. Every finite being produces *some* effects in the things that surround it, and many of them exercise their causality in producing themselves after a fashion—as the act of living exercises itself upon materials the living thing needs to build up its own body. It builds *itself;* it is not merely the passive recipient of the activity of other things. Thus, by exercising a real causality each being bears a true resemblance to God as efficient cause. It is a likeness, however, that is marked by a fundamental unlikeness. Infinite and finite causality differ mainly in this: God, as Being, causes being simply—He can produce from non-being; finite beings, on the contrary, need the wherewithal upon which to exercise their causality —they cannot produce from non-being and can only act in such wise that what is begins to exist in this or that new way.

> . . . every agent acts forasmuch as it is in act: wherefore action must needs be attributed to an agent according to the measure of its actuality. Now a particular thing is actual in a particular manner, and this in two ways. First by comparison with itself, because its substance is not wholly act, since such things are composed of matter and form: for which reason a natural thing acts not in respect of its totality, but in respect of its form whereby it is in act. Secondly, in comparison with things that are in act: because no natural thing comprises the acts and perfections of all the things that are in act: but each one has an act confined to one genus and one species, so that none has an activity extending to being as such, but only to this or that being as such, and confined to this or that species: for an agent produces its like. Wherefore a natural agent produces a being not simply, but determines a pre-existent being to this or that species, of fire, for example, or of whiteness and so forth. Wherefore the natural agent acts by moving something, and consequently requires matter as a subject of change or movement, and thus it cannot make a thing out of nothing.[23]

Finite things, then, act as causes in *their* order of being in a way similar to God's acting as cause in *His* way of being. So things imitate God as causes: He is present to them as a kind of model of causality. He is their exemplar not as form, but as being and efficient cause—not, in-

deed, that all finite things knowingly and intentionally pattern themselves on God. They do so, rather, in their being. And if it should be
that their being is a *knowing* being—as, indeed, it is in the case of
human being—then it can be said that when a man acts as a knowing
and willing being he is consciously and deliberately acting in his own
order as God does in His. Indeed, St. Thomas expresses the central
theme of his whole moral doctrine in these very terms.

> Since, as Damascene states (*De Fide Orthod.* ii), man is said to be
> made to God's image, insofar as the image implies *an intelligent*
> *being endowed with free-will and self-movement:* now that we
> have treated of the exemplar, i.e. God, and of those things which
> come forth from the power of God in accordance with His will; it
> remains for us to treat of His image, i.e. man, inasmuch as he too
> is the principle of his actions, as having free-will and control of his
> actions.[24]

Therefore, God is present to each man, as He is to everything else,
as exemplar.

Finally, all finite things naturally incline to what is good for them;
in causing things to be and to act for an end suited to their natures,
God created in them a natural appetite for Himself. As St. Thomas puts
it, all things by their natures implicitly desire and seek God.

> All things naturally tend to God implicitly, but not explicitly. That
> this may appear clearly it should be observed that a secondary cause
> can influence its effect only insofar as it receives the power of the
> first cause. The influence of an efficient cause is to act; that of a
> final cause is to be sought or desired. A secondary agent acts only
> by the efficacy of the first agent existing in it; similarly a secondary
> end is sought only by reason of the worth of the principal end ex-
> isting in it inasmuch as it is subordinated to the principal end or
> has its likeness.
>
> Accordingly, because God is the last end, He is sought in every
> end, just as, because He is the first efficient cause, He acts in every
> agent. But this is what tending to God implicitly means. For the
> efficacy of the first cause is in the second as the principles of rea-
> soning are in the conclusions. But to reduce conclusions to their
> principles or secondary causes to their first causes belongs only to
> the power of reasoning. Hence only a rational nature can trace
> secondary ends back to God by a sort of analytic procedure so as
> to seek God Himself explicitly. In demonstrative sciences a conclu-
> sion is correctly drawn only by a reduction to first principles. In the
> same way the appetite of a rational creature is correctly directed

only by an explicit appetitive tendency to God, either actual or habitual.[25]

Only man, because he is a rational being, can explicitly harmonize his ends with God as the end of his activities. The good of man, his completeness and happiness as man, will be found in freely seeking God. In so doing he attains moral rectitude or the ordered activity of a free being. So either implicitly or explicitly God is present to all finite beings as the *final* cause of their being. Throughout St. Thomas' philosophical analysis of finite things as beings, therefore, God is present either as efficient, exemplary, or final cause. The world of things as *beings* proclaims the *being* of God. He is the principle of their being.

Consequently, when St. Thomas approaches the task of proving God's existence, he has but to turn to the evidence revealed by his philosophical understanding of the being of things and arrange that evidence in the form of demonstrations. For such demonstrations were the accepted way of formulating evidence in his day. The need to do so was imposed on him by the structural demands of philosophy itself. For in addition to being a *Christian* theologian, St. Thomas was also a theologian in the sense that Aristotle was a theologian (i.e. a man doing the highest work of philosophy).

> If, then, there is something in what the poets say, and jealousy is natural to the divine power, it would probably occur in this case above all, and all who excelled in this knowledge would be unfortunate. But the divine power cannot be jealous (nay, according to the proverb, "bards tell many a lie"), nor should any other science be thought more honourable than one of this sort. For the most divine science is also most honourable; and this science alone must be, in two ways, most divine. For the science which it would be most meet for God to have is a divine science, and so any science that deals with divine objects; and this science alone has both these qualities; for (1) God is thought to be among the causes of all things and to be a first principle, and (2) such a science either God alone can have, or God above all others. All the sciences, indeed, are more necessary than this, but none is better.[26]

As such he was concerned with understanding his Christian faith insofar as that is possible to man using his own native powers. Now one of the methods developed for doing that consisted in bringing the instruments of science (as the men of the Middle Ages understood "science") to bear on the content of faith—in other words, in formulating conclusions rationally drawn from revealed premises. That is the task of a Christian theologian, in this sense of the term "theology." But theology, like any other science, first has to try to find convincing reasons *that* its subject exists before it tries to discover what it can about the *nature* of its subject. St. Thomas, then, was faced with the task of proving the existence of God as the subject of theology. Now how did he do it?

Well, first let us see something of the structure of his proofs. As we saw in an earlier chapter, proof or demonstration is intended to result in a conclusion or statement that a person can accept with certainty and conviction. Now, according to St. Thomas, some proofs convince us *why* the conclusion is true, while others show us *that* it is so.

> Demonstrations can be made in two ways: One is through the cause, and is called *propter quid,* and this is to argue from what is prior absolutely. The other is through the effect, and is called a demonstration *quia;* this to argue from what is prior relatively only to us. When an effect is better known to us than its cause, from the effect we proceed to the knowledge of the cause. And from every effect the existence of its proper cause can be demonstrated, so long as its effects are better known to us; because, since every effect depends upon its cause, if the effect exists, the cause must pre-exist. Hence the existence of God, in so far as it is not self-evident to us, can be demonstrated from those of His effects which are known to us.[27]

He gives many examples of what he has in mind. Here is one: without applying any of the principles of geometry, a person might be sure that light is reflected by a mirror so that a definite relation obtains between the line with which the light strikes the mirror and the line along which it is reflected. He would know *that* this is so. If, however, he were to study the lines simply as lines and not as lines of light, he would be able to apply the principles of geometry and know *why* the lines were related as they were. So St. Thomas, following Aristotle, distinguishes between a proof resulting in the knowledge *on account of which* something is so and a proof concluding *that* something is so. The main reason these two differ is that the former uses a *cause* to prove its conclusion (the geometrician uses the definition of line to prove his conclusions about lines), whereas the latter uses *effects* to reach its conclusions. In this latter kind of proof, then, a person starts with effects and reaches a conclusion *that* something is so about those effects; one does not use the cause because he does not know the nature of the cause. And if he should come to a conclusion about the cause in virtue of its effects, it will never be a conclusion about the *nature* of the cause, but only that the effect indicates *that* there is a cause. Now the demonstrations St.

Thomas formulates to establish God's existence are of this kind: they result in the conclusion *that* God exists; they do not yield a conclusion about *what* He is.

St. Thomas' demonstrations, then, in each case begin with some effect. As we have just noted, demonstrations *that* something is so always begin with what is better known to us—usually a thing of which we are sensibly certain—and result in a conclusion about what is not so well known to us—even though in itself it may be knowable in the highest degree. Obviously St. Thomas could not demonstrate that God exists by using His nature or a definition of God as a means of demonstration because that would assume the very point in question, i.e. that God does exist and that we know His nature. And these assumptions have not yet been established. So St. Thomas starts with effects. He is prompt to point out, however, that there is a very great difference between effects such as one experiences, for example, in seeing light and feeling heat caused by the sun and the effects one examines to discover God.

> Univocal predication is impossible between God and creatures. The reason of this is that every effect which is not a proportioned result of the power of the efficient cause receives the similitude of the agent not in its full degree, but in a measure that falls short; so that what is divided and multiplied in the effects resides in the agent simply, and in an unvaried manner. For example, the sun by the exercise of its one power produces manifold and various forms in these sublunary things. In the same way, as was said above, all perfections existing in creatures divided and multiplied pre-exist in God unitedly. Hence, when any name expressing perfection is applied to a creature, it signifies that perfection as distinct from the others according to the nature of its definition; as, for instance, by this term "wise" applied to a man, we signify some perfection distinct from a man's essence, and distinct from his power and his being, and from all similar things. But when we apply *wise* to God, we do not mean to signify anything distinct from His essence or power or being. And thus when this term *wise* is applied to man, in some degree it circumscribes and comprehends the thing signified; whereas this is not the case when it is applied to God, but it leaves the thing signified as uncomprehended and as exceeding the signification of the name. Hence it is evident that this term *wise* is not applied in the same way to God and to man. The same applies to other terms. Hence, no name is predicated univocally of God and of creatures.[28]

In the case of creatures, then, there is an adequate proportion between effect and cause, or there may be such a proportion, in that both are finite; in the case of God that kind of proportion does not exist because He is infinite and His effects are finite. This discrepancy must be borne in mind in evaluating any conclusions that are drawn from effects. Indeed, it is one of Kierkegaard's main objections to all proofs. St. Thomas and Kierkegaard are agreed, then, in rejecting the possibility of approaching God through univocal likeness.

St. Thomas' proofs are usually structured in the following way: first, a statement about the effects that are to be examined, for example, that the senses do in fact present us with moving things; second, an analysis of those effects designed to point out their need of a cause; third, the conclusion that a *first* cause is required; fourth, a nominal definition that it is this primary cause that we call "God"; finally, the conclusion that God exists.

> When the existence of a cause is demonstrated from an effect, the effect takes the place of the definition of the cause in proving the cause's existence. This is especially the case in regard to God because, in order to prove the existence of anything, it is necessary to accept as a middle term the meaning of the name, and not its essence, for the question of its essence follows on the question of its existence. Now the names given to God are derived from His effects, as will be shown later. Consequently, in demonstrating the existence of God from His effects, we may take for the middle term the meaning of the name *God*.[29]

The number of proofs given by St. Thomas varies in his different works. He is most often identified with the Five Ways given at the beginning of his major theological work, the *Summa Theologiae*. Each starts with a different effect found to exist in things: motion, an order between cause and effect, necessity in the being of things, a gradation of more or less in things, and inclination to an end. In the *Summa Contra Gentiles*, a work that he wrote on the Christian faith for discussion with men trained in Arabic thought, he gives four proofs: a proof from motion, one from efficient cause, one from the more or less true, and a fourth from the order in nature. And in his *Compendium Theologiae* St. Thomas gives one proof, the proof from motion.

Now without examining each of these proofs in detail, several general comments are in order. First, they are *metaphysical* proofs. This means that they are about being and consist primarily in the analysis of being. Indeed, that is the reason we found God haunting our every step in our effort to understand St. Thomas' doctrine of being. St. Thomas' proofs do *not* start with thought, idea, nature, definition, phenomena given in sensible intuition, or moral experience. Their principle or starting-point is some way in which things exist. Second, since they do consist in an analysis of being, they are *not* basically concerned with developing a series of intermediaries between the effect observed and the first cause. St. Thomas' investigation of being has shown that finite things *do* cause being in this or that way, and that kind of causality could be traced back through a long line of intermediaries. But the primary question concerns being *simply:* why does any motion *at all* exist? Since no finite being can cause being *simply*, but only this or that way of being, then if things do exist it must be because a non-finite being exists capable of causing being simply. Thus, for example, if motion *does* exist, it can only be because there is a being to cause the very *being* of motion and not merely moving in this or that way. A merely moving cause gives way to a cause of being as such. Third, the real thrust of St. Thomas' metaphysical proofs should not be missed because of historical incidentals. For example, it is historically true that St. Thomas has used proofs already formulated by Aristotle, Moses Maimonides, Avicenna and John Damascene. But the proofs take their unique meaning from St. Thomas' own understanding of being. The basic philosophical principles that St. Thomas' predecessors used to construct their proofs have been re-worked to bear the burden St. Thomas finds it necessary to impose on them. It is also historically true that St. Thomas has used illustrations in his proofs, and they are drawn from a medieval science that we no longer consider valid. But his proofs are not physical proofs, they are metaphysical. Whether fire is an element or the lower heavens are moved by the higher is not the vital issue; what *is* vital is that finite existing things require a cause of their existing.

Now what do the proofs establish about that cause? Well, any proof beginning with effects is limited, as we have shown, to providing a knowledge *that* something is so. So these proofs only tell us *that* God exists. St. Thomas insists that even the lack of proportion between God and His effects does not stand in the way of the proofs reaching that conclusion.

> From effects not proportioned to the cause no perfect knowledge of that cause can be obtained. Yet from every effect the existence of the cause can be clearly demonstrated, and so we can demonstrate the existence of God from His effects; though from these we cannot know God perfectly as He is in His essence.[30]

There is no proportion in the sense that cause and effect are of the same nature; St. Thomas' proof, however, is not based on nature or essence but, rather, on the act of existing that needs a cause. It does not require that there be some degree of identity between God's existence and the existence of His effects. That, too, would be a proof from cause rather than from effect. His proofs only require that there be a proportion between God and His act of being, and things and their act of existing. The fact that things *do* exist suffices to convince St. Thomas that such a proportion does in fact exist.

> Neither, on the other hand, are names applied to God and creatures in a purely equivocal sense, as some have said. Because if that were so, it follows that from creatures nothing at all could be known or demonstrated about God; for the reasoning would always be exposed to the fallacy of equivocation. Such a view is against the Philosopher, who proves many things about God, and also against what the Apostle says: *The invisible things of God are clearly seen being understood by the things that are made* . . . (*Rom.* i, 20). Therefore it must be said that these names are said of God and creatures in an *analogous* sense, that is, according to proportion.[31]

In saying that we have a knowledge of God's existence, St. Thomas is careful to point out that we do *not* thereby gain an insight into His nature. If God is His existence, knowing His existence would seem to suggest that we come to know His essence. But according to St. Thomas this is not so. A proof *that* something is so does not suddenly change character and provide us with a knowledge *why* it is so. We do not know God's essence, we merely know that there is a God. Or, as St. Thomas puts it with even greater precision, we know that the proposition "God is" is true.

> *To be* can mean either of two things. It may mean the act of being, or it may mean the composition of a proposition effected by the mind in joining a predicate to a subject. Taking *to be* in the first sense, we cannot understand God's being (or His essence); but only in the second sense. We know that this proposition which we form about God when we say *God is,* is true.[32]

And we know this from His effects.

Yet we do say "God is good," and "God is wise." Does this suggest that we do act as though we *did* know *what* God is? Not at all. Knowing that God is their cause, we very often assign names to God in virtue of our experiencing His creatures. Sometimes the names are only used metaphorically, as when we say: "God smiled on us;" for we do not intend to attribute to the divine nature any of the physical characteristics we find in our experience of a friend's smile. But when we say "God is good," we do attribute something to Him as belonging to His nature. We do so, however, without knowing what goodness is *in God*. To speak of God as good is to speak of Him insofar as our intellects can know Him from His creatures. It is to know goodness as it is found in things, to have a finite intellect's understanding of what goodness is, and to realize at the same time that a finite thing cannot be of the same species as God. In saying "God is good," we do mean that He is good, but not with the goodness whereby we understand that a finite thing is good; God is good as an excelling source of goodness. The word "good" does signify the divine nature but imperfectly and without our knowing what goodness is in God. As St. Thomas puts it:

> According to the preceding article, our knowledge of God is derived from the perfections which flow from Him to creatures; which perfections are in God in a more eminent way than in creatures. Now our intellect apprehends them as they are in creatures, and as it apprehends them thus does it signify them by names. Therefore, as to the names applied to God, there are two things to be considered —viz. the perfections themselves which they signify, such as goodness, life, and the like, and their mode of signification. As regards what is signified by these names, they belong properly to God, and more properly than they belong to creatures, and are applied primarily to Him. But as regards their mode of signification, they do not properly and strictly apply to God; for their mode of signification befits creatures.[33]

In short: what the term signifies *does* belong to God; it does *not* belong to Him in the *way* it signifies.

In virtue of the lack of proportion between God and His effects, no term has the same meaning when applied to God and any finite thing; nor is it totally different. For St. Thomas realized as well as Kierkegaard that it would then be impossible to argue from God's effects. But there is some proportion, according to St. Thomas. When we speak of God as good or wise, we speak of Him by analogy, or by recognizing a proportion between what goodness is in creatures and what it is in God.

> Therefore it must be said that these names are said of God and creatures in an *analogous* sense, that is, according to proportion.
>
> This can happen in two ways: either according as many things are proportioned to one (thus, for example, *healthy* is predicated of medicine and urine in relation and in proportion to health of body; of which the latter is the sign and the former the cause), or accord-

ing as one thing is proportioned to another (thus, *healthy* is said of medicine and an animal, since medicine is the cause of health in the animal body). And in this way some things are said of God and creatures analogically, and not in a purely equivocal nor in a purely univocal sense. For we can name God only from creatures. Hence, whatever is said of God and creatures is said according as there is some relation of the creature to God as to its principle and cause, wherein all the perfections of things pre-exist excellently. Now this mode of community is a means between pure equivocation and simple univocation. For in analogies what is said is not, as it is in univocals, one and the same; yet it is not totally diverse as in equivocals; but the name which is thus used in a multiple sense signifies various proportions to some one thing: *e.g. healthy*, applied to urine signifies the sign of animal health; but applied to medicine, it signifies the cause of the same health.[34]

Proceeding in this way, St. Thomas tells us that the most proper name we can use of God is "Being;" and in order to stress the primacy of that term and the fact that it signifies something of God that surpasses all essence and everything that we can know, St. Thomas says that we should speak of God as a "Subsistent Act of Being".

> . . . from what has been already proved, God is being itself, of itself subsistent. Consequently, He must contain within Himself the whole perfection of being. For it is clear that if some hot thing has not the whole perfection of heat, this is because heat is not participated in its full perfection; but if this heat were self-subsisting, nothing of the virtue of heat would be wanting to it. Since therefore God is subsisting being itself, nothing of the perfection of being can be wanting to Him. Now all the perfections of all things pertain to the perfection of being; for things are perfect precisely so far as they have being after some fashion. It follows therefore that the perfection of no thing is wanting to God.[35]

Now we have no way of coming to know the nature of that act; the best we can do is remove everything we do know of finite acts of existing. But even then we can only say that we realize that God *is* and that He is *not* as trees, stones, animals, and men *are*. We must, then, remove from our knowledge of God everything that we learn from things; in the final analysis we have to use the *negative way*, the way of removal, in speaking of God.

Now, in considering the divine substance, we should especially make use of the method of remotion. For, by its immensity, the divine substance surpasses every form that our intellect reaches. Thus we are unable to apprehend it by knowing *what it is*. Yet we are able to have some knowledge of it by knowing *what it is not*. Furthermore, we approach nearer to a knowledge of God according as through our intellect we are able to remove more and more things from Him. For we know each thing more perfectly the more fully we see its differences from other things; for each thing has within itself its own being, distinct from all other things. So, too, in the case of the things whose definitions we know. We locate them in a genus, through which we know in a general way what they are. Then we add differences to each thing, by which it may be distinguished from other things. In this way, a complete knowledge of a substance is built up.

However, in the consideration of the divine substance we cannot take a *what* as a genus; nor can we derive the distinction of God from things by differences affirmed of God. For this reason, we must derive the distinction of God from other beings by means of negative differences. And just as among affirmative differences one contracts the other, so one negative difference is contracted by another that makes it to differ from many beings. For example, if we say that God is not an accident, we thereby distinguish Him from all accidents. Then, if we add that He is not a body, we shall further distinguish Him from certain substances. And thus, proceeding in order, by such negations God will be distinguished from all that He is not. Finally, there will then be a proper consideration of God's substance when He will be known as distinct from all things. Yet, this knowledge will not be perfect, since it will not tell us what God is in Himself.[36]

Knowledge of *what* God is in Himself and *how* He exists in Himself can only come from Revelation. Philosophy can bring us to the confines of faith; it can arouse in our intellects a desire to know God in a more perfect way. But it can never take us across the chasm.

Now does that limited and imperfect philosophical knowledge of God stand as a threat to human freedom, as Sartre has charged? Sartre and Kierkegaard share two basic fears: first, reason must make man an object of thought rather than a subject who can choose. If that is so, man will not only lose all individuality in becoming one of the mass, but he will have to act as an object acts: logically and in a way determined by certain purely rational rules. Second, God will become an Absolute conceived as presiding over the whole world of objects, an Absolute engaged in the game of manipulating his puppets. Now none of this is true in St. Thomas' view. We have seen that the human intellect does have to abstract, but only so that it can judge and know;

what is real exists, and intellect and reason serve only as a tool man needs to know things as they exist. Being is *neither* an abstraction *nor* an absolute idea; and man is not an object nor a concrete instance of a logical idea. Reason does abstract, and that is precisely why we *cannot* stop with reason if we are to know things, men and God. And for the very reason that men and things are beings and have existence, they have and retain their uniqueness. A man is a being, and one of the mass only by abstraction; he is not an object but a person, i.e. a unique, existing reality. True, he does act logically, especially when he is in search of knowledge. But he engages in that search because he wants to do so, not because any logical determination of his nature makes him do it. How, indeed, could Sartre's man gain any speculative knowledge without doing the same? Existing as he does, freely and intelligently, a man does *not* lose his freedom because he has a nature. It is his nature to be free, to choose, to make himself more fully a man.

Nor does God threaten man's freedom. God is not an Absolute; He is Being. Now because He is Being, He can be known in some way by man (who is also a being) through the things He has made (they, too, being beings); but precisely as Being, He can never be fully or adequately known by a human intellect. Philosophy is not a threat to Revelation and does not pretend to invade the divine transcendence. Similarly, when God creates things, He does so freely; His creative act is not a logical emanation imposed upon Him. When He created man like Himself, it was by making man a free being, capable of acting freely. God *did* give man a nature. He made him a physical, sensing being, and He gave him a reason; but it was not to destroy his freedom. Indeed, the only freedom that an *animal* body could destroy would be the freedom of a pure intelligence. But *our* freedom is a *human* freedom, the freedom of an *incarnate* intelligence, a freedom of choice. God gave man a nature so that he could exist and be free, and, being free, make himself the kind of man he deems best. But whatever he makes of himself, God will always be present as the cause of his being free. St. Thomas' Christian philosophy does, therefore, lead a person's mind to God; but to a God who does *not* threaten freedom or destroy man's true humanity. Indeed, his philosophy provides the most fundamental kind of philosophical under-pinning for man and his freedom. And that was its purpose.

In philosophizing, then, St. Thomas was in search of the most profound understanding of reality that human powers could provide. He was certain from Revelation that the world had a beginning in time, that man had fallen from God's favor by sin, that God had redeemed him through the Incarnation of His Son, that a Trinity of Divine Persons is constantly present to him in every act he performs. These truths and many more were freely given to St. Thomas by his Christian faith; they were not mere statements, but personal convictions resulting from his own experience of God's taking possession of him through His grace. They were in no sense philosophical conclusions. Most men would have been content to pattern their lives on such experiences; many did, indeed, strive to re-live them at every moment. But St. Thomas felt himself called to a life of contemplation and teaching; he was convinced that dedication to the life of reason compelled him to elaborate his Christian experiences in rational terms. His own re-living of Christian faith would take the form of continuing rational speculation. But the formulation of divine science in theological concepts requires a disciplined reason; a Christian need not be a theologian, but if he feels that he has to be one, he must prepare himself for his work.

That preparation may take the form of learning the languages of the Scriptures, the history of the peoples involved in the biblical stories, or the physical settings of the Bible left to us in archaeological remains. In virtue of the Christian experience that preceded him, St. Thomas was persuaded that God had taught us about Himself in the things He had made; knowledge of the things of nature would provide precious clues to the theologian. So St. Thomas set about preparing himself in that way. But as he proceeded with his scientific studies, he found himself compelled to pose a whole host of questions to the things he found round about him in the world of nature. What are things? Where did they come from? What is man? Is he capable of doing right or wrong? Where did he come from? Where is he going? Is there a single cause of everything that exists? What is it like? Questions of that sort are not strange to modern eyes. We may not be prompted to ask them by Christian faith, but many of us are urged to do so by contemporary physics, psychology, anthropology and sociology. Modern man is still wondering whether or not he is free; he still asks: is God dead? So philosophy still has a job to do whether the philosophical questions originate in Christian curiosity, as they did for St. Thomas, or in scientific perplexity, as they did for Jean-Paul Sartre.

St. Thomas turned to the philosophers for enlightenment, readied himself with philosophical discipline and knowledge, and became progressively more dissatisfied with the answers he received from reality seen through the concepts of his predecessors. Some of them claimed that things were but so many modifications of matter, the particles constituting them entering into many and varied mixtures; others insisted that they were participations in ideas or forms immersed in matter. Making things parts of a vast natural system or shifting products of impersonal, universal forces did not seem to take things seriously precisely as individual things; indeed, atoms, ideas and forms seemed much more real than things. And the explanations of their origin seemed more relative than absolute. That was not enough for St. Thomas. He was convinced that if he were to understand things in their profoundest reality, it had to be by considering the *thing* as most real; the question of origin must be answered in the most radical way possible. St. Thomas found his answer in understanding things as beings, each with its own act of existing; he found their origin to be most radical because he discovered that there is no reason within the nature of such things that they exist.

The same search led St. Thomas to a new interpretation of man. Once again he turned to Plato, Aristotle, Avicenna and Averroes to discover what man is. He found once again a great many inadequacies in the accounts these eminent philosophers provided. Man lacked unity, it was not clear that reason really belonged to *him*, he did not appear to do his own thinking, he did not seem to be free but to move under the impetus of a higher body or intelligence. In short: the various philosophical interpretations given of man by his predecessors did not present him as a *complete entity*, one capable of understanding and acting with his own initiative and responsibility. St. Thomas discovered man's deepest meaning when he reflected on his contemplative and moral activities as *ways of being* and saw that he was an intelligent, free being acting with his own causality and responsibility. Then the enormity of man's wrong-doing became clear—in moral action man might imitate God as cause or strive to create a new order of being.

It soon became clear to St. Thomas, however, that a world of existing entities, each subsistent and capable of its own causal action, and of free, intelligent beings, each striving to imitate God's causality, could not have originated in the way conceived by any previous philosopher. For although all entities are marked by some differences, they still share in one characteristic, i.e. the act of existing; not that their individual acts bear much resemblance, as acts, one to the other, but each thing does exercise such an act. A common, *proportional likeness* of that kind differs radically from a *univocal* sharing in atomic composition, form or matter and could hardly be explained by a multiplicity of gods manipulating matter, as the old philosophers would have it. Nor could a *single* God, even though an intelligent God, whose concern was merely for nature as a whole rather than for each individual entity, have the intimate, individual relationship with each thing required of a unique, subsistent entity. The world that opened up philosophically to St. Thomas' gaze gradually revealed its cause in a God with His own unique, subsistent being—a truly transcendent God, a God present to each thing by His very substance.

Thus St. Thomas, as a Christian and a theologian, found it necessary to create a philosophy of being, man and God, if he were to gain the understanding of faith that he sought. The philosophers he had at his disposal were great aids to him and helped to prepare him for philosophical understanding of reality; but in his estimation their insights and explanations were not radical enough. So he fashioned a new philosophy of being, and he used the tools of the philosophers to do so. St. Thomas' philosophy remains thoroughly philosophical even as it serves the needs of a Christian theologian. Perhaps those inspired by his example may be able to use insights provided by later philosophers and scientists to enrich the theological understanding of our own day. But philosophy will only provide the Christian of today with understanding comparable to that gained by St. Thomas if it remains true to itself, i.e. strictly philosophical.

# Notes

## NOTES TO CHAPTER I

(For the use of abbreviations, see *Note to the Reader*)

1. Nigel Dennis, *Cards of Identity* (Harmondsworth, Penguin Books, 1960), pp. 80–81.
2. Lewis Carroll, *Through the Looking-glass* (New York, The Modern Library, n.d.), p. 201.
3. Martin Heidegger, *Über den Humanismus* in *Platons Lehre von der Wahrheit*, trans. by Lawrence Lynch (Bern, A. G. Franke, 1947), pp. 72–73.
4. Lewis Carroll, *op. cit.*, pp. 204–05.
5. Funk & Wagnalls, *The Practical Standard Dictionary* (New York, Funk & Wagnalls Co., 1922), p. 1017B.
6. *Ibid.*, p. 1017B.
7. *Ibid.*, p. 835A.
8. John Dewey, "Scholasticism" in Baldwin's *Dictionary of Philosophy and Psychology* (New York, Macmillan Co., 1928), pp. 491–92.
9. Friedrich Paulsen, *Immanuel Kant*, trans. by J. E. Creighton and Albert Lefevre (New York, Charles Scribner's Sons, 1902), p. 11.
10. Bertrand Russell, *History of Western Philosophy* (London, G. Allen & Unwin Ltd., 1946), p. 456.
11. Will Durant, *The Age of Faith* (New York, Simon and Schuster, 1950), p. 982.
12. Gordon Leff, *Medieval Thought* (Harmondsworth, Penguin Books, 1958), p. 92.
13. Barthélemy Hauréau, *Histoire de la Philosophie Scolastique*, trans. by Lawrence Lynch (Paris, Durand, 1872–1880), p. 36.
14. Maurice de Wulf, *Histoire de la philosophie médiévale*, trans. by Lawrence Lynch (Paris, Félix Alcan, 1895), p. xi.
15. *Ibid.*, pp. xii–xiii.
16. *Ibid.*, p. xviii.
17. Will Durant, *op. cit.*, p. 960.
18. Aristotle, *On the Soul*, Bk. 3, ch. 5, 430a15–18. In all notes, for the sake of convenience, Aristotle will be quoted from *The Basic Works of Aristotle* edited by Richard McKeon (New York, Random House, 1941). Cf. p. 592.

19. Aristotle, *Physics*, Bk. 8, ch. 1, 250b11–15. Ed. McKeon, p. 354.
20. *Ibid.*, 252b4–6. Ed. McKeon, p. 359.
21. St. Thomas, *In VIII Physica*, lect. 2.
22. St. Thomas, *S.T.* I, 46, 1.
23. Canon Van Steenberghen, *Epistemology*, trans. by Martin J. Flynn (New York, Wagner, 1949), p. ix.
24. Etienne Gilson, *The Christian Philosophy of St. Thomas Aquinas*, trans. by L. K. Shook (New York, Random House, 1956), pp. 366–67.
25. Jacques Maritain, *A Preface to Metaphysics* (London, Sheed and Ward, 1948), p. 24. (Also Mentor edition.)
26. Bertrand Russell, *op. cit.*, pp. 484–85.

## NOTES TO CHAPTER II

1. Martin Heidegger, *An Introduction to Metaphysics*, trans. by Ralph Mannheim (New York, Doubleday & Co., 1961), Anchor Books, pp. 6–7.
2. Etienne Gilson, *The Spirit of Mediaeval Philosophy*, trans. by A. H. C. Downes (London, Sheed and Ward, 1950), pp. 8–9.
3. Maurice Nédoncelle, *Is There a Christian Philosophy?*, trans. by Illtyd Trethowan, O.S.B. (New York, Hawthorn Books, 1960), pp. 85–99.
4. Emile Bréhier, 'La Notion de Philosophie Chrétienne' in *Bulletin de la Société française de Philosophie* XXXI, (1931), p. 50.
5. Emile Bréhier, 'Y-a-t-il une Philosophie Chrétienne?' in *Revue de Métaphysique et de Morale*, XXXVIII, no. 2 (1931), p. 140. Trans. by Lawrence Lynch.
6. *Ibid.*, p. 141.
7. Etienne Gilson, 'La Notion de Philosophie Chrétienne' in *Bulletin de la Société française de Philosophie*, XXXI (1931), p. 48.
8. *Ibid.*, pp. 40ff.
9. St. Paul, *Epistle to the Colossians*, II, 8.
10. Tertullian, *On the Prescription of Heretics*, ch. 7., trans. by T. H. Bindley (London, S. P. C. K., 1914), pp. 43–44.
11. Peter Damian, *De sancta simplicitate*, P. L. 145, 697B–C.
12. Peter Damian, *The Book 'The Lord be with you'*, ch. 1., trans. by Patricia McNulty (London, Faber and Faber, 1959), p. 54.
13. St. Bernard, *Sermons: III Sermon for Pentecost*, trans. by a priest of Mount Melleray (Dublin, Browne and Nolan, 1923), Vol. 2, pp. 310–11.
14. Thomas à Kempis, *The Imitation of Christ*, Bk. 1, ch. 2, trans. by Albert Hyma (New York, Century Co., 1927), p. 5.
15. St. Paul, *Epistle to the Romans*, I, 20.
16. St. Augustine, *Confessions*, Bk. 7, ch. 9, par. 13, trans. by E. B. Pusey (London, J. M. Dent & Sons, 1949), pp. 129–30.
17. Plotinus, *Enneads*, V, 1, 7., trans. by Joseph Katz in *The Philosophy of Plotinus* (New York, Appleton-Century-Crofts, 1950), pp. 16–17.

18. St. John, I, 1–5.
19. St. Augustine, *op. cit.*, Bk. 7, ch. 20, par. 26, p. 142.
20. Isaias, VII, 9.
21. St. Anselm, *Proslogion*, ch. 2, trans. by Sidney Norton Deane (LaSalle, Ill., Open Court Publishing Co., 1948), pp. 7–8.
22. St. Thomas, *S.T.* I, 2, 1; *S.C.G.* I, 10–11.
23. Immanuel Kant, *Critique of Pure Reason*, Transcendental Dialectic, Bk. 2, ch. 3, sec. 4, trans. by N. K. Smith (London, Macmillan, 1929), pp. 500ff.
24. Etienne Gilson, *History of Christian Philosophy in the Middle Ages*, part 6, ch. 1 (New York, Random House, 1955), pp. 235ff.
25. St. Thomas, *S.T.* II–II, 1, 4.
26. St. Thomas, *S.T.* II–II, 4, 2.
27. Dionysius, *Divine Names* IV. P. G. 3, 872.
28. St. Thomas, *S.T.* II–II, 4, 3.
29. St. Thomas, *On Truth*, 14, 4.
30. St. Thomas, *S.T.* II–II, 1, 5.
31. St. Thomas, *S.T* I, 1, 2.
32. St. Thomas, *S.T.* I, 46, 2.
33. St. Thomas, *S.T.* II–II, 1, 5 ad 2.
34. St. Thomas, *S.T.* I, 1, 1 ad 2.
35. St. Thomas, *On Truth*, 14, 3.
36. St. Thomas, *S.T.* II–II, 1, 5 obj. 3.
37. Etienne Gilson, 'Les Philosophantes' in *AHDLM* XIX (1952), p. 135.
38. M.-D. Chenu, 'Philosophes,' in *Revue des Sciences philosophiques et théologiques* XXVI (1937), pp. 27–40. Cf. also Etienne Gilson, *Thomas Aquinas and Our Colleagues* (Princeton, Princeton University Press, 1953), p. 15.
39. Etienne Gilson, *op. cit.*, p. 15.
40. St. Thomas, *On Boethius' 'De Trinitate'*, II, 3. Trans. by Sister Rose Emmanuella Brennan, p. 60.
41. *Ibid.*, II, 3, p. 59.
42. Roger Bacon, *Opus Minus*, ed. J. S. Brewer (London, Longmans, Green, Longman and Roberts, 1859), pp. 322ff.
43. *Ibid.*, p. 323.
44. Martin Heidegger, *op. cit.*, pp. 6–7.
45. Jean-Paul Sartre, *L'être et le néant* (Paris, Librairie Gallimard, 1943), pp. 653–54. Cf. also pp. 707–08.

## NOTES TO CHAPTER III

1. George Santayana, *Realms of Being* (New York, Charles Scribner's Sons, 1942), Introd., pp. 7–8.
2. Gabriel Marcel, 'On the Ontological Mystery' in *The Philosophy of Ex-*

*istence,* trans. by Manya Harari (New York, Philosophical Library, 1949), pp. 29–30.

3. Francis Bacon, *Great Instauration,* ed. E. A. Burtt in *English Philosophers from Bacon to Mill* (New York, Modern Library, 1939), p. 15.

4. Bertrand Russell, *Human Knowledge: its scope and limits* (London, George Allen and Unwin Ltd., 1948), pp. 159–60. (Also New York, Simon and Schuster.)

5. *Ibid.,* p. 160.

6. *Ibid.,* p. 161.

7. *Ibid.,* p. 160.

8. Bertrand Russell, 'The Philosophy of Logical Atomism' in *Logic and Knowledge* (London, George Allen and Unwin Ltd., 1956), p. 179. Cf. also 'Logical Atomism', *ibid.,* p. 341. (Also New York, Macmillan.)

9. *Ibid.,* p. 178.

10. *Ibid.,* pp. 323–24.

11. *Ibid.,* p. 232. Cf. also *Human Knowledge: its scope and limits,* p. 468.

12. Bertrand Russell, *Mysticism and Logic* (London, George Allen and Unwin Ltd., 1959), pp. 30–31. (Also New York, Barnes and Noble, and Doubleday.)

13. St. Thomas, *S.T.* I–II, 57, 2.

14. St. Thomas, *S.T.* II–II, 1, 5 ad 2.

15. Claude Bernard, *An Introduction to the Study of Experimental Medicine,* trans. by Henry Copley Green (New York, Dover Publications Inc., 1957), pp. 219–20.

16. St. Thomas, *S.T.* I, 12, 7.

17. St. Thomas, *S.T.* I–II, 67, 3.

18. St. Thomas, *On Boethius' 'De Trinitate',* VI, 2. Trans. by Armand Maurer, p. 65.

19. *Ibid.,* VI, 1, p. 54.

20. *Ibid.,* VI, 1, p. 55.

21. *Ibid.,* VI, 2, p. 63.

22. *Ibid.,* VI, 2, p. 64.

23. St. Thomas, *S.T.* II–II, 47, 11.

24. St. Thomas, *S.T.* I–II, 54, 2 ad 2.

25. St. Thomas, *S.C.G.* II, 79, #2.

26. St. Thomas, *S.T.* I, 2, 2.

27. St. Thomas, *In II Post. Anal. Arist.,* lect. 20.

28. St. Thomas, *On Truth,* 4, 1 ad 8.

29. St. Thomas, *S.T.* I–II, 57, 2.

30. St. Thomas, *S.T.* I, 33, 1 and ad 1.

31. St. Thomas, *S.T.* I, 4, 1 ad 3.

## NOTES TO CHAPTER IV

1. R. J. Forbes, "Power", in *A History of Technology*, ed. Charles Singer, et al. (Oxford, Clarendon Press, 1956), Vol. II, p. 606.
2. Auguste Comte, *The Positive Philosophy*, trans. by Harriet Martineau (London, G. Bell & Sons, Ltd., 1896), p. 1.
3. Moritz Schlick, "The Turning Point of Philosophy," in *Erkenntnis*, I, 1, trans. by Chas. H. Monson, Jr. in *Philosophy, Religion and Science* (New York, Charles Scribner's Sons, 1963), p. 189.
4. Ludwig Wittgenstein, *Philosophical Investigations*, I, 97, trans. by G. E. M. Anscombe (Oxford, Basil Blackwell, 1953), p. 44e.
5. *Ibid.*, I, 109, p. 47e.
6. Martin Heidegger, *Being and Time*, Introd., II, 22, trans. by John Macquarrie and Edward Robinson (New York, Harper & Row, 1962), p. 22.
7. Martin Heidegger, *An Introduction to Metaphysics*, trans. by Ralph Mannheim (New York, Doubleday & Co., 1961), Anchor Books, p. 104. Cf. also *Being and Time*, Introd., II, 25–26, pp. 46–49.
8. *Ibid.*, p. 41.
9. St. Thomas, *S.T.* I, 115, 6.
10. St. Thomas, *S.T.* I, 22, 2.
11. Aristotle, *Physics*, Bk. 2, ch. 1, 193a31–b7. Ed. McKeon, pp. 237–38.
12. Avicenna, *De Prima Philosophia*, tract 5, ch. 5, trans. by Lawrence Lynch (Venice, 1520, reproduced by the Franciscan Institute, St. Bonaventure, N. Y., 1948), pp. 164–65.
13. *Ibid.*, tr. 5, ch. 1, pp. 133–34.
14. *Ibid.*, tr. 5, ch. 1, p. 135.
15. St. Thomas, *S.C.G.* I, 25.
16. St. Thomas, *S.T.* I, 8, 1.
17. St. Thomas, *S.T.* I, 4, 1 ad 3.
18. St. Thomas, *S.T.* I, 50, 2 ad 3.
19. St. Thomas, *S.C.G.* II, 50, #3.
20. St. Thomas, *S.T.* I, 45, 4.
21. St. Thomas, *S.T.* I, 75, 5 ad 4.
22. St. Thomas, *S.C.G.* II, 52, #2.
23. St. Thomas, *On the Power of God*, 3, 8.
24. St. Thomas, *S.T.* I, 45, 5 ad 1.
25. St. Thomas, *S.T.* I, 45, 1.
26. St. Thomas, *S.T.* I, 46, 2.
27. St. Bonaventure, *II Sentences*, d. 1, p. 1, a. 1, q. 2, trans. by Lawrence Lynch (Paris, Vives, 1864), Vol. II, p. 244B.
28. Siger of Brabant, *Quaestio de aeternitate mundi*, ed. W. J. Dwyer, C.S.B., trans. by Lawrence Lynch (Louvain, Editions de l'Institut Supérieur de Philosophie, 1937), pp. 41–42.
29. St. Thomas, *S.T.* I, 46, 2. Cf. also *S.C.G.* II, 38, #11–12.

30. St. Thomas, *S.C.G.* II, 35, #3.
31. St. Thomas, *S.T.* I, 104, 4.
32. St. Thomas, *On the Power of God*, 5, 5. Cf. also *S.T.* I, 65, 1 ad 1, and *On the Power of God*, 5, 3.
33. St. Thomas, *S.C.G.* II, 30, #1–2.
34. *Ibid.*, II, 30, #4.
35. *Ibid.*, II, 30, #8–9.
36. *Ibid.*, II, 30, #11–15.
37. St. Thomas, *On the Power of God*, 7, 2.
38. *Ibid.*, 3, 4.
39. St. Thomas, *S.C.G.* III, 21, #5.
40. *Ibid.*, III, 69, #18.
41. St. Thomas, *S.T.* I, 103, 1 ad 1.
42. St. Thomas, *S.T.* I, 82, 4.
43. St. Thomas, *On Truth*, 21, 2.
44. Alfred North Whitehead, *Process and Reality* (New York, Harper & Row, 1960), Torchbooks, pp. 128–29.
45. *Ibid.*, p. 339.

## NOTES TO CHAPTER V

1. Vercors (Jean Bruller), *You Shall Know Them* (Toronto, McClelland & Stewart Ltd., 1953), p. 171.
2. Harvey Cox, *The Secular City* (New York, Macmillan Co., 1965), p. 63.
3. Jean-Paul Sartre, *Being and Nothingness*, Part 4, ch. 1, #1, trans. by Hazel Barnes (New York, Philosophical Library Inc., 1956), Citadel Press edition, p. 416.
4. Rollo May, *Existence: A New Dimension in Psychiatry and Psychology*, Part I, Introduction (New York, Basic Books Inc., 1958), pp. 3–4.
5. Eugen Kahn, "An Appraisal of Existential Analysis", in the *Psychiatric Quarterly* and *Psychiatric Quarterly Supplement*, XXXI, pp. 203–37, April 1957; pp. 417–44, July 1957.
6. R. Descartes, *Meditations*, II, trans. by E. S. Haldane and G. R. T. Ross (Cambridge, Cambridge University Press, 1911–12), Dover Publications, Vol. 1, p. 149.
7. R. Descartes, *Discourse on Method*, *op. cit.*, Vol. 1, p. 101.
8. Nicolas Malebranche, *Entretiens sur la Métaphysique et sur la Religion*, Ent. 1, trans. by Lawrence Lynch (Paris, Vrin, 1945), p. 68.
9. R. Descartes, *Discourse on Method*, *op. cit.*, Vol. 1, p. 101.
10. R. Descartes, *Meditations*, VI, *op. cit.*, Vol. 1, p. 190.
11. R. Descartes, *Principles of Philosophy*, prin. CXCVII, *op. cit.*, Vol. 1, p. 294.

12. *Ibid.*, prin. XLVIII, Vol. 1, p. 238.
13. R. Descartes, *Meditations,* VI, *op. cit.,* Vol. 1, p. 191.
14. John Locke, *Essays on Human Understanding,* Bk. 2, ch. 2, par. 1–2. Ed. E. A. Burtt, pp. 253–54.
15. David Hume, *An Enquiry Concerning Human Understanding,* Sect. 1, Ed. E. A. Burtt, p. 591.
16. John Locke, *Essay on Human Understanding,* Bk. 2, ch. 8, par. 11. Ed. E. A. Burtt, p. 266.
17. *Ibid.,* Introd., par. 8. Ed. E. A. Burtt, p. 247.
18. *Ibid.,* Bk. 2, ch. 8, par. 13–14. Ed. E. A. Burtt, pp. 266–67.
19. *Ibid.,* Bk. 2, ch. 23, par. 1–2. Ed. E. A. Burtt, pp. 294–95.
20. David Hume, *An Enquiry Concerning Human Understanding,* Sect. 5, part 1. Ed. E. A. Burtt, p. 609.
21. *Ibid.,* Sect. 7, part 2. Ed. E. A. Burtt, p. 630.
22. Immanuel Kant, *Critique of Pure Reason,* Transcendental Dialectic, ch. 3, appendix, "Regulative Employment of the Ideas", trans. by N. Kemp Smith (London, Macmillan & Co., 1929), p. 534.
23. Ernst Cassirer, *An Essay on Man* (New York, Doubleday & Co., 1954), Anchor Books, pp. 39–40.
24. St. Thomas, *S.T.* I, 12, 4 ad 3.
25. St. Thomas, *S.C.G.* II, 1, #1.
26. St. Thomas, *S.T.* I, 104, 1.
27. St. Thomas, *S.T.* I, 76, 1 ad 1. Cf. Aristotle, *Physics,* Bk. 2, ch. 2, 194b14. Ed. McKeon, p. 240.
28. St. Thomas, *On Truth,* 24, 1 ad 19.
29. St. Thomas, *S.T.* I, 11, 1.
30. St. Thomas, *S.C.G.* II, 47, #4.
31. St. Thomas, *S.T.* II–II, 58, 2.
32. St. Thomas, *In 3 Sententiae,* 28, 1, 7 ad 4. (Not available in translation.)
33. St. Thomas, *S.C.G.* III, 42, #9.
34. St. Thomas, *S.T.* I, 85, 5.
35. St. Thomas, *S.T.* I, 14, 16.
36. St. Thomas, *S.T.* I, 79, 12.
37. St. Thomas, *On Truth,* 16, 1.
38. St. Thomas, *S.T.* I, 79, 8.
39. St. Thomas, *S.T.* I, 84, 2.
40. St. Thomas, *S.C.G.* III, 81, #1.
41. St. Thomas, *S.T.* I, 55, 2.
42. St. Thomas, *S.C.G.* II, 68, #3.
43. St. Thomas, *S.T.* I, 75, 6.
44. St. Thomas, *S.T.* I, 87, 3.
45. St. Thomas, *S.T.* I, 85, 2.
46. St. Thomas, *On Truth,* I, 1.
47. St. Thomas, *S.T.* I, 29, 3 ad 2

## NOTES TO CHAPTER VI

1. Friedrich Nietzsche, *Twilight of the Idols*, "Skirmishes of an Untimely Man," #38, trans. by Walter Kaufmann, in *The Portable Nietzsche* (New York, Viking Press, 1964), p. 542.
2. Jean-Paul Sartre, *The Flies*, Act 3, trans. by Stuart Gilbert (London, Hamish Hamilton, 1946), p. 96. (Also New York, Knopf.)
3. Johann Gottlieb Fichte, *The Vocation of Man*, trans. by Roderick M. Chisholm (New York, Library of Liberal Arts, 1956), pp. 19–20.
4. Benedictus Spinoza, *Ethics*, Part I, prop. 17, trans. by A. Boyle (London, J. M. Dent & Sons Ltd., 1938), pp. 15–16. (Also New York, Dutton.)
5. David Hume, *An Enquiry Concerning Human Understanding*, Sect. 8, part 2. Ed. E. A. Burtt, p. 644.
6. Johann Gottlieb Fichte, *op. cit.*, p. 26.
7. Immanuel Kant, *Fundamental Principles of the Metaphysic of Morals*, trans. by T. K. Abbott (New York, The Liberal Arts Press, 1949), p. 63.
8. Friedrich Nietzsche, Notes published as part of *The Will to Power*, #1052, in Kaufmann, *op. cit.*, p. 459.
9. Jean-Paul Sartre, *Descartes*, trans. by Lawrence Lynch (Paris, Les Classiques de la Liberté, 1946), pp. 34–36.
10. Jean-Paul Sartre, *Being and Nothingness*, "The Pursuit of Being," trans. Hazel Barnes (New York, Citadel Press, 1964), p. lxiv.
11. *Ibid.*, p. lxvi.
12. *Ibid.*, p. 409.
13. *Ibid.*, pp. 416–17.
14. Jean-Paul Sartre, *Existentialism*, trans. by Bernard Frechtman (New York, Philosophical Library, 1947), p. 26.
15. Jean-Paul Sartre, *Being and Nothingness*, pp. 514–15.
16. *Ibid.*, pp. 540–41.
17. Jean-Paul Sartre, *The Flies*, Act 3, *op. cit.*, p. 97.
18. St. Thomas, *S.T.* I, 29, 2. It should be noted that at the beginning of this text St. Thomas is quoting Aristotle but goes on to change the meaning to his own way of thinking. Thus, οὐσία is *not* substance in St. Thomas' sense. As he says below, substance is being that gives being to accidents; and in Aristotle οὐσία is not St. Thomas' *essence*. In Aristotle οὐσία is form and for St. Thomas the essence of material entities is matter as well as form.
19. St. Thomas, *S.T.* I, 29, 1.
20. St. Thomas, *S.C.G.* III, 50, #2.
21. St. Thomas, *On Truth*, 21, 2.
22. St. Thomas, *S.C.G.* III, 3, #5.
23. St. Thomas, *On Truth*, 21, 1.
24. St. Thomas, *S.C.G.* III, 24, #7.

25. St. Thomas, *S.T.* I, 5, 1 ad 1.
26. St. Thomas, *S.T.* I–II, 1, 2.
27. St. Thomas, *S.T.* I, 5, 1; *S.T.* I, 6, 2 ad 2; *S.C.G.* I, 37, #4; *On Truth,* 22, 1.
28. St. Thomas, *S.T.* I–II, 13, 3.
29. St. Thomas, *S.C.G.* III, 16, #3.
30. St. Thomas, *S.T.* I–II, 8, 1.
31. St. Thomas, *S.T.* I, 80, 1. Cf. also *S.T.* I–II, 8, 1.
32. St. Thomas, *S.T.* I, 83, 1.
33. St. Thomas, *On Truth,* 22, 4.
34. St. Thomas, *S.T.* I, 78, 4.
35. St. Thomas, *S.T.* I, 59, 1.
36. St. Thomas, *S.T.* I, 82, 2.
37. St. Thomas, *S.T.* I–II, 13, 1.
38. St. Thomas, *S.T.* I–II, 13, 3.
39. St. Thomas, *S.T.* I–II, 83, 1.
40. St. Thomas, *S.C.G.* III, 3, #7.
41. St. Thomas, *S.T.* I, 83, 3.
42. St. Thomas, *S.T.* I–II, 13, 6.
43. St. Thomas, *S.T.* I–II, 9, 1 ad 3.
44. St. Thomas, *On Truth,* 22, 12.
45. St. Thomas, *S.T.* I–II, 14, 1 ad 1.
46. St. Thomas, *S.T.* I–II, 14, 2 ad 1.
47. St. Thomas, *S.T.* I–II, 14, 2.
48. St. Thomas, *S.T.* I–II, 10, 3.
49. St. Thomas, *S.T.* I–II, 55, 1.
50. St. Thomas, *S.C.G.* III, 25, #9. Cf. also *S.C.G.* III, 2, #9.
51. Immanuel Kant, *Fundamental Principles of the Metaphysic of Morals, op. cit.,* p. 20. Cf. also *ibid.,* pp. 33–36 and *Critique of Practical Reason,* Part I, Bk. 1, ch. 1, #8, theorem 4, remark 2, trans. by L. W. Beck (New York, The Liberal Arts Press, 1956), pp. 36–38.
52. St. Thomas, *S.T.* II–II, 47, 10.
53. St. Thomas, *S.T.* II–II, 47, 10 ad 2.
54. St. Thomas, *S.T.* I–II, 57, 4.
55. St. Thomas, *S.T.* I–II, 57, 5.
56. St. Thomas, *S.T.* I–II, 90, 1 ad 2.
57. St. Thomas, *S.T.* I–II, 90, 4.
58. St. Thomas, *S.T.* I–II, 91, 2.
59. St. Thomas, *S.T.* I–II, Prologue.
60. St. Thomas, *S.T.* I–II, 10, 1.
61. St. Thomas, *S.T.* I–II, 94, 2.
62. St. Thomas, *S.T.* I–II, 94, 2.
63. St. Thomas, *S.T.* I–II, 94, 4.
64. St. Thomas, *S.T.* I–II, 94, 5.
65. St. Thomas, *S.T.* I–II, 95, 1.

## NOTES TO CHAPTER VII

1. Teilhard de Chardin, *The Future of Man*, ch. 17, trans. by Norman Denny (London and Toronto, Collins, 1964), pp. 254–55.
2. Jean-Paul Sartre, *Being and Nothingness*, Part 3, ch. 1, trans. by Hazel Barnes (New York, Citadel Press, 1964), p. 278.
3. *Ibid.*, Part 1, ch. 3, part B, p. 404.
4. Jean-Paul Sartre, *In Camera* [*No Exit* is the title of U.S. edition], trans. by Stuart Gilbert (London, Hamish Hamilton, 1946), p. 166. (Also New York, Knopf.)
5. Jean-Paul Sartre, *Being and Nothingness*, Part 3, ch. 3, part B, trans. by Hazel Barnes, p. 405.
6. Karl Marx, "Theses on Feuerbach," ed. Lewis S. Feuer in *Marx and Engels* (New York, Anchor Books, 1959), pp. 244–45.
7. Friedrich Engels, "Letters on Historical Materialism," *ibid.*, p. 399.
8. Friedrich Engels, "Letter to Heinz Starkenburg," London, January 25, 1894, *ibid.*, p. 411.
9. Karl Marx, *A Contribution to the Critique of Political Economy*, Preface, *ibid.*, p. 43.
10. Thomas Hobbes, *Leviathan*, Part I, ch. xiv. Ed. E. A. Burtt, p. 163.
11. *Ibid.*, Part I, ch. xiii, p. 161.
12. *Ibid.*, Part II, ch. xvii, p. 176.
13. *Ibid.*, Part II, ch. xxi, pp. 196–97.
14. *Ibid.*, Part II, ch. xxi, pp. 197–98.
15. John Locke, *Concerning Civil Government*, ch. 2. Ed. E. A. Burtt, p. 404.
16. *Ibid.*, ch. 7, p. 441.
17. *Ibid.*, ch. 11, p. 461.
18. John Stuart Mill, *On Liberty*, ch. 1. Ed. E. A. Burtt, p. 951–52.
19. *Ibid.*, ch. 1, pp. 955–56.
20. *Ibid.*, ch. 1, p. 958.
21. Jean-Paul Sartre, *Being and Nothingness*, Part 3, ch. 3, sect. 1, trans. by Hazel Barnes, p. 343. Cf. also *L'être et le néant* (Paris, Librairie Gallimard, 1943), p. 685.
22. St. Thomas, *On Truth*, 21, 1.
23. St. Thomas, *S.T.* I–II, 28, 2.
24. John Locke, *Concerning Civil Government*, ch. 2. Ed. E. A. Burtt, pp. 408–09.
25. St. Thomas, *S.T.* I, 96, 4.
26. St. Thomas, *S.T.* II–II, 47, 15 ad 3; cf. also *On Truth*, 17, 1.
27. St. Thomas, *On Kingship*, ch. 1, #6, trans. by I. Th. Eschmann (Toronto, The Pontifical Institute of Mediaeval Studies, 1949), p. 5.
28. It is worth remembering that Hobbes examined the same text of Aristotle on which St. Thomas bases his argument and concluded that a state of war is natural to men, society is artificial.

Here are the parallel texts of Aristotle and Hobbes on this point:

Now, that man is more of a political animal than bees or any other gregarious animal is evident. Nature, as we often say, makes nothing in vain, and man is the only animal whom she has endowed with the gift of speech. And whereas mere voice is but an indication of pleasure or pain, and is therefore found in other animals (for their nature attains to the perception of pleasure and pain and the intimation of them to one another, and no further), the power of speech is intended to set forth the expedient and the inexpedient, and therefore likewise the just and the unjust. And it is characteristic of man that he alone has any sense of good and evil, of just and unjust, and the like, and the association of living beings who have this sense makes a family and a state.
Aristotle, *Politics,* Bk. 1, ch. 2, 1253a7–18. Ed. McKeon, p. 1129.

It is true that certain living creatures, as bees and ants, live sociably one with another, which are therefore by Aristotle numbered amongst political creatures; and yet have no other direction than their particular judgments and appetites; nor speech, whereby one of them can signify to another what he thinks expedient for the common benefit: and therefore some men may perhaps desire to know why mankind cannot do the same. To which I answer:

First, that men are continually in competition for honor and dignity, which these creatures are not; and consequently amongst men there ariseth on that ground, envy and hatred, and finally war; but amongst these not.

Secondly, that amongst these creatures, the common good differeth not from the private; and being by nature inclined to their private, they procure thereby the common benefit. But man, whose joy consisteth in comparing himself with other men, can relish nothing but what is eminent.

Thirdly, that these creatures, having not, as man, the use of reason, do not see, nor think they see, any fault in the administration of their common business: whereas amongst men, there are very many that think themselves wiser, and able to govern the public better, than the rest; and these strive to reform and innovate, one this way, and another that way; and thereby bring it into distraction and civil war.

Fourthly, that these creatures,

though they have some use of voice
in making known to one another
their desires and affections; yet they
want that art of words by which
some men can represent to others,
that which is good in the likeness
of evil, and evil in the likeness of
good, and augment or diminish the
apparent greatness of good and
evil; discontenting men and trou-
bling their peace at their pleasure.

Fifthly, irrational creatures cannot distinguish between *injury* and
*damage;* and therefore as long as
they be at ease, they are not of-
fended with their fellows; whereas
man is then most troublesome when
he is most at ease; for then it is
that he loves to shew his wisdom,
and control the actions of them
that govern the commonwealth.

Lastly, the agreement of these
creatures is natural; that of men is
by covenant only, which is artificial: and therefore it is no wonder
if there be somewhat else required,
besides covenant, to make their
agreement constant and lasting:
which is a common power, to keep
them in awe, and to direct their
actions to the common benefit.
Thomas Hobbes, *Leviathan,* Part
II, ch. xvii. Ed. E. A. Burtt, pp.
175–76.

29. St. Thomas, *In I Perihermeneias Aristotelis,* lect. 4–5.
30. St. Thomas, *On Kingship,* ch. 1, #7, *op. cit.,* p. 5.
31. Avicenna, *De Anima (Sextus Naturalium),* V, 1, fol. 22rB, trans. by I. Th.
    Eschmann in *St. Thomas on Kingship,* pp. 94–95.
32. St. Thomas, *On Kingship,* ch. 1, #8, *op. cit.,* pp. 5–6.
33. *Ibid.,* ch. 1, #4, pp. 3–4.
34. John Locke, *Concerning Civil Government,* ch. 9, #123. Ed. E. A. Burtt,
    p. 453.
35. Thomas Hobbes, *Leviathan,* Part II, ch. xviii. Ed. E. A. Burtt, pp. 179–
    180. Cf. also pp. 181–82.
36. St. Thomas, *S.T.* I, 96, 4.

37. St. Thomas, *S.T.* I, 96, 3.
38. St. Thomas, *S.T.* II–II, 58, 6.
39. St. Thomas, *S.T. I,* 21, 1. Cf. also *S.T.* II–II, 61, 3; *In V Ethic. Nicom. Arist.,* lect. 4–6.
40. Aristotle, *Nicomachean Ethics,* Bk. 5, ch. 4, 1132a1–6. Ed. McKeon, p. 1008.
41. St. Thomas, *S.T.* II–II, 61, 2.
42. Aristotle, *Nicomachean Ethics,* Bk. 5, ch. 3, 1131a30–b9. Ed. McKeon, pp. 1006–07.
43. St. Thomas, *S.T.* I, 20, 2 ad 3.
44. St. Thomas, *S.T.* II–II, 23, 1.
45. St. Thomas, *In I Ethic. Nicom. Arist.,* lect. 1, #5. Cf. also *S.C.G.* IV, 35.
46. St. Thomas, *S.C.G.* III, 17, #5–6. Cf. also *In I Ethic. Nicom. Arist.,* lect. 2, #30.
47. St. Thomas, *S.T.* II–II, 26, 3.
48. St. Thomas, *In I Ethic. Nicom. Arist.,* lect. 2, #30.
49. St. Thomas, *S.C.G.* III, 17, #6.
50. Aristotle, *Nicomachean Ethics,* Bk. 8, ch. 7, 1158b30–1159a8. Ed. McKeon, p. 1066.
51. *Ibid.,* Bk. 10, ch. 8, 1178b24–1179al. Ed. McKeon, p. 1107.
52. St. Augustine, *The City of God,* Bk. 15, ch. 2, trans. by Marcus Dods (New York, Hafner Publishing Co., 1948), Vol. II, pp. 51–52.

## NOTES TO CHAPTER VIII

1. Martin Heidegger, *Über den Humanismus,* in *Platons Lehre von der Wahrheit,* trans. by James M. Robinson in *The Later Heidegger and Theology* (New York, Harper & Row, 1963), pp. 33–34.
2. Søren Kierkegaard, *Journals,* #1054, trans. by Alexander Dru (London, Oxford University Press, 1938), p. 374.
3. Friedrich Nietzsche, *The Joyful Science,* #125, trans. by Oscar Levy (London, George Allen and Unwin Ltd., 1929), Vol. X, p. 167.
Cf. also: This [i.e. the soul of despair] knows how the case stands with the actual claims to validity which the abstract [legal] person puts forward, as also with the validity of this person in pure thought [in Stoicism]. It knows that a vindication of such validity means really being altogether lost; it is just this loss become conscious of itself, and is the surrender and relinquishment of its knowledge about itself. We see that this "unhappy consciousness" constituted the counterpart and the complement of the perfectly happy consciousness, that of comedy. All divine reality goes back into this latter type of consciousness; it means, in other words, the complete relinquishment and emptying of substance. The former, on the contrary, is conversely the tragic fate that befalls certainty of self which

aims at being absolute, at being self-sufficient. It is consciousness of the loss of everything of significance in this certainty of itself, and of the loss even of this knowledge or certainty of self—the loss of substance as well as of self; it is the bitter pain which finds expression in the cruel words, "God is dead." G. W. F. Hegel, *The Phenomenology of Mind*, trans. by J. B. Baillie (London, George Allen and Unwin Ltd., 1961), pp. 752–53.

4. Jean-Paul Sartre, *The Flies*, Act 2, scene 1, trans. by Stuart Gilbert (London, Hamish Hamilton, 1946), p. 59. "What . . . a change has come over everything, and, oh, how far away you seem. Until now I felt something warm and living around me, like a friendly presence. That something has just died. What emptiness! What endless emptiness! As far as eye can reach. Night is coming on. The air is getting chilly, isn't it? But what was it . . . what . . . died just now?"

5. Immanuel Kant, *The Critique of Pure Reason*, The Transcendental Dialectic, Bk. 2, ch. 3, section 2, trans. by N. Kemp Smith (London, Macmillan, 1929), p. 493.

6. *Ibid.*, The Transcendental Aesthetic, section 1, #3, p. 72.

7. *Ibid.*, The Transcendental Doctrine of Judgment, ch. 3, pp. 267ff. Cf. especially p. 270.

8. G. W. F. Hegel, *The Phenomenology of Mind, op. cit.* [Note 3.], Part VII, Revealed Religion, pp. 757–59.
Hegel discusses religion within the following framework:
The first realization of spirit is just the principle and notion of religion itself—religion as immediate and thus Natural Religion. Here spirit knows itself as its object in a "natural" or immediate shape. The second realization is, however, necessarily that of knowing itself in the shape of transcended and superseded natural existence, i.e. in the form of self. This therefore is Religion in the form of Art. For the shape it adopts is raised to the form of self through the productive activity of consciousness, by which this consciousness beholds in its object its own action, i.e. sees the self. The third realization, finally, cancels the onesidedness of the first two: the self is as much an immediate self as the immediacy is a self. If spirit in the first is in the form of consciousness, and in the second in that of self-consciousness, it is in the third in the form of the unity of both; it has then the shape of what is completely self-contained [An-und-Fürsichseins]; and in being thus presented as it is in and for itself, this is Revealed Religion. Although spirit, however, here reaches its true shape, the very shape assumed and the conscious presentation are an aspect or phase still unsurmounted; and from this spirit has to pass over into the life of the Notion, in order therein completely to resolve the form of objectivity, in the notion which embraces within itself this its *own* opposite. (*op. cit.*, pp. 693–94.)

9. Ludwig Feuerbach, *The Essence of Christianity*, ch. 7, trans. by George Eliot (New York, Harper & Row, 1957), Torchbook, p. 75. Cf. also pp. 38–39.

10. Immanuel Kant, *op. cit.*, The Transcendental Dialectic, Bk. 2, ch. 3, section 4, p. 505.
11. St. Thomas, *S.T.* I, 2, 1 ad 2.
12. Søren Kierkegaard, *Journals*, #1054, *op. cit.*, p. 374.
13. G. W. F. Hegel, *Philosophical Propadeutik*, Introduction, trans. by G. E. Mueller in *Hegel: Encyclopedia of Philosophy* (New York, Philosophical Library, 1959), pp. 277–78.
14. G. W. F. Hegel, *ibid.*, #471, pp. 283–84.
15. Søren Kierkegaard, *Journals*, #88, *op. cit.*, p. 35.
16. Søren Kierkegaard, *Journals*, #1027, *op. cit.*, pp. 357–58.
17. Søren Kierkegaard, *Philosophical Fragments*, ch. 3, trans. by David F. Swenson and Howard V. Hong (Princeton, Princeton University Press, 1962), p. 53.
18. Søren Kierkegaard, *op. cit.*, pp. 57–58.
19. St. Thomas, *S.C.G.* I, 11, #1–2.
20. St. Thomas, *S.T.* I, 2, 2 ad 3.
21. St. Paul, *Epistle to the Romans*, I, 20. (King James version)
22. St. Thomas, *S.T.* I, 8, 3 ad 1. Cf. also *S.T.* I, 8, 1.
23. St. Thomas, *On the Power of God*, 3, 1.
24. St. Thomas, *S.T.* I–II, Prologue.
25. St. Thomas, *On Truth*, 22, 2. Cf. also *S.C.G.* III, 19.
26. Aristotle, *Metaphysics*, Bk. 1, ch. 2, 983al–10. Ed. McKeon, pp. 692–93.
27. St. Thomas, *S.T.* I, 2, 2. Cf. also *S.T.* I, 2, 2 ad 2; *S.C.G.* I, 12; *In I Post. Anal. Arist.*, lect. 23–25.
28. St. Thomas, *S.T.* I, 13, 5. Cf. also *S.T.* I, 13, 6 and *S.C.G.* I, 29.
29. St. Thomas, *S.T.* I, 2, 2 ad 2.
30. St. Thomas, *S.T.* I, 2, 2ad 3.
31. St. Thomas, *S.T.* I, 13, 5.
32. St. Thomas, *S.T.* I, 3, 4 ad 2.
33. St. Thomas, *S.T.* I, 13, 3. Cf. also *S.T.* I, 13, 2.
34. St. Thomas, *S.T.* I, 13, 5. Cf. also *S.T.* I, 13, 6.
35. St. Thomas, *S.T.* I, 4, 2. Cf. also *S.T.* I, 3, 4; *S.T.* I, 13, 11; *S.C.G.* I, 22.
36. St. Thomas, *S.C.G.* I, 14.

# Biographies

The following brief notes will help to identify many of the individuals mentioned or quoted in the text, or in the extracts from other publications. All saints are located at the word "saint."

PETER ABELARD (1079–1142), theologian and philosopher, was born at Le Pallet in Brittany. He studied logic at Paris under Roscelin and William of Champeaux, and subsequently taught it at Melun, Corbeil and Paris. His love for Heloise, as recounted in his *Historia Calamitatum*, became one of the famous love stories of the Middle Ages. He was in constant difficulties as a consequence of his theological views, but made important philosophical contributions in logic and ethics. His most important works are: *Theologia Christiana, Sic et Non, Scito te ipsum, Dialectica*, and commentaries on some of the logical works of Aristotle, Porphyry and Boethius. Cf. E. Gilson, *History of Christian Philosophy in the Middle Ages* (New York, 1955), pp. 153–63.

ARISTOTLE (384–322 B.C.), Greek philosopher, psychologist, logician, political thinker, biologist and rhetorician, was born at Stagira. Although he studied with Plato for some 20 years (367–347 B.C.), Aristotle's thought gradually turned more to biology than to mathematics. After Plato's death, he spent two years on the island of Lesbos studying natural history, especially marine biology. His interest in politics probably led Philip of Macedon to bring Aristotle to Pella to tutor the young Alexander. When Alexander the Great came to power, Aristotle became head of his own school in the Lyceum, so-called because of its proximity to the temple of Apollo Lyceus in Athens. His followers came to be called Peripatetics as a result of a custom at the school of strolling about as they studied and discussed. Aristotle's later teaching in Athens gave strong emphasis to experimental, scientific investigation. Most of the extant writings of Aristotle represent lectures delivered in his school at Athens. Works of his early period with Plato now remain only in fragments, two of the most famous being the *Protrepticus* and *On Philosophy*. The main works that we now possess date from the period 355–347 B. C. and include his logical treatises (*Categories, On Interpretation, Topics, Sophistic Elenchics, Prior* and *Posterior Analytics*), his physical works (*Physics, On Heavens, On Generation and Corruption*, and *Meteorology*), works on psychology (*On the Soul, Parva Naturalia*), works recording his biological investigations (*History of Animals*), the *Metaphysics,* his ethical treatises (*Eudemian Ethics* and *Nicomachean Ethics*), the *Politics,* and, finally, his writings in what we would call literary criticism (the *Rhetoric* and *Poetics*). Cf. W. D. Ross, *Aristotle* (London, 1949), and W. Jaeger, *Aristotle* (Oxford, 1948).

AVERROËS (1126–1198), outstanding exponent of Arabic thought in philosophy, astronomy, medicine and law, was born in Cordova, Spain. He was a judge in Seville (1169) and Cordova (1171). He was banished to Lucena from 1195 to 1198 for his philosophical views, but was restored to favor in 1198. His main original work was a reply to Algazel's *Incoherence of the Philosophers* and bore the title *Incoherence of the Incoherence.* It represents a concerted defense of Neo-platonic and Aristotelian philosophy. Most of his remaining works were extended commentaries on the works of Aristotle: the great commentaries, the middle commentaries and compendia. Latin translations of the commentaries exercised considerable influence over Christian philosophical thought in Western Europe both during the Middle Ages and Renaissance.

AVICENNA (980–1037) was an Islamic philosopher and physician who wielded great influence in both the Moslem world and in Christian Europe during the late Middle Ages. He was born in a small village near Bukhara but left when the Sumanid empire collapsed in 999. In 1020 he was vizier in Hamadan. His most important medical work was *The Canon of Medicine.* His chief philosophic work, the *Sufficientia,* was really a philosophical encyclopedia including as it did sections on logic, the natural sciences, psychology and metaphysics. The various parts of this great collection were translated into Latin, beginning with the work of Dominicus Gundissalinus late in the 12th century. His most mature thought is contained in his *Demonstrations and Affirmations,* a work that also covers almost the entire range of philosophy. Cf. F. Rahman, *Avicenna's Psychology* (London, 1952).

ROGER BACON (*ca.* 1220–1292), English theologian, philosopher, experimental scientist and educational reformer, was born either at Ilchester in Somerset or at Bisley in Gloucester of a wealthy family. He studied and later taught in the faculty of arts at Paris. His early interest in the more philosophical aspects of Aristotle's work was replaced by an all-consuming interest in experimental research about 1247. His new interest probably resulted from his contact with Robert Grosseteste and Adam Marsh at Oxford. His energies for ten years were devoted to languages, mathematics, optics, alchemy and astronomy. In 1257 he entered the Order of Friars Minor. In 1266 he wrote to Pope Clement IV suggesting changes in the courses of studies in the universities which, he felt, were needed for the Church's welfare. In response to the Pope's urging he wrote his *Opus Majus, Opus Minus* and *Opus Tertium* to explain his plans. His great plea was for a greater role for the experimental sciences in the universities. Bacon completed his *Compendium Philosophiae* in 1272. In addition to these original works he also commented extensively on Aristotle's writings (especially the *Metaphysics* and *Physics*) and on the *Liber de Causis*. His last work, completed in 1292, was the *Compendium studii theologiae*. Cf. Stewart C. Easton, *Roger Bacon and His Search for a Universal Science* (Oxford, 1952).

HENRI BERGSON (1859–1941), French philosopher, was born in Paris. After his studies at the Ecole Normale Supérieure, he taught philosophy at various lycées—Angers, Clermont-Ferrand, Henri IV. In 1900 he assumed his teaching-post at the Collège de France and in 1914 was elected to the Académie Française. After various diplomatic assignments in Spain and the United States during World War I he became chairman of the League of Nations committee on intellectual co-operation. The Nobel Prize for literature was awarded to him in 1928. His great contribution to philosophy was his re-thinking of being in dynamic terms; no longer were reality, time and freedom to be thought of as static images of the eternal but, rather, as realities marked by change and duration. His best-known works are *Matter and Memory, Creative Evolution,* and *The Two Sources of Morality and Religion.*

BOETHIUS, Anicius Manlius Severinus Boethius (480–524), Roman theologian, philosopher, scholar and statesman, was a member of the powerful Roman family of the Anicii. After his father's death he was raised by Symmachus, Roman senator, and married his daughter Rusticiana. Boethius held a series of high political posts, was consul in 510, a senator and head of civil services 520–522. He was accused of plotting against Theodoric and in favor of the Eastern Emperor, Justin I. He was imprisoned, probably at Pavia, and put to death in 524. In spite of such an eventful political life, his great cultural contribution was to grammar, mathematics, music, philosophy and theology. Especially important are his translations and commentaries on Porphyry's *Isagoge* and on Aristotle's *Categories, Perihermeneias* and *Prior Analytics.* Five theological tracts have survived, the most influential being *De Trinitate, Contra Eutychen et Nestorium,* and *Quomodo substantiae.* He is justly renowned as the author of *On the Consolation of Philosophy,* written while he was in prison. Cf. H. M. Barrett, *Boethius: some aspects of his times and work* (Cambridge, 1940).

CARDINAL CAJETAN (1468–1534), whose proper name was Tommaso de Vio, took the name 'Gaetanus' from his birthplace, Gaeta, in the kingdom of Naples. He became a Dominican in 1484, studied at the University of Padua and taught metaphysics there. In 1508 he became general of his order and cardinal-archbishop of Palermo in 1517. He was made legate to Germany in 1518 and it was before him that Martin Luther appeared at the Diet of Augsburg. He helped draw the bull excommunicating Luther in 1519. In theology and philosophy he tried to follow and interpret St. Thomas Aquinas, but his work is marked by the Averroism he experienced at Padua. He is best known in philosophy for his commentaries on Aristotle (*Categories, Posterior Analytics, On the Soul*) and St. Thomas (*Summa Theologiae, De Ente et Essentia*). His own work *De Analogia Nominum* has had considerable influence.

RENÉ DESCARTES (1596–1650), French philosopher, geometrician and physicist, was born at La Haye in Touraine. At the age of eight he was sent to the celebrated Jesuit college of La Flèche where he studied for some eight years. He was particularly impressed by the teaching of mathematics at the college and he also became interested in the mechanical arts while there. In 1612 he went to the University of Poitiers and graduated in law in 1616. After joining the army of Prince Maurice of Nassau he met Isaac Beeckman at Breda and returned to his work in science. His famous discovery of a universal science is said to have come in a dream at Neuberg on St. Martin's Eve, November 10, 1619; physics should be reduced to geometry and the other sciences connected thereto. During his travels in Germany, France and Switzerland throughout the following few years he pursued his ambition of making experiments and observations and reducing them to geometry. By 1629 he felt that his method was established and so he proceeded to expound it in his *Rules for the Direction of the Mind*. His next 20 years were spent in Holland. His *Discourse on Method* appeared in 1637 and his great philosophical work, *Meditations on First Philosophy*, in 1642. The *Principles of Philosophy* was dedicated to Princess Elizabeth of the Palatinate, his protectress, and appeared in 1644. He was invited to Sweden by Queen Christina to instruct her in his new views and he died in Stockholm. His new method in physics and philosophy was inspired by the clarity he found in geometric concepts, definitions and demonstrations. Rather than seek a different method for each of the sciences and philosophy appropriate to different subject-matter, Descartes would devise *one* method, a geometric method, for all sciences. The consequence for philosophy was his fundamental doctrine of clear and distinct ideas, a doctrine that has left its mark on his views of knowledge, body and mind, the material world and God. Cf. N. K. Smith, *Studies in Cartesian Philosophy* (New York, 1962).

JOHN DEWEY (1859–1952), philosopher, psychologist and educator, was born at Burlington, Vt. After graduation from the University of Vermont in 1879 he taught in rural schools for two years before going on to further studies at Johns Hopkins University. After receiving his doctorate he taught at Minnesota, Michigan and Chicago before going to Columbia University in 1904. There followed a most distinguished career in philosophy at Columbia and in several foreign countries, including the U.S.S.R. Much of his research and teaching in philosophy and psychology was directed toward reform in the American educational system. He approached problems in the field of education largely in the light of principles of mental activity and growth revealed by psychological research. A successful theory of education must, he felt, be based on a sound philosophy of human development and on an accurate analysis of the aims and needs of the society to be served by that educational system. Our experience must be constantly reconstructed and not merely recapitulated.

Many of his ideas became embodied in what came to be called "progressive education," an education that was largely student-centered rather than subject-centered. His philosophy as a whole was termed "Pragmatism," although he himself preferred "Instrumentalism." He felt that the experimental method of science provided the best way to solve philosophical, moral and social problems. His most important writings include *Psychology, Democracy and Education, Reconstruction in Philosophy, Human Nature and Conduct, Experience and Nature, The Quest for Certainty,* and *Logic: The Theory of Inquiry.* Cf. Paul Schilpp, *The Philosophy of John Dewey* (Evanston and Chicago, 1939).

DONATUS (Aelius Donatus) was a famous Roman grammarian and rhetorician of the mid-4th century A.D. His *Ars minor,* written for young students, provides basic instruction in the eight parts of speech. His *Ars major* is in three parts and is concerned with the elements of grammar, the various parts of speech and the beauties of language. In addition to these works Donatus also wrote commentaries on Terence and Vergil. His grammatical writings were widely used throughout the Middle Ages.

JOHN DUNS SCOTUS (1266–1308), known as *Doctor Subtilis,* theologian and philosopher, was born in the village of Maxton in Scotland. After becoming a member of the Order of Friars Minor in 1281, he studied at Oxford and Paris and lectured on the *Sentences* of Peter Lombard. He lectured at Oxford, Paris and Cologne, where he died on November 8, 1308. Scotus' thought is firmly imbedded in the Franciscan tradition of his day and is marked by a deep regard for St. Augustine and the scientific tradition of the Oxford Franciscans. He is generally critical of St. Thomas, but Henry of Ghent and Godfrey of Fontaine also came under his censure. He was best known for his doctrine of matter, the positive entity of *haecceity* or *thisness* setting one singular thing off from another, the univocal concept of being and the *a posteriori* proof of God's existence, the central role accorded to the will, and the formal distinction between the divine essence and attributes. His works include commentaries on the *Sentences* given at Oxford (*Opus Oxoniense*) and Paris (published in the form of reports of his Paris lectures and accordingly entitled *Reportata Parisiensa*), *Quaestiones Quodlibetales* and *Quaestiones subtilissimae in Metaphysicam.* The long-established tradition assigning the *De rerum Principio* to Scotus is without foundation. Cf. C. R. S. Harris, *Duns Scotus,* 2 vols. (Oxford, 1927); D. E. Sharp, *Franciscan Philosophy at Oxford* (London, 1930); E. Gilson, *Jean Duns Scot. Introduction à ses positions fondamentales* (Paris, 1952), also *History of Christian Philosophy in the Middle Ages* (New York, 1955), pp. 454–64.

WILLIAM JAMES DURANT (1885–        ), American historian of ideas, was born in North Adams, Mass. He was educated at St. Peter's College in Jersey City and Columbia University. Before becoming an instructor in philosophy at Columbia University in 1917, he had been a professor of Latin and French at Seton Hall College in South Orange, N.J. for four years. Durant became interested in social, and especially labor problems, as director of the Labor Temple School in New York from 1914 to 1927. His work in philosophy resulted in his writing the very popular *Mansions of Philosophy* in 1929, and the *Story of Philosophy*, which was revised in 1933. Later he undertook the more ambitious task of presenting the great cultures of history—oriental, Greek, Roman, early and medieval Christian, Reformation—in one many-volumed series.

GILES OF ROME (Aegidius Romanus c. 1245–1316), Italian theologian and philosopher, was the intellectual leader of the Augustinian hermits and a pupil of St. Thomas Aquinas at Paris 1269–1272. He was involved in the ecclesiastical condemnation of certain theses of St. Thomas in 1277 and was suspended from teaching 1277–1285. He was general of his order from 1292–1295 and archbishop of Bourges 1295–1316. He died at Avignon. His controversy with Henry of Ghent over the distinction between essence and existence made him a well-known figure. He also gained renown for his political views, especially regarding the pope's direct political power over temporal rulers. His many writings include commentaries on Aristotle's works, on the *Liber de Causis* and on the *Sentences* of Peter Lombard as well as the *Theoremata de esse et essentia* and the *De potestate ecclesiastica*. Cf. E. Gilson, *History of Christian Philosophy in the Middle Ages* (New York, 1955), pp. 420–23, 735–37.

ETIENNE GILSON (1884–        ), French theologian, philosopher and historian of ideas was born in Paris. After completing his philosophical studies at the Sorbonne, he became a professor at the University of Lille in 1913. Before being appointed Professor of Medieval Philosophy at the Sorbonne in 1921, he taught for two years at the University of Strasbourg. Gilson came to America to lecture at Harvard in 1928 and helped to found the Pontifical Institute of Medieval Studies at Toronto in 1929. In 1951 he retired as professor at the Collège de France after 19 years of teaching there. He is a Fellow of the French Academy and an officer in the Légion d'Honneur. His life-time of study has been dedicated to the careful study and reconstruction of the philosophical activities of medieval thinkers from Augustine to Ockham. In later years his attention has fallen almost exclusively on re-discovering the authentic thinking of St. Thomas Aquinas. His writings cover a span of 45 years and include most notably *The Philosophy of St. Bonaventure, The Christian Philosophy of St. Augustine, The Unity of Philosophical Experience, Being and Some Phi-*

*losophers, History of Christian Philosophy in the Middle Ages, Painting and Reality, Elements of Christian Philosophy,* and the *Spirit of Thomism.*

GODFREY OF FONTAINES, known as *Doctor venerandus,* was originally from Liège, but the date of his birth is not certain. He studied at Paris, first philosophy and then theology. He was a master of theology some time before 1285 and attained the regency in 1285–6. He was a canon at Liège, Tournai and Paris before becoming provost of St. Severin in Cologne. Godfrey was deeply involved in the controversy over the mendicant orders between 1282 and 1290. He was in Rome in 1300 and back in Paris in 1301. Godfrey died October 29 in either 1306 or 1309. The writings that we have consist mainly of a long series of 'quodlibetal' questions. Cf. E. Gilson, *History of Christian Philosophy in the Middle Ages* (New York, 1955), pp. 424–25, and 739–40.

BARTHÉLEMY HAURÉAU (1812–1896), French historian of theological, philosophical and literary works of the Middle Ages, was a deputy in the National Assembly before becoming director of the manuscript department of the Bibliothèque Nationale. He devoted all of his energies in the library to the task of cataloguing and making abstracts of the library's holdings of medieval manuscripts. He made a collection of the *incipits* or opening words of many manuscripts and after his death his notes were arranged to form a manuscript-catalogue. His works include: *Histoire de la philosophie scolastique* (Paris, 1872–80).

GEORG WILHELM FRIEDRICH HEGEL (1770–1831), German philosopher, was born at Stuttgart. As a schoolboy at Stuttgart he developed a deep interest in classical antiquity. He studied classics and philosophy at Tübingen, where he took his Ph.D. in 1790. There followed a period of theological study, but his friendship with J. C. F. Hölderlin soon revived his passion for Greek literature. His reading of Kant rekindled his interest in religion, but now a more thoroughly rational religion. Hölderlin obtained a tutorship for him at Frankfurt-am-Main in 1796 and he was able to pursue his studies in Greek philosophy and to devote himself to a newly-found interest in Christianity—he was especially intrigued by the theology of the Holy Spirit. He began, too, serious reading in history. One result of these studies was his *Spirit of Christianity.* Love and spirit came to play a greater role in his thinking than Kantian reason. In 1801 he went to Jena, where Schelling was a professor, and soon produced a work *On the Difference between Fichte's and Schelling's System of Philosophy.* He began a teaching career at Jena and was made extraordinary professor in 1805. Two years later in 1807 he produced his first great work, *Phenomenology of Spirit.* There followed a period as editor of the *Bamberger Zeitung* before he was made rector of a gymnasium at Nuremberg. At Nuremberg he produced his *Science of Logic,* part I (Objective Logic) in 1812, part 2 (Subjective Logic) in 1816. Subsequently he held professorships at Erlangen, Berlin and Heidelberg, and produced the *Encyclopedia of the Philosophical Sciences,* and the *Philosophy of Right.* His later work is represented almost exclusively by series of lectures on aesthetics, philosophy of history, history of philosophy and religion. He died while at work on the revision of the *Science of Logic.*

MARTIN HEIDEGGER (1889–      ), German philosopher, continues to exercise a profound influence over contemporary phenomenology and existential thinking. He was born at Messkirch in the Black Forest, and studied philosophy at Freiburg under Edmund Husserl. He was made professor of philosophy at Marburg in 1923. His first work, *Being and Time,* was published in 1927 and quickly brought him renown. In 1928 he succeeded Husserl in the chair of philosophy at Freiburg and was made rector of the university in 1933. He resigned in 1934 to resume his teaching. His writings constitute a formidable array and all of them focus on the question of Being (*Sein*). He has designated his own thinking as a fundamental thinking of the truth of Being (*Sein*), rather than traditional ontology or more contemporary philosophical anthropology. Phenomenological analysis or interpretation of *Dasein* (There-being) provides the key to the interpretation and thinking about Being (*Sein*). Cf. William Richardson, *Martin Heidegger: Through Phenomenology to Thought* (The Hague, 1963).

HENRY OF GHENT (Henricus de Gandavo d. 1293) was known as 'Doctor Solemnis.' After studies at Ghent and Cologne, he was made a canon at Tournai in 1267 and archdeacon of Bruges in 1276. As a master of theology at Paris he became renowned for his theological and philosophical views. His indebtedness to St. Augustine was very real, including the sceptical questions about man's capacity for knowledge Augustine had inherited from Cicero. Henry's own distrust of natural knowledge leaves its mark not only on his philosophy but on his theology as well. His thought influenced Duns Scotus in the 14th century. He is the author of a *Summa Theologiae,* as well as various *Quodlibetal* questions. Cf. E. Gilson, *History of Christian Philosophy in the Middle Ages* (New York, 1955), pp. 447ff.

THOMAS HOBBES (1588–1679), English philosopher, was born at Westport, Wiltshire. At the age of four he was sent to the church school in Westport and later to a private school. In 1603 Hobbes entered Magdalen Hall, Oxford and upon graduation became a private tutor to William Cavendish, later second Earl of Devonshire. He devoted himself to classical studies, but some time between 1621 and 1625 met Francis Bacon and became interested in philosophy. He found himself attracted to work in philosophy and science while on travels to France and Italy in 1630 and 1634; geometry aroused his enthusiasm in a special way. Visits to Mersenne and Galileo finally determined him on the project of expounding motion geometrically. However, when he returned to England he found serious political upheavals threatening and threw himself into a defense of the monarchy. When he felt himself in danger in 1640, Hobbes fled to Paris and remained there for eleven years. In 1651 he returned and was soon involved in his famous controversies with John Bramhall, Seth Ward and John Wallis. He returned to favor under Charles II for a time, but in 1666 the commons proposed to take action against atheism and *Leviathan* (1651) was cited for investigation. The bill was dropped but Hobbes could no longer get permission to publish, so he returned to his classical studies. He died at Hardwick Hall in Derbyshire. In addition to *Leviathan*, Hobbes also wrote *On the City, On Body, On Man* and numerous polemical works. Cf. Sir Leslie Stephen, *Hobbes* (London, 1904); John Laird, *Hobbes* (London, 1934); C. B. Macpherson, *The Political Theory of Possessive Individualism, Hobbes to Locke* (Oxford, 1962), and R. Peters, *Hobbes* (London, 1956).

DAVID HUME (1711–1776), British historian, economist and philosopher, was born in Edinburgh. He entered Edinburgh University in 1723 and later studied law for a very short period. In 1743 after a few years in business he went to France for three years of study and writing that saw the beginning of his first work *A Treatise of Human Nature*. It gained him little attention, but his *Essays, Moral and Political*, written in 1741–2 had a far different reception. After an unsuccessful effort to get the chair of philosophy at Edinburgh in 1744, he spent the next years as a tutor and secretary. This leisure time enabled him to continue his philosophical writing. In 1752 Hume became keeper of the Advocates Library in Edinburgh and he took up the serious study of history. Between 1754 and 1762 he produced six volumes of his *History of England*. In 1763 he became secretary of the British embassy in Paris and in 1766 was made undersecretary of state. Upon his return to London he brought Jean-Jacques Rousseau, then a refugee from persecution in France, with him. Hume retired to Edinburgh in 1769 and devoted his energies to re-editing his earlier works. He died in Edinburgh after a long illness. Apart from his histories and essays in economics, his main philosophical writings were his *Enquiry Concerning Human Understanding, A Treatise of Human Nature* and the *Enquiry Concerning the Principles of Morals*. Cf. E. C. Mossner, *Life of David Hume* (Austin, Texas, 1954) and N. Kemp Smith, *The Philosophy of David Hume* (London, 1941).

EDMUND HUSSERL (1859–1938), German philosopher and father of phenomenology, was born at Prossnitz in Moravia on April 8, 1859. He began his mathematical studies at various German universities before moving to Vienna in 1884. There he met Franz Brentano and his attention was turned to the philosophical foundations of mathematics. Husserl became a *Privatdozent* at Halle in 1887 and later professor at Göttingen and Freiburg-im-Breisgau. His later work was carried on at Freiburg until his retirement in 1928. Husserl died there on April 27, 1938. He first devised his phenomenological method about 1896 and first applied it to numbers and logical concepts. Later it developed into a systematic descriptive analysis of other phases of consciousness. His most notable writings were the *Logical Investigations, Ideas for a Pure Phenomenology* and *Cartesian Meditations*.

IMMANUEL KANT (1724–1804), German philosopher and father of critical, transcendental philosophy, was born at Königsberg, East Prussia. Pietism was the prevailing influence in his family and his early education was at the Collegium Fridericianum, a famous Pietist school. In 1740 he went to the University of Königsberg and very soon became deeply influenced by the philosophies of Leibniz and Wolff. He earned his living at this period as a private tutor and *Privatdozent* at Königsberg. In 1770 he became professor of logic and metaphysics there and remained active in that capacity until near his death. Apart from his early pre-critical essays, Kant is most famous for his three *Critiques* (*Critique of Pure Reason, Critique of Practical Reason,* and *Critique of Judgment*), the *Prologomena to any Future Metaphysic, Groundwork of the Metaphysics of Morals,* and *Religion within the Bounds of Mere Reason*. Cf. Stephen Körner, *Kant* (Harmondsworth, 1955); N. Kemp Smith, *A Commentary on Kant's Critique of Pure Reason* (London, 1918), and H. J. Paton, *The Categorical Imperative* (London, 1947).

SØREN AABYE KIERKEGAARD (1813–1855), Danish theologian and philosopher, was born at Copenhagen. He was raised in the shadow of his father's guilt, the consequence of his cursing God, and he lived under the constant fear of death. After his father died in 1838 he had his soul-searing engagement with Regina Olsen, followed by the breaking of the engagement and years of remorse. Kierkegaard left Copenhagen briefly to visit Berlin, where he attended Schelling's lectures. After returning to Copenhagen he devoted the rest of his life to criticizing the contemporary forms of Christianity he encountered, and to inspiring people to become Christians. His later life was marked by constant polemic—with Meïr Goldschmidt and the periodical *Corsair,* and with bishops Mynster and Martensen. Kierkegaard died in Copenhagen. He is remembered best for his *Journals, Either- Or, Concluding Unscientific Postscript, Philosophical Fragments* and *Sickness unto Death*. Cf. J. E. Hohlenberg, *Søren Kierkegaard* (London, 1954) and Walter Lowrie, *Kierkegaard* (London, 1938).

JOHN LOCKE (1632–1704), English philosopher, was born at Wrington, Somersetshire. After early studies at Westminster School, he entered Christ Church, Oxford, in 1646. Locke lectured on Greek, rhetoric and philosophy from 1661 to 1664. Reading Descartes spurred him to even greater interest in and devotion to philosophy. He was attracted to the experimental work in medicine and chemistry being done by Thomas Sydenham and Robert Boyle. Shortly after 1666 he met the first Earl of Shaftesbury and became his confidential secretary, making his home at Exeter House for many years. It was in friendly discussions held at Exeter House that Locke conceived the inspiration for his *Essay on Human Understanding*, eventually published in 1690. The downfall of Shaftesbury in 1675 forced Locke from England, and he spent the next three years in France. In 1683 he returned to Holland for five years and completed the *Essay* while there. A year after William of Orange landed in England, Locke returned and continued his writing, particularly on political matters and questions of toleration. In 1691 he retired to Oates Manor in Essex and spent 14 years writing, although in poor health, and in various public services. Many of his letters dealt with liberty and tolerance, as well as with interpreting and defending views expressed in the *Essay*. In addition to the *Essay Concerning Human Understanding*, Locke wrote three *Letters on Toleration* (a fourth was incomplete at his death), *Two Treatises of Government* and *Some Thoughts Concerning Education*. Cf. H. R. Fox Bourne, *The Life of John Locke* (London, 1876); R. I. Aaron, *John Locke* (London, 1955); and J. W. Gough, *John Locke's Political Philosophy* (London, 1950).

GABRIEL MARCEL (1889–    ), French philosopher and man of letters, was born at Paris. He was educated at the Lycée Carnot and the Faculty of Letters in Paris. After receiving the Agrégé in philosophy he taught at various lycées, Lycée Vendôme (1911–12), Lycée Condorcet (1915–18), and Lycée Sens (1919–22). Marcel then forsook formal teaching and worked in various capacities with the publishing houses of Plon and Grasset. He became the drama critic for *Nouvelles littéraires* and contributed numerous critical articles to other literary journals. Marcel is a member of the Institute (Academy of moral and political sciences), was Gifford lecturer at Aberdeen 1949–1950, and has been awarded several prizes for literature—the Grand Prix de littérature de l'Académie Française in 1949 and the Grand Prix national des lettres in 1958. Marcel is an officer of the Légion d'Honneur. In addition to numerous plays, themselves philosophically important, he has written *Metaphysical Journals, Being and Having, Homo Viator, The Mystery of Being, Man against Mass Society*, and *The Decline of Wisdom*.

JACQUES MARITAIN (1882–    ), French Catholic theologian and philosopher, was born in Paris. His first philosophical studies were made under Prof. Dereux at the Lycée Henri IV. Later at the Sorbonne he continued his studies in philosophy and the natural sciences; Victor Delbos, Gabriel Séailles, Lucien Lévy-Bruhl, Emile Durkheim and Henri Bergson were numbered among his illustrious professors. It was his friend Charles Péguy who first brought Maritain to Bergson's classes. Léon Bloy first kindled an interest in Christianity in Maritain, and he became Bloy's spiritual godchild. Maritain has taught at the Institut Catholique in Paris, the Pontifical Institute of Medieval Studies in Toronto and at Princeton University. Maritain left France in 1940 to continue his writing and teaching in New York during World War II. After the war he became French ambassador to the Holy See from 1945 to 1948. His main philosophical work has centered on the thought of St. Thomas Aquinas, and it has been his continuing inspiration to re-think the philosophical questions of his day in the light of Aquinas' principles. Maritain's writings span a period of 46 years, some of the more influential ones being *Art and Scholasticism, Three Reformers, The Degrees of Knowledge, Integral Humanism, Education at the Crossroads, Man and the State, Creative Intuition in Art and Poetry,* and *Moral Philosophy.*

KARL HEINRICH MARX (1818–1883), German philosopher and economist, was born at Treves in Germany. After preliminary studies at Treves, Marx went to the universities at Bonn and Berlin, studying history, law and philosophy. He began work with the *Rheinische Zeitung* and in October 1842 became one of the editors of that journal. His interest in socialism was aroused by articles in his paper and in 1843 Marx went to Paris to study the intellectual phase of the socialist movement at first hand. He became convinced that only a political solution could help the proletariat. It was in Paris that Marx met Friedrich Engels and thereby began his long collaboration with that writer. The Prussian government requested that Marx and his small group be dismissed from France, so Marx went to Brussels where he published *The Poverty of Philosophy* as a rejoinder to Proudhon. In 1847 Marx and Engels wrote their *Communist Manifesto.* When revolution broke out in France in 1848 Marx was in France for a short time but soon left for Cologne. Shortly after his arrival he was forced to leave Germany and settled in London, where he was to remain and do the rest of his writing. In 1859 Marx published his *Critique of Political Economy* and then thoroughly revised the material to produce *Capital* in 1867. The International Working Men's Association was founded in London in 1864 and Marx became its head; he remained in that capacity until its dissolution in 1876. Ill health interfered with his researches and he finally died on March 14, 1883. Cf. Isaiah Berlin, *Karl Marx, His Life and Environment* (London, 1948); Erich Fromm, *Marx's Concept of Man* (New York, 1961); Eugene Kamenka, *The Ethical Foundations of Marxism* (New York, 1962), and Robert C. Tucker, *Philosophy and Myth in Karl Marx* (Cambridge, 1961).

JOHN STUART MILL (1806–1873), British philosopher and economist, was born in Pentonville, London. His education was received entirely from his father, James Mill, and at the age of eight he began studying Latin, algebra and geometry; by the age of twelve he read Plato in Greek and had begun the serious study of logic. The year 1820–1821 was spent in France with the family of Sir Samuel Bentham, brother of Jeremy. When he returned he began reading psychology and Roman law. Mill entered the examiner's office of the East India Co. in 1823 and from 1836 to 1856 had charge of the company's relations with native states. Mill's interest in logic and moral philosophy led to numerous articles in the

*Traveller, Morning Chronicle, Westminster Review, Examiner,* and *Edinburgh Review.* Many such articles were collected in his *Dissertations and Discussions.* Upon the dissolution of the East India Co. in 1858 he retired and spent some years at his villa at St. Véran near Avignon, where his wife had died. Mill came out of retirement in 1865 to stand as parliamentary candidate for Westminster. He took an active part in the debates on the Reform bills of 1866–1867. He was elected rector of St. Andrew's University in 1867. After his defeat in the election of 1868 Mill retired once more to Avignon where he continued to live and write until his death. In addition to innumerable articles his main philosophical works are *The System of Logic, On Liberty, Utilitarianism, Examination of Sir William Hamilton's Philosophy,* and *Auguste Comte and Positivism.* As an economist he is best known for his *Principles of Political Economy.* Cf. M. S. Packe, *The Life of John Stuart Mill* (London, 1954) and Richard P. Anshutz, *The Philosophy of John Stuart Mill* (Oxford, 1953).

WILLIAM OF OCCAM or OCKHAM (c. 1280–1349), known as *Venerabilis Inceptor,* was probably born at Ockham in Surrey. After joining the Franciscans about 1300, he studied the arts at Oxford prior to 1310 and later (1312–1318) theology. He lectured on the *Sentences* of Peter Lombard from 1318 to 1320 and became a doctor of theology in 1319. In 1323 he was called to Avignon to defend himself against charges of heresy and was confined to his convent from 1324 to 1328. In 1328 he entered into a further conflict with Pope John XXII over the Spirituals in the Franciscan order, and he fled with Michael of Cesena, General of the Franciscans, to the court of Louis of Bavaria. His defense of the independence of kingly authority as against the pope's temporal authority brought him into continuous conflict with Rome and he was expelled from his order in 1331. He died at Munich in 1349 while striving for reconciliation with the pope. In philosophy he was famous for his attack on abstract speculation and his insistence on the fundamental reality of singular things known by perceptive or intuitive knowledge. This basic insight led him to criticize prevailing views of nature, matter, abstraction, the habits and the ordering of the sciences. His principle of economy in demonstration has come to be called "Ockham's Razor." Among his best-known works are a commentary on the *Sentences, Summa totius logicae, Quodlibeta septem, Octo quaestiones de potestate papae* and *Defensorium contra errores Johannis XXII papae.* Cf. L. Baudry, *Guillaume d'Occam. Sa vie, ses oeuvres, ses idées sociales et politiques,* Vol. I (Paris, 1950); E. Gilson, *History of Christian Philosophy in the Middle Ages* (New York, 1955), pp. 489–98.

PLATO (428–7 B.C.—348–7 B.C.) was born at Athens of an influential family, the son of Ariston and Perictione. His mother's family was ardent in its support of Pericles; Socrates was an old family friend. Plato's early interest was in a political career, but Socrates' fate deterred him from such a future. After Socrates' death Plato spent several years travelling in Greece, Egypt and Italy. About 387 he returned and founded the Academy as a center of philosophical study. The main departure from speculative work came in 367 when Dionysius I of Syracuse died and Dion, his brother-in-law and a friend of Plato's, arranged for him to come as tutor to Dionysius' successor. The project of training and influencing the young leader did not bear fruit but continued in one way or another —including a second visit to Syracuse in 361–360—until Dion's death in 354. Closely allied with Plato's work in philosophy and his political activity was the stimulus he and the Academy gave to mathematics. Thaetetus, Eudoxus and most of the creative mathematicians of the day were members of the Academy. From the *Apology* to the *Laws* some 50 years of speculation intervened and produced some 36 major works. Perhaps the best known and most widely read are the *Republic, Timaeus, Phaedo, Symposium, Meno, Parmenides, Theaetetus* and *Philebus*. Cf. A. E. Taylor, *Plato: The Man and His Work* (London, 1948); P. Shorey, *What Plato Said* (Chicago, 1934); J. Burnet, *Greek Philosophy,* part I (London, 1932).

PLOTINUS (205–270 A.D.) was the founder and one of the most influential philosophers of what has come to be called the Neo-platonist school. He was probably born in Egypt, although his education and cultural development was Greek. He studied philosophy at Alexandria under Amonius Saccas. In 243 he accompanied Gordion III's expedition to the East, hoping to learn something of Indian philosophy. Gordion's death in Mesopotamia, however, prevented the plan from being accomplished. Plotinus returned and went to Rome, where he spent the rest of his life teaching and writing. He died at the age of 66 after a lengthy illness. His great work was to extend and unify Plato's speculations about the soul and the good, and to develop Platonism in the direction of a religious philosophy. It was this turn that made it so attractive to St. Augustine and medieval Christian theologians. His writings were collected by his devoted disciple Porphyry, and arranged in groups of nine treatises. Hence, they have come to us under the title of *The Enneads*. Cf. A. H. Armstrong, *Plotinus* (London, 1953); J. Katz, *Plotinus' Search for the Good* (New York, 1950).

PRISCIAN (Priscianus Caesariensis, lived about 500 A.D.) is one of the most famous of Latin grammarians. He was born at Caesarea and taught at Constantinople. His most important work, the *Institutiones Grammaticae*, is a long exposition of Latin grammar from basic sounds and word-formation to more complex syntax. It was widely used in the Middle Ages and became a model not only for work in grammar but logic as well. Cf. J. E. Sandys, *History of Classical Scholarship*, Vol. 1 (New York, 1958).

PROCLUS (410–485 A.D.) was the representative of Neo-platonism best known to Christian thinkers in medieval Europe. He was born at Constantinople, studied philosophy under Olympiodorus at Alexandria and Syrianus at Athens. He became head of the Academy at Athens and held that esteemed post until 485. Proclus was a great systematizer, and it was his main accomplishment to organize and abridge the work and conclusions of Iamblicus and his predecessors in the Academy. The work that wielded the greatest influence through the so-called *Liber de Causis* was Proclus' *Elements of Theology,* a presentation of Neo-platonic metaphysics in 211 propositions. He also wrote an *Elements of Physics, Platonic Theology,* commentaries on several dialogues of Plato, and a few shorter essays. Cf. E. R. Dodds, ed., *Proclus: The Elements of Theology* (Oxford, 1933); L. J. Rosan, *The Philosophy of Proclus* (New York, 1949).

ROSCELIN (Roscellinus Compendiensis c. 1050–1125), theologian and philosopher, was born at Compiègne. After making his initial studies at Soissons and Reims, he taught at Compiègne, Loches, Besançon and Tours. Almost nothing he wrote has come down to us, his teachings being reported for refutation in the works of Abelard and St. Anselm. In Philosophy he is identified with the positions that the universal is a *flatus vocis,* i.e. the sound of the spoken word; in theology he is remembered for a doctrine of the Trinity as three substances, condemned at the Council of Soissons in 1092. Cf. Fr. Picavet, *Roscelin philosophe et théologien d'après la legende et d'après l'histoire* (Paris, 1911).

BERTRAND ARTHUR WILLIAM, Lord Russell (1872–      ), British mathematician and philosopher, was born at Trelleck. He was educated at Trinity College, Cambridge where he earned his degree in mathematics and moral science. He was awarded the Sylvester Medal of the Royal Society in 1934, the De Morgan Medal of the London Mathematical Society in 1934, and received the Nobel Prize in Literature in 1950. His early studies in mathematics have resulted in highly original and valuable contributions to the philosophical understanding of mathematical entities and to the development of mathematical logic; his first training in moral science has matured into a continuing social concern for world peace and a parallel condemnation of nuclear warfare. His literary activity has been truly astounding and now covers a period of 70 years! One of his early works, done with Alfred North Whitehead, the *Principia Mathematica,* has had a decisive influence on modern logic. Among his other works some of the more notable are the *Philosophy of Leibniz, Our Knowledge of the External World, Introduction to Mathematical Thinking, The Analysis of Matter, The Scientific Outlook, Education and the Social Order, Freedom and Organisation, An Inquiry into Meaning and Truth, History of Western Philosophy, Human Knowledge, Its Scope and Limits, Common Sense and Nuclear Warfare* and *Has man a future?*

SAINT ALBERT THE GREAT (Albert of Cologne 1200–1280), theologian, philosopher and scientist was born at Lauingen in Swabia. He joined the Order of Preachers in 1223 at Padua and subsequently taught at Cologne and Paris. In 1248 he was at Cologne to establish a *studium generale* for the Dominicans and had St. Thomas Aquinas as one of his disciples there. He was later provincial of the German province of Dominicans, bishop of Regensburg, papal legate preaching the Crusade in Germany. His numerous writings include works in theology, philosophy and natural science. Some of the more important ones are the following: *De Bono*, *Summa de Creaturis*, *Summa Theologiae* and expository works explaining the writings of Aristotle, Boethius and Dionysius the Areopagite. Cf. E. Gilson, *History of Christian Philosophy in the Middle Ages* (New York, 1955), pp. 277–94; S. M. Albert, *Albert the Great* (Oxford, 1948).

SAINT ANSELM (1033–1109), theologian, philosopher and archbishop of Canterbury, was born at Aosta in Piedmont. Following a quarrel with his father in 1047 he left Aosta to cross the Alps and travelled through France to settle ultimately at the monastery of Bec—the prior being Lanfranc, a countryman of Anselm's. Anselm became a monk in 1063 and when Lanfranc became abbot of Caen in 1063, Anselm was elected Prior. In 1078 he was made Abbot of Bec. It was one of his responsibilities to visit the monastery's properties in England, and on one such visit assisted in the founding of St. Werburgh's monastery in Chester as a dependent of Bec. In 1093 William II nominated him for the archbishopric of Canterbury and much against his will Anselm was consecrated in December 1093. Disputes at once arose concerning the recognition of Urban II and Anselm's liberty to visit Rome. In 1097 Anselm visited Rome and stayed in Italy until William's death. In 1100 Henry I recalled him but the struggle over investiture rights continued. A short period of exile followed 1103–1106 when he returned to his see and remained there until his death April 21, 1109. His main writings include *Cur Deus Homo, De Veritate, Monologion, Proslogion, Liber Apologeticus* and *De Libero Arbitrio*. Cf. J. Clayton, *Saint Anselm, a critical biography* (Milwaukee, 1933).

SAINT AUGUSTINE (Aurelius Augustinus, 354–430), theologian, philosopher and bishop of Hippo, was born at Tagaste, Numidia (in North Africa). At the age of twelve he was sent to the school of grammar at Madaura where he learned Latin and some Greek. He later studied rhetoric at Carthage. Still not a Christian, Augustine accepted the practice of concubinage common to students of his day and became the father of a son, Adeodatus. He became interested in Manichaeism and followed the practices of that cult for some nine years. However, when Faustus came to Carthage, Augustine found him less than a challenging head of the sect and soon lost interest in it. Instead, he became attracted to Cicero and a form of scepticism. Augustine went to Rome to teach rhetoric and finally reached Milan in 384. There, largely through the direction of his mother Monica, Augustine came under the influence of St. Ambrose, bishop of Milan. He wrote to Ambrose from Cassiciacum asking to be baptized a Christian, to which Ambrose acceded at Easter 387. Augustine resolved to return to Africa, but Monica died en route at Ostia. Augustine and Adeodatus then settled at Tagaste. On a visit to Hippo he was acclaimed by the people and recommended to the bishop for ordination in 391. He was made bishop in 395. During his 35 years as bishop of Hippo Augustine became famous for his defense of Catholic doctrine against Manichaeans, Arians and Donatists. His writings are extensive, but the most familiar are his *Confessions, City of God, Against the Academics, On the Happy Life, On the Immortality of the Soul, On Music, On the Trinity* and *On Free Choice*. Cf. V. J. Bourke, *Augustine's Quest of Wisdom* (Milwaukee, 1945) and Etienne Gilson, *The Christian Philosophy of Saint Augustine* (New York, 1960).

SAINT BONAVENTURE (Giovanni di Fidanza, 1221–1274), Italian theologian and doctor of the Church (the "Seraphic Doctor") was born at Bagnorea near Viterbo. He became a Franciscan in 1243 and studied at Paris at the same time as St. Thomas Aquinas. In 1253 he assumed the teaching chair reserved for Franciscans at Paris, was appointed general of his order in 1257 and made a doctor of theology. He attended the Council of Lyons as cardinal and bishop of Albano. He died during the council July 14, 1274 and was canonized by Pope Sixtus IV in 1482. In his theology and philosophy. St. Bonaventure placed himself firmly in the tradition of St. Augustine. His numerous writings include a long commentary on Peter Lombard's *Sententiae*, the *Breviloquium,* and the *Itinerarium mentis in Deum*. Cf. E. Gilson, *The Philosophy of St. Bonaventure* (New York, 1938).

SAINT JOHN OF DAMASCUS (Johannes Damascenus, John Damascene), widely-read and influential theologian of the Eastern Church, was born at an undetermined date early in the eighth century at Damascus. His father Sergius, although a Christian, held high office under the Saracen caliph and John succeeded him. Some time after 730 he entered the monastery of St. Sabas near Jerusalem and spent most of his remaining years there in prayer, meditation and writing. He was ordained, travelled briefly through Syria struggling with the iconoclasts who opposed the use of images in worship, and even visited Constantinople. He died about 752. Before entering upon the monastic life he wrote several treatises in defense of images. His most important treatise, *The Fountain of Knowledge*, was, however, written later as a monk and is composed of three parts: a) *Philosophical Chapters,* often called the *Dialectic,* briefly examines many of the main concepts encountered in the various parts of philosophy; b) *On Heresies* gives a brief account of the various heresies that had arisen in the Church; c) *An Accurate Exposition of the Orthodox Faith* is an attempt to produce a well-integrated system of theology based on the councils and the Fathers. About 1150 it was translated into Latin by Burgundio of Pisa and subsequently had wide circulation, under the title *De Fide Orthodoxa,* among the theologians of the Western Church during the 13th. and 14th. centuries. It is published in the *Patrologia Graeca* of Migne in volume 94, col. 517ff.

SAINT THOMAS AQUINAS (1225–1274), theologian, philosopher and doctor of the Church (*Doctor communis* and *Doctor angelicus*), was born of a distinguished Lombard-Norman family at Roccasecca. His first studies were made at nearby Monte Cassino, and he later moved to Naples where he studied under Peter the Irishman and Martin of Denmark. After becoming a Dominican he was sent to Cologne to study under Albertus Magnus. He first taught at Paris in 1252, later at the papal court in 1259. He was recalled to Paris in 1269 to combat Averroism. In 1272 he was appointed to the house of studies at Naples. He was summoned to the Council of Lyons in 1274 but died on the way at Fossa Nuova on March 7, 1274. His main works include the *Scriptum in IV libros Sententiarum magistri Petri, Summa Contra Gentiles, Summa Theologiae,* disputed questions *On Truth, On the Power of God, On Evil,* 12 'quodlibetal' questions, commentaries on several works of Aristotle, biblical commentaries and a variety of smaller works. Cf. Martin Grabmann, *Thomas Aquinas* (New York, 1928); Frederick Copleston, *Aquinas* (Harmondsworth, 1955); Joseph Pieper, *Guide to St. Thomas* (New York, 1962); Etienne Gilson, *The Christian Philosophy of St. Thomas Aquinas* (New York, 1956).

JEAN-PAUL SARTRE (1905–      ), French philosopher, novelist and playwright, was born at Paris. After completing his early studies at the Lycée in La Rochelle, he returned to Paris to do his advanced work. He gained the Agrégé in Philosophy in 1930 and taught at Le Havre and the French Institute in Berlin before joining the staff of the famous Lycée Henri IV in Paris. At the beginning of World War II he was mobilized into the French army and taken prisoner in 1940. After nine months in captivity he came back to France and worked in the resistance movement. After the war he returned to teaching for a brief period, then retired to devote his full time to writing and directing his review *Les Temps Modernes.* Sartre has always managed to combine serious writing in academic philosophy with highly dramatic plays and novels that convey his philosophical ideas in much more exciting form. Thus, for example, *Being and Nothingness* appeared along with *The Flies* and *No Exit* in 1943. Earlier philosophical works included *Imaginaire* and *Imagination.* His last major work appeared in 1960 under the title *Critique de la Raison dialectique.* Sartre's own brand of phenomenology has earned him the title of father of French existentialism, although it must be admitted that his own thinking constitutes but one limited aspect of that manner of philosophizing.

SIGER OF BRABANT, French philosopher, was a native of the Duchy of Brabant, but the exact dates of his birth and death are not known. From 1266–1276 he was prominent in the disputes in the Faculty of Arts at

Paris. His version of Aristotelianism, combining as it did Aristotle with Avicenna, Averroës and Proclus, has been variously titled "Latin Averroism," "Latin Aristotelianism" and "Heterodox Aristotelianism," and faced continuing criticism and final condemnation in his own day. Bonaventure and Aquinas were his two great foes, and he was formally condemned on December 10, 1270 and March 7, 1277. He was stabbed to death at Orvieto before 1284. His most controversial doctrines centered on his view of the world as eternal and necessary, the necessary emanation of all beings from God, and a unique soul and intellect for all men. His main works include *Quaestiones in Metaphysicam, Impossibilia, Quaestiones de Necessitate et Contingentia Causarum, De Aeternitate Mundi* and *Quaestiones in tertium De Anima*. Cf. Fernand van Steenberghen, *Aristotle in the West* (Louvain, 1955); E. Gilson, *History of Christian Philosophy in the Middle Ages* (New York, 1955), pp. 389–99.

BENEDICTUS DE SPINOZA (1632–1677), Dutch philosopher, was born in Amsterdam of a family of prosperous merchants. He probably attended the school for Jewish boys in Amsterdam. His father died in 1654 and although, after much litigation, Spinoza should have inherited the family wealth, he allowed his step-sister to do so and managed with great financial strain to support himself by learning to grind lenses. He continued his studies and he soon came to hold views that prompted his dismissal from the synagogue in July 1656. Spinoza was banished from Amsterdam and for a time taught school with a Jesuit friend, Francis van den Enden. At this time he became interested in Descartes' philosophical speculations and began re-thinking them in his own way. In 1660 he went into seclusion at Rijnberg near Leyden and wrote *On the Improvement of the Understanding* and a *Short Treatise on God, Man, and his Well-being*. By 1662 he had completed a plan for a systematic exposition of his own views and there soon followed the full *Ethics* and the *Tractatus theologico-politicus*. Spinoza contracted a severe pulmonary condition from his work with lenses and died at the Hague on Feb. 20, 1677. Cf. Stuart Hampshire, *Spinoza* (London, 1956); George H. R. Parkinson, *Spinoza's Theory of Knowledge* (Oxford, 1954); Harry A. Wolfson, *The Philosophy of Spinoza* (Cambridge, 1948), and Ruth L. Saw, *The Vindication of Metaphysics* (London, 1951).

FRANCISCO SUAREZ (1548–1617), Spanish theologian and philosopher, was born at Granada on January 5, 1548. He entered the Society of Jesus in 1564 and subsequently taught theology at Valladolid, Alcala, Salamanca and Rome. In philosophy his interpretation of St. Thomas' thought was influenced by his reading of Scotus, Ockham and the later commentators; in theology he was involved in the Molinist controversy concerning grace and predestination and taught a doctrine that came to be called congruism. His influence in political philosophy was extensive and in many ways he prepared the way for Hugo Grotius and Samuel Pufendorf. He was famous for a lengthy treatise he wrote against James I when the latter demanded an oath of allegiance from all his subjects. It bore the title *Defensio Catholicae fidei contra anglicanae sectae errores.* Other works included the *Disputationes Metaphysicae* and *Tractatus de legibus ac deo legislatore.* Cf. J. H. Fichter, *Man of Spain: Francis Suarez* (New York, 1940).

ALFRED NORTH WHITEHEAD (1861–1947), British philosopher and mathematician, was born at Ramsgate in Kent on Feb. 15, 1861. He studied mathematics at Cambridge and became a fellow of Trinity College. He taught mathematics at University College in the University of London before going to Harvard in 1924 as professor of philosophy. During his stay at Harvard Whitehead worked out his organic philosophy in which he tried to correct an over-emphasis on the role of mathematics in philosophy by bringing his thinking into close touch with the biological and behavioral sciences. He collaborated with Bertrand Russell in the writing of *Principia Mathematica* and exerted a great influence on the development of mathematical logic. He died at Cambridge, Massachusetts. Whitehead's most influential philosophical works are *The Concept of Nature, Process and Reality, Science in the Modern World* and *The Aims of Education.*

WILLIAM OF CHAMPEAUX (Guglielmus de Campellis, 1070–1121), French theologian and philosopher was born at Champeaux near Melun. He studied under Manegold of Lautenbach, Anselm of Laon and Roscelin. Abelard was one of his pupils at the cathedral school of Notre Dame. About 1108 he retired to the Abbey of St. Victor in Paris to teach theology and logic. During his last years he was bishop of Châlons-sur-Marne. In philosophy he is best remembered for his part in the twelfth century debates over the nature of universals. Initially he taught the reality of each species, but under attack by Abelard he defended the position of non-difference, i.e. that a name can be predicated of several individuals because in the aspect designated by the name they are not different. Most of his works that remain are theological in character: *De sacramento altaris, Sententiae seu quaestiones* and glosses on *De Interpretatione* (now lost).

CHRISTIAN WOLFF (1679–1754), German philosopher and mathematician, was born at Breslau. He studied mathematics, physics and philosophy at the University of Jena and in 1703 became *Privatdozent* at Leipzig. In 1706 Leibniz was instrumental in having him appointed professor of mathematics and natural philosophy at Halle. His aim of founding theological truth in mathematical certitude soon brought him into conflict with the Pietists. The controversy continued for some ten years and was finally appealed to Frederick William I, whereupon Wolff was ordered to leave Prussia, guilty of having advocated a rigid determinism. He was welcomed at Marburg and later (1740) recalled to Halle by Frederick the

Great. In 1743 he became chancellor of the university. Apart from his works in mathematics, his best-known philosophical writings are *Rational Speculations on the Powers of Human Understanding, On God, the World and Man's Soul, On the Operations of Nature,* and *On the Social Life of Man.* His ideas were systematized in his ten-volume series of philosophical manuals that became a model for this genre of philosophical writing.

# Suggested Reading

Bourke, Vernon, *Ethics* (New York, Macmillan, 1951).

Chesterton, G. K., *St. Thomas Aquinas* (New York, Sheed and Ward, 1933).

Collins, James, *The Existentialists* (Chicago, H. Regnery, 1952).

———, *The Mind of Kierkegaard* (Chicago, H. Regnery, 1953).

Gilson, Etienne, *History of Christian Philosophy in the Middle Ages* (New York, Random House, 1955).

———, *The Unity of Philosophical Experience* (New York, Charles Scribner's Sons, 1937).

———, *The Christian Philosophy of St. Thomas Aquinas* (New York, Random House, 1956).

———, *Elements of Christian Philosophy* (Garden City, N. Y., Doubleday, 1960).

Grabmann, Martin, *Thomas Aquinas* (New York, Longmans, Green & Co. (now McKay) 1928).

Lauer, Quentin, *The Triumph of Subjectivity* (New York, Fordham University Press, 1958).

Maritain, Jacques, *St. Thomas Aquinas* (London, Sheed and Ward, 1933).

———, *Existence and the Existent* (New York, Pantheon, 1948).

———, *Approaches to God* (New York, Harper & Row, 1954).

———, *Man and the State* (Chicago, University of Chicago Press, 1951).

Nédoncelle, Maurice, *Is there a Christian Philosophy?* (New York, Hawthorne Books, 1960).

Pieper, Joseph, *Guide to St. Thomas* (New York, Pantheon, 1962).

———, *Fortitude and Temperance* (New York, Pantheon, 1948).

———, *Justice* (New York, Pantheon, 1955).

———, *Prudence* (New York, Pantheon, 1959).

———, *Happiness and Contemplation* (New York, Pantheon, 1958).

Regis, Louis-Marie, *Epistemology* (New York, Macmillan, 1953).

Sillem, Edward, *Ways of thinking about God: Thomas Aquinas and the Modern Mind* (New York, Sheed and Ward, 1961).

Spiegelberg, Herbert, *The Phenomenological Movement*, 2 Vols. (The Hague, Nijhoff, 1960).

Walz, Angelus Maria, *St. Thomas Aquinas* (Westminster, Md., Newman Press, 1951).

Warnock, G. J., *English Philosophy since 1900* (New York, Oxford University Press, 1966).

Warnock, Mary, *Ethics since 1900* (New York, Oxford University Press, 2nd ed., 1966).

# Index and Glossary

Entries for some names are selective, and a few unusual terms have been given brief explanations to assist the reader.

Abelard, Peter, 11, 251
Alkindi, 15
appetite, 150–52
Aquinas, cf. St. Thomas Aquinas
Aristotle, xiii, xiv, 13, 14, 16, 17, 30, 31, 38, 39, 40, 78, 187, 193, 194, 199, 200, 201, 245, 251
Averroes, 15, 17, 252
Avicenna, 15, 78, 79, 80, 188, 252

Bacon, Francis, 46
Bacon, Roger, 15, 38, 252
being, 40, 76, 77, 144, 145
beliefs, 48
Bergson, Henri, 19, 253
Bernard, Claude, 55
Boethius, 18, 253
Bréhier, Emile, 25

Cajetan, Cardinal, 19, 253
Cassirer, Ernst, 113
causality, 84, 85, 89, 91, 92, 96, 112, 113, 116, 146, 218, 219
Comte, Auguste, 69, 70
Cox, Harvey, 101
creation, 81, 140, 141

Damian, Peter, 26
Dasein (in M. Heidegger that being which stands in the midst of Being revealing its sense or meaning; vulgarly, man), 40, 74
demonstration (proof through syllogism resulting in a necessary conclusion), 61–62, 222–225

Descartes, René, 104, 105, 106, 107, 108, 127, 254
Dewey, John, 7, 254
De Wulf, Maurice, 9, 11
Donatus, Aelius, 18, 255
Duns Scotus, John, 10, 255
Durant, William J., 8, 13, 256

Engels, Friedrich, 176
en-soi (in J. P. Sartre, being that merely is; things of nature incapable of freely fashioning their being), 101
essence (characteristics that endure throughout a being's existence), 81, 82, 83, 148
eternity of the world, 16–18, 85, 86, 88
existence (esse, first act of a being), 80–83, 91, 95, 99, 117, 124, 125, 127, 132, 210, 213, 228
existence (Existenz, the way human being projects itself towards its being), 99
existent, 77, 84, 85
existential analytics (as practiced by M. Heidegger it is fundamental, ontological thinking about Being), 103
existential analysis (in existential psychotherapy it is a therapeutic tool brought to bear on man in his concrete situation), 103

faith, 31–36

fate, 68, 74, 75, 97

Feuerbach, Ludwig, 208

Fichte, Johann Gottlieb, 137

final cause (end or purpose), 93–96, 149, 156, 157, 196, 197

free choice, 157–161

freedom, 102, 130, 131, 133, 135–141, 154–156, 162, 171, 178–182

friendship, 184, 185, 195, 196

Giles of Rome, 10, 256

Gilson, Etienne, 5, 19, 21, 24, 25, 26, 256

God, 15, 30, 41, 90, 92, 105–107, 136, 139, 143, 171, 172, 199, 201, 203, 205–209, 213–219, 223, 226, 227, 230

Godfrey of Fontaines, 10, 257

good, 147, 153, 155, 157–159

Hauréau, Barthélemy, 9, 257

Hegel, G. W. F., 207, 211, 247, 248, 257

Heidegger, Martin, 5, 23, 40, 41, 72, 73, 74, 204, 258

Henry of Ghent, 10, 258

Hobbes, Thomas, 177, 178, 179, 245, 246, 258

human being, 99, 100, 114, 115, 117, 118, 123, 125, 129, 142, 183

human nature, 76, 106, 107, 108, 130, 176, 177, 187, 189, 191

Hume, David, 110, 112, 113, 136, 137, 359

Husserl, Edmund, 19, 259

intellect, 14, 15, 33, 118–122, 125, 132

ju-jus (talisman, usually engraved object deemed capable of warding off evil), 100

justice, 192–195

Kahn, Eugen, 103

Kant, Immanuel, 113, 138, 163, 205, 206, 209, 210, 260

Kierkegaard, Søren, 204, 211, 212, 213, 214, 260

law, 165–173

Locke, John, 109, 110, 111, 128, 179, 180, 181, 185, 186, 190, 191, 260

*logos* (word, form, law or essence; the necessary properties of a thing), 73

Malebranche, Nicolas, 105

man, 12

Marcel, Gabriel, 41, 45, 261

Maritain, Jacques, 21, 261

Marx, Karl, 176, 262

mathematics, 52, 58, 59

May, Rollo, 102, 103

metaphysics (usually interpreted as being the knowledge of being as such), 100, 101, 104

Mill, John Stuart, 179, 181, 182, 198, 262

nature, 76, 78, 135, 167, 168, 186

necessity, 89, 90

Nietzsche, Friedrich, 134, 139

Occam (Ockham), William, 12, 263

*olon* (totality, the whole of reality, the being that embraces all being), 144

ontological argument, 30

οὐσία (entity or substance, variously conceived but usually refers to a thing's primary being), 242

Paulsen, Friedrich, 7

person, 131, 145

philosophy, 36–38, 46, 49, 51, 53, 65, 66, 69–71, 74, 76, 97, 98, 212, 229–233

*physis* (nature; principles or forces, other than artificial ones, at work influencing the behavior of things), 73

Plato, 12, 14, 74, 232, 263

Plotinus, xiv, 28, 29, 264
*pour-soi* (in J. P. Sartre, the being that is to-be; free being that is responsible for its being; human reality), 101, 174, 175
principle, 63, 64, 81, 97, 122
Priscian, 18, 264
Proclus, 14, 264, 265
providence, 74, 75
prudence, 163–165

quiddity (from Latin *quid*, what; hence, essence or definition), 78, 79

Roscelin, 11, 265
Russell, Lord Bertrand, 7, 22, 41, 44, 47–52, 67, 265

St. Albert the Great, 12, 15, 265–266
St. Anselm, 29, 266
St. Augustine, 28, 29, 39, 44, 202, 266
St. Bernard, 27
St. Bonaventure, 85, 267
St. John of Damascus, 225, 267
St. Paul, 26, 27, 29
St. Thomas Aquinas, xv, xvi, 10, 12, 16, 18–19, 39, 74–77, 81, 87–89, 96, 97, 114, 115, 146–149, 164, 167, 183–187, 190–193, 209, 215–218, 220–227, 231–233, 242, 268
Sartre, Jean-Paul, 41, 101, 134, 139–143, 174–176, 183, 205, 268
Scholastic philosophy, 4, 6, 8, 9–13

science, 34, 55–64, 72, 92, 104, 211, 221, 222
*Sein* (in M. Heidegger the dynamic, future-looking being that makes beings be), 73, 74
*Seiendes* (in M. Heidegger beings viewed substantively as embodying Being), 73
sensation, 107–109, 128–129
Siger of Brabant, 31, 37, 86, 87, 268–269
society, 178, 179, 168–189, 196, 201, 202
Spinoza, Benedictus, 135, 136, 269
Suarez, Franciscus, 19, 269–270

tendency, 95, 146, 147
Tertullian, 26
theology, 34, 35
Thomas à Kempis, 27
Thomism, 19–20

universals, 11

virtue, 162, 163

Whitehead, Alfred North, 95, 270
will, 33, 151, 152, 159
William of Champeaux, 11, 270
wisdom, 53, 54, 64
Wittgenstein, Ludwig, 71
Wolff, Christian, 30, 270–271